CONFIDING

ALSO BY SUSAN BAUR

The Dinosaur Man

CONFIDING

A PSYCHOTHERAPIST AND HER PATIENTS SEARCH FOR STORIES TO LIVE BY

SUSAN BAUR

HarperCollins*Publishers*

HarperCollins books may be purchased for educational, business, or sales promotional use. For information, please write: Special Markets Department, HarperCollins Publishers, Inc., 10 East 53rd Street, New York, NY 10022.

FIRST EDITION

Designed by Alma Hochhauser Orenstein

Library of Congress Cataloging-in-Publication Data
Baur, Susan.
    Confiding : a psychotherapist and her patients search for stories to live by / Susan Baur. — 1st ed.
        p. cm.
    ISBN 0-06-018238-5
    1. Personal construct therapy—Case studies. 2. Mental illness—Case studies. 3. Self-perception—Case studies. I. Title.
RC489.P46B38   1994
616.89'14—dc20   93-42081

94 95 96 97 98 ❖/RRD 10 9 8 7 6 5 4 3 2 1

For Betty Carroll Fuller,

who has been telling me stories for seventeen years while
we've run together through fog, heat, and winter cold.

CONTENTS

ACKNOWLEDGMENTS

Because this book tries to combine the most personal stories of the mentally ill with broader essays on psychology, I find myself wanting to thank two different groups of people for teaching me two different kinds of things. Surely the teachers of the science had the easier task. Among them I would like to thank Bill Hallstein for his help throughout, Lydia Kapell for helping to run the experiment reported in chapter 6, and Alan Flashman for his contribution to chapter 12, "Mapping the Family Story." Mark Morgan Osborne is another whose help has been invaluable.

Although the demands of confidentiality check the urge to thank publicly all who have shared with me their vivid observations of "life on the inside," I want the clients who come and go through what I call the Hillsdale Clinic and Mountain Valley Hospital to know that I appreciate the stories they have told me. Certainly I count among the treasures of my life the times that I have witnessed the undisguised expression of bravery in the face of terror and peace in the face of great sadness. I am continually amazed by the resilience of us all.

My friends Julie McWhinnie, Bob Anderson, and Peggy Stein have helped immensely. To Domenic Cimino go special thanks for the times we talked over the chapters and for the imaginative advice he provided. David Giragosian and Pat Markert have read portions of the manuscript, and they have supported the project throughout. As before, my agent and editor, Miriam Altshuler of Russell & Volkening and Kathy Banks, have been truly indispensable.

INTRODUCTION

The task of the mentally ill is no different from the task of others: to experience the world and tell the story.

I once had a lovely, tormented young woman in treatment whose thoughts were so disordered that she found it impossible to follow a conversation for more than a minute. The sad-eyed Yolanda would sit in her chair, hands clasped, round face scanning the ceiling, and seemingly search for a formula that would decode her thoughts.

"Clouds of sticky little voices say sweety-peety things of love," she said in confusion. "It's too cutesie-tootsie. I mean sweety-peety. I mean . . . oh, I don't know what!" Sometimes she would get so thoroughly trapped in her own words that in desperation she would grab a pencil and take a "sin tense a part in an ef (or if?) fort to h-old on."

Once, after failing to decipher her own ideas, she turned to me with a sigh and patiently started all over again.

"I want to be an angel," she said carefully, "because then I could give the gift of some other understanding."

The hardest job I have at the Hillsdale Clinic is to show my patients that they can give that gift—are already giving it, in fact—as they tell me startling stories of ordinary virtues. My second hardest job is to help these gifts sneak back into the community. To the extent that I fail, the whole community loses something of value. All of us slide further toward the intolerance, distrust, and despair that seem increasingly characteristic of our times.

Hillsdale is no more receptive to the unexpected gifts that sometime lie within irrationality than other parts of the Western world, and unless changes are under way in our society as a whole, there is no reason to expect to find any new understanding here. Yet it seems to me that glimpses have begun to appear. Even as funding is cut back and clinics close, small shifts in attitude seem to be opening new doors—at least a crack. You can see the theory behind the new ideas in certain professional journals, and you can hear the ideas discussed by people like Yolanda who drift through the door of the Hillsdale Clinic like leaves, year after year.

This change in attitude stems from a shift in what we consider to be useful knowledge. In simplest terms, the shift is from the belief that objective truth is the one and only goal to belief in the more inclusive idea that meanings come from many perspectives and continually evolve over time. At least in the social sciences, we are gradually becoming less like chemists and more like historians. In this new era of thought, variously called Post-Objectivism or Postmodernism, we are reacting against the narrowness and exclusivity of the current reign of rationality which, among many, many other things, defines minorities such as the mentally ill as useless.

Until recently, the cultural zeitgeist proclaimed that the single voice worth listening to was that of reason. With a steadfast faith in an orderly world where the truth of everything could be discovered given enough time and enough accurate observations, the kind of person who was respected was goal-directed, rational, efficient, hardworking, and level-headed. This person, who not surprisingly was often a white male, discovered useful and wonderful things about the natural world but did no favors for the social sciences by treating lives and institutions as if they were elements and compounds. The "laws of human nature" that were thus apparently discovered and that stated that certain ways of living are normal and others abnormal are turning out to be not laws, but the reflections of our society's preferences at certain points in history. For example, Piaget put forward the idea that as children mature, their thinking progresses from a magical to a logical, abstract plane. This is still seen by some developmental psychologists as the goal toward which every normal mind aspires. Growing up means learning to think straight about real things, and only young children, psychotics, superstitious natives, and perhaps poets remain stuck in the rambling, storytelling kind of thinking that expresses more interest in imaginative possibilities than in facts.

Postmodernists, with their appreciation of the many ways there are to know and think, question whether divisions like this hold everywhere and forever, and they further maintain that our preference for a quality like logic over the quality of imagination reflects a cultural bias, not a law. Given this shift in perspective, the search for universal laws is being gradually replaced by the more complicated task of studying meaning. An improbable coalition of psychologists, sociologists, theologians, anthropologists, historians, and literary men and women are beginning to ask how this or that person or this or that group makes sense of itself and how this "making sense" helps them to function in the world. For these students of the human condition, narrative—the stories we tell about ourselves and our worlds—is becoming the root metaphor for knowing. As each of us constructs a personal reality, it is organized as we put it into words. It is as if we construct a world for ourselves from the fragments of information at our disposal and then find we are held back or pushed ahead by the very constructions we create with our stories. To put this another way, the stories I tell about myself not only state that this and that has happened to me, but also that I'm a certain kind of person. I am one who characteristically copes or suffers or goes to sleep. Taken together, the anecdotes about my daily doings that I share with friends or simply tell myself give me an identity as well as an itinerary. And this identity or characteristic way of reacting to the world has a momentum that turns the raw experience of everyday life into more of my victories or losses or sleepy afternoons.

If my story is adequate to my needs, it will not stay the same over the years. Constantly updated by new information or, as in therapy, revised by a new appreciation of old information, my understanding of myself will evolve. Such a continually reworked story leads to new experiences, which in turn produce new information and require further reworkings. Of course, every teller understands that his or her experience is not exactly the same as the story that purports to describe it, but in good times, the teller and the tale promote each other. Moments of living alternate regularly with moments of putting experience into words, and storyteller and story spiral upward and downward through the years. Recognition that the silent personal narrative we construct—or have constructed for us by our families—actually gives direction to our lives has placed the old-fashioned story in a bright new light.

Take, for example, my client Kathleen. She is a wonderful, red-haired woman in her late forties who believes that silicon chips have been implanted under her scalp by the Central Intelligence Agency. The advantage of having chips, she tells me, is that she receives reports of ski conditions from throughout the cosmos, which she passes on to friends. The disadvantage is that the CIA can track Kathleen, and whether she ambles all morning along the old railroad tracks that lead southward from Hillsdale toward Franklin and the larger cities or whether she holes up in her rented room for days on end, the agency listens to her breathe the way a cat might listen to the quick and shallow respiration of a mouse.

Kathleen *lives* by this story. It is the framework on which every event of every day is hung. As her therapist, if I want her to interact more regularly with other people or wear bright clothes when she walks the back roads at night, then I encourage her to elaborate or modify her CIA story so that it makes room for visits to Edna's Donut Shop and the addition of a reflecting vest to her wardrobe.

An even clearer example of the formative power of a story is provided by the irrepressible Johnny Paradise, a lanky, middle-aged ex-convict who arrived in a hospital for the criminally insane with nothing of any value to offer in that rough society. Gradually he constructed an identity as a storyteller, and by the time I met him, he was describing himself as a storytelling "store," which was analogous to a food store or a liquor store.

He explained to me that, "Stores are people, man, walking talking supplies." His buddy Cherubino, who worked in the chow
hall and stole coffee, was a coffee store. Cherubino's cousin was
what might be called a revenge store: "We send Vinnie to castrate the rats." Johnny had a Bible and a great imagination.
"So," he told me, smiling broadly, "I start telling them stories."
Soon he became known as the con who could take a man's mind
off anything, even the electric chair.

In Johnny's case, the story he tells of being a storyteller not
only supports him like a life raft but gives him the power to
wheel and deal with others in his community. As long as he is
believed, his wild tales allow him more options for thinking,
feeling, and behaving than he would have had had he based his
story on his original thought of "Maybe I have nothing."

Such expansions in a person's story do not depend on the
narrator alone, however. To start telling more potent stories
about your experience is not solely a matter of personal ability
and ambition. Stories are told, and an understanding of the self
attempted, within the framework that our culture provides its
families, and not everyone has the same plots to choose from.
Although Joseph Campbell believed he had found the basic plot
for our time—the "monomyth," as he called it—in the story of
the individual hero who single-handedly overcomes adversity
and achieves his goal, this is not a viable template for everyone.
The mentally ill, for example, not to mention women, blacks,
gays, the handicapped, and other minorities, have a hard time
fitting their lives into the kind of plot that has been fashioned by
free white males over the past several centuries. Indeed, when
Johnny Paradise left the hospital—or prison, as they all called
it—his identity as an itinerant storyteller rather than a wage
earner did not earn him respect.

Psychiatrists, psychologists, social workers, and counselors
take an active hand in modifying plots. Their therapeutic treatments still largely flow from the "laws" of human nature that
were thought to have been discovered in this century and that
reflect our cultural preferences. Taking for granted that rational,
objective, level-headed people are the truly complete people,
most members of the "tinkering trades" still seek to move their

clients back into the dominant culture by shaping the stories their clients bring to them.

Students of behavior modification are notorious for surreptitiously testing the power of their specialty by performing a simple experiment in the classroom. On an agreed upon day, they nod with discreet enthusiasm whenever their professor moves to the right hand side of the room, and they avert their eyes and seem to lose interest when he or she moves to the left. The simple exercise inevitably draws the teacher to the right side of the room and holds him or her there for most of the hour. Unconsciously using similar techniques (in addition to whichever therapeutic methods they favor), clinicians draw their clients back into the mainstream. When a therapist only has ears for the monomyth; that is, when phrases such as "I guess I'll try to get a job," or "I'm showering every day now, Doc," get a warm smile and a nod, the therapist is inadvertently maintaining a status quo that denies respect and attention to many kinds of thinking.

Therapy is "a contest of singers," maintains the Jungian psychologist James Hillman. He points out that until recently therapists have not been sufficiently aware that their views of the people they treat represent merely one perspective among dozens. Also, therapists have been slow to acknowledge that their perspective is not an inherently privileged one. In certain situations, for example, a therapist's understanding is *less* useful and *less* welcome than that of a friend's. But, says Hillman, we are beginning to see that therapy is "a collaboration between fictions." Both client and therapist use their skills as novelists as well as historians or detectives as they labor to get a story to work right and feel right. After a long tug of war, a new story, invariably called "How Things Really Were," is pulled from a mixture of old facts and new dreams. Hopefully this new account is more intelligent, more inclusive, and more cohesive than the story originally brought into therapy. If it is also more imaginative, it may lead its narrator in directions he or she had not yet dared explore. In simplest terms, then, this is what much of the new therapy is like. The therapist as historian, humbled by the new understanding that any account of a client's life (like any story of Kennedy's assassination) is but one of a hundred possible versions, collaborates with the eyewitness. And the eyewitness returns at the end of the long therapy day with a clearer understanding of a more organized life.

Hillman suggests that this yearning for a clearer plot is the new goal in therapy. In the past, he says, the majority of clients hoped that therapy would give them love or a cure or at least instruction. Obligingly, therapists functioned as providers of parental concern for the needy, dispensers of medication or magic for the broken, and as bubbling wells of information for those who wished to learn. But now, Hillman surmises, most individuals come to therapists for a plot to live by. They come as if to a professional biographer, one who is part careful historian, part inspired poet, and part gatekeeper for the dominant culture. And they leave, not with "The Story of My Life" but, it is hoped, with a better, richer version of *a* story.

When a therapist agrees to do the slow and careful work needed to modify the plot of a life, then such a clinician must sink into that life—"sink yourself into their position," as Bruno Bettelheim used to say—and listen so hard that he or she actually *participates in* that person's confusions, terrors, hopes, and perverted pleasures. This is what I am calling "dangerous listening." It is dangerous because this kind of responsiveness exposes one to the subversive qualities of the mentally ill, their unwillingness as well as their inability to conform to traditional expectations, to think logically, or even to want to get well. Dangerous listening wholeheartedly accepts the emotions expressed by these rebellious individuals but declines to be drowned in what appears to the client to be the unalterable facts of the matter, be they "facts" about the CIA, about what a person can or cannot do, or about how life must be lived with an alcoholic spouse. In other words, dangerous listening involves both client and therapist not only in every known emotion but also in every known way of thinking. Both find inside themselves at least traces of all ways of being-in-the-world. Both are shaken and changed. They are united. And for the schizophrenics or manics telling their stories, this dangerous listening finally provides an opportunity to maintain their inherent differences *and* find common ground with members of the dominant culture.

I am not, of course, recommending that mental illness be considered a viable way of living or that it be left alone to develop without treatment. But I am agreeing with those who have found that the seriously mentally ill, especially schizophrenics, find it much easier to recover in societies where different ways of thinking are respected—and deviance less feared. As every therapist knows, when a story changes, an individual changes. It is also true that when enough stories change, our world changes too.

Because narrating is intimately related to knowing and is our way of taking the flow of experience and making it intelligible, it is not surprising to find that children as young as three have learned to make up stories.[1] Chattering away to themselves at night, they explain such things as why it gets dark, why parents sometimes leave, and why toys like to roll off the bed.

In *Acts of Meaning*, Jerome Bruner points out that stories rain down on children relentlessly from the moment of their birth. In one study, the normal chatter of mothers, relatives, and children was recorded in black households in a ghetto in Baltimore. In every hour of conversation an average of eight and a half stories were told. Many were the tales of violence and confrontation that black mothers hope will prepare their children for life on the street.

"And she says, 'Look at that big nosed B-I-T-C-H.' And I turned and I says, 'Uh, you talkin' to me?' I said 'ARE YOU TALKIN' TO ME?' I says, 'Well, you fat slob, I put you in a skillet and strip you down to normal size, if you mess with me.'"[2]

Later, when children retell these stories, or stories of their own, they will modify them to conform to what they hear around them; that is, they will quickly learn which kinds of sto-

---

1. It is now generally believed that our inability to remember much about our lives prior to age three or four is the direct result of our inability to put experience into words and thus put it into a form that can be stored in memory.

2. Jerome Bruner, *Acts of Meaning* (Cambridge: Harvard University Press, 1990), p. 84.

ries are understood and welcomed and which are not. In most cases their explanations of what goes on in the world will increasingly reflect what the culture expects of them. Even as adults they will continue to negotiate the subtle points of what it means to be happy, sad, sick, or well with an eye toward telling a story that fits their feelings as well as it fits them into the rest of the world.

A personal story that is sufficient to explain an individual's present situation and allow him or her to face the future is one that is coherent, comprehensive, and convincing. By coherent, I mean that the events of the life have been thought about and arranged so that causes are connected to effects, the present seems to flow naturally from the past, and the life seems to hold together in a unified fashion. To be, in addition, comprehensive, the story must have been progressively elaborated to incorporate as many points of view as possible. Unlike the story of a Johnny-one-note, it must be complex. Finally, a convincing story is one that is understandable. It is not so idiosyncratic that it cannot be told. When the therapists who think in terms of plots and stories talk about improving a person's story, they are referring to these qualities of coherence, comprehensiveness, and convincingness. They are also hoping to encourage the narrator to be more active, more unified or self-possessed, and more critical than ingenuous. Sometimes they also encourage a more precise or factual account, but not necessarily.

Increasingly it is understood that the adequacy of a personal narrative cannot be judged exclusively by its factual accuracy. Naturally, this is a matter of degree. Most of the time we try to get the gist and the feeling of a story right and let the details slide, both because this saves time and because our memories work this way. A memory stores and retrieves gists and feelings much more efficiently than isolated facts, and research in all areas of psychology has shown repeatedly that our memories are notoriously imprecise. In some ways this is useful, for it allows us to reinterpret the past in light of our present needs without stumbling over too much contradictory evidence. It gives us some slack. Nevertheless, if the facts of experience are allowed too much scope, as they are in lies and delusions, the account loses its currency in the wider world. It becomes a private language—and it becomes impotent.

Most of the stories related in *Confiding* are not coherent, comprehensive, and convincing. There are accounts so full of lies and delusions that they twist themselves into angry isolation, and there are others that are mangled by family members until no one knows where one person's experience ends and the next's begins. There are thin, reluctant stories that rigidly cling to a single theme, and there are tumultuous exaggerations that change so dramatically with the speaker's mood and the nature of the audience that the narrator's identity falls apart. There are stories that deteriorate, and others that climb against all odds into a wider, happier world.

The true negotiation of idiosyncratic realities is not an easy or a particularly agreeable process, and among the discoveries made recently by social psychologists is one that documents our preference for spending vastly more energy supporting what we already know rather than incorporate new views into our picture of the world.

As Angie Savalonis discovered in describing her troubles over the course of her career as a schizophrenic, most doctors saw and heard what they were looking for and what already made sense to them. Like the rest of us, her doctors sought information that further confirmed their views. Using these selective observations, they then formulated explanations. Finally, they mistook these partial explanations for "the real Angie Savalonis." The more extraneous information they were able to ignore, the clearer and more persuasive their descriptions of Savalonis-as-schizophrenic became. But with the exclusion of the unfamiliar and the unexpected—that is, with the exclusion of *the patient's own stories*—her case history ceased to describe a person. The tightest, most elegant cases inevitably describe stereotypes.

Such reductions present more than one disadvantage. In terms of stories, they omit all common experience that doctors and patients can discuss as equals. As the patient's and the doctor's stories diverge, the patient becomes in a very real sense a lonely foreigner who does not speak the language. Like Miss

Savalonis, such a person is not able to find solace either in the community or even in her own story, which has no value if it cannot be told to an understanding listener. As a stereotype, the patient is alienated from herself as well as from others.

One of the results of the widespread acceptance of Campbell's monomyth has been to winnow out the thinkers from the dreamers or, more accurately, the productive from the nonproductive. While we have rewarded the rational, quick-thinking worker, we have progressively excluded those who cannot or will not work consistently and think logically. Take my sixty-eight-year-old patient Louella Brady, whose illness occasionally gives her the energy to drape a red scarf and a feather boa around her graceless midsection and shuffle over to County Road to stick out her thumb for a ride. She has recently been placed in a boarding facility, ostensibly because she will receive better care there, but actually because her neighbors complained of her antics. They didn't want to hear Louella ranting at God, and they didn't want to see her conducting services on her lawn for fallen sparrows. It embarrassed them to see her on County Road under the shady maples throwing back her shoulders for the boys.

In Hillsdale, homeless women and their children have also been herded out of sight. They have disappeared behind the bland facade of a huge yellow house that reminds me of a funeral home. Down the same side street we have tucked away the addicted and the retarded. In fact, we have special "homes" for all these people now—the deaf, the alcoholic, the criminal, the mentally ill, the old, the poorest of the poor, and the retarded. The care of every one of these individuals has been relinquished by a family and picked up by the state. There are advantages, of course, especially economic ones for the streamlined, pared-down working families that remain at the center of our community. But there is also the sense that we have unlearned something, that as the winnowing has proceeded, we have lost a power or an ability that now paradoxically threatens the security we thought we were protecting.

Judith Freeman in her review of Bret Lott's *Jewel* states that the suspense of the novel comes in wondering "what will result from accepting . . . , the 'giant blessing and curse of a retarded child?'" What is produced by a "family's devotion to the weakest of its members"?[3] Selflessness is what Freeman suggests, nobility of spirit, dignity, courage, and above all allegiance. By working patiently to find the humanity in Brenda Kay, who has Downs syndrome, the members of Jewel's family reaffirm that their own worth is not contingent upon time and fortune. They regain the security of knowing that their family and their community will cherish all its children all the time. It is the kind of security that many of us feel we have lost.

Stories lobbed into the community of Hillsdale by the profoundly depressed, the schizophrenic, and the rocketing manic are at the center of this collection. There are the graceful complaints of Charlie Isabella, who has chosen to watch shadows climb across his bedroom wall each afternoon rather than rejoin the world of the living. And, by way of contrast, there are the caffeine highs of Johnny Paradise, who would sneak a quart of coffee from the clinic's kitchen, then explode into my office exaggerating everything.

Even though the stories in this collection deal with some strange topics—a seductive guardian angel; perversion; torture; and a quoit-throwing dwarf who ejaculates on the hour like a demented cuckoo clock—they illustrate many surprisingly common themes. Angie Savalonis explains her unhappiness as punishment for some dreadful action she must have taken. The family of a profoundly troubled young man believes that if an illness is ignored, it will disappear. And Lloyd Bartlett, who for twenty-five years has been trapped between two warring bands of delusional Indians, tells a charming story that shows in exaggerated detail how all stories evolve over time, how they change depending on the receptivity of the listener, and how they are fought over by the individual and those closest to him—each of whom claims to have the true version.

Confiding is as much about listening as about stories. I

---

3. Judith Freeman, "Blessed Are the Ordinary," review of Bret Lott's *Jewel*, in *New York Times Book Review*, 1 March 1992, p. 21.

remember one gray autumn afternoon when I felt so besieged by
the spinning Johnny Paradise and the screaming Miss Savalonis
that I decided to get out of the clinic and drive to a coffee shop
with "my three o'clock," the mysterious word-bound Yolanda.

"Out for coffee with Y.," I wrote later. "Before coffee, she
was fairly quiet and spoke semi-coherently about a boyfriend."

"I had a boyfriend and he or people use hand gestures, you
know, because that's the way you might say part of the conversation, but it's many messages that push and pull. So people say,
'You're thinking too hard.' If I'd changed my behavior . . . if I
could get a big feeling of power from the turkey or other
designs, then the sentences would give me more security and I'd
get over the hump."

After coffee, Yolanda's relentless monologues became even
more voluble. Her sentences made false starts. They struggled to
stay on course. They twisted their way toward their targets then
collapsed into writhing heaps around a word like "boy." Driving back to the clinic along a tired road already narrowed by
fallen leaves, I could imagine what it must feel like for therapists
who find only frustration, confusion, and rejection in psychotic
monologues. I could imagine falling off Yolanda's twisting sentences and just not bothering to climb back on. For a moment I
was aware of the enormous energy it takes to accept confusion—not to dismiss it as meaningless, not to turn it into a symbol of something that is easier to understand, but to suffer it as
you would a hard rain.

Other kinds of listening are explored here as well. There is
the distracted listening of defensive relatives who can't bring
themselves to hear the painful parts of a story and of busy doctors who believe they already know how the story goes. There
are also imaginary conversations of great complexity where the
self listens to itself and often learns a great deal. Finally, there is
the listening that unites, that returns the teller and the listener to
a common and familiar world.

The stories in *Confiding* are arranged according to a pattern.
All but one story/chapter or case history is followed by a companion chapter on a psychological point of interest related to
storytelling. One is on the psychology of confiding, another on

our natural gullibility, and a third on the ways that imaginary companions help us clarify our most private stories. For example, in the fourth case history we see Mr. Bartlett and his overweight sidekick, Bobby Two-Ton Eagle, promiscuously weaving "their" dreams of glaciers, canyons, and roaring cataracts into the often frustrating boredom of Hillsdale. This chapter is followed and augmented by one that examines the ways we all use imaginary social interactions.

Here, then, is a collection of stories from men and women whose very lives depend on rebuilding accounts that contain enough self-respect and hope to make their lonely struggles worth continuing. Without listeners, these people cannot know that there is an incandescent quality to their stories, a kind of honest speaking from the heart that is so beautiful, so to the point of being alive, so nakedly descriptive of the human condition, that it has the power, just as our voice does, to break hearts and mend them in a single day.

The stories which I describe in *Confiding* are based on my actual experiences. However, I have had to make many changes to disguise and protect the identity of my patients and others. To that end, details such as physical traits and specific life experiences have been changed, and in one instance combined. Any similarity to real individuals arises from the commonality of experiences of people who suffer from mental illness.

Dr. Susan Baur
February 1994

RIDING THE GLASS ROLLER COASTER

> *When life ends badly, the great temptation is to construe it as a long, inevitable journey to ruin. But the death is not the life.*
>
> KATHA POLLITT[1]

THE FIRST TIME I MET THE EIGHTEEN-YEAR-OLD, JIVING, CONNIVING Chuck Willet I was much too shocked to take notes. In fact, I was too surprised to remember later what he looked like. I thought that a picture of him might come back to me—at least enough of one to recognize him the next time I saw him in the waiting room—but initially I had only a memory of eyes that rolled upward until they disappeared into his head, a smile that I instantly (and uncomfortably) recognized as my son's, and an armful of new, no-nonsense scars. I find it easy to remember long, flamelike scars. He showed me the older ones, too, like silvery gratings or ventilators, but they were not in serious places. They did not look like fire.

"You understand," he'd whispered hoarsely, straining his enormous muscular frame toward me, "I had to let out the pain."

1. Katha Pollitt, *New York Times Book Review*, 18 August 1991, p. 22.

It was that sort of thing that curtailed note-taking—the dis-tractions. In spite of them I recall him saying that a celestial spirit gave him blowjobs and that he was enraged with Jesus for only pretending to take away the worst of the pain.

"Oversold. God spelled backwards—back wards, get it, doc-tor?—is man's best friend and *that's bad*!" He jumped to his feet, and he was tall—really, really tall. He began dancing like a video star to his own rap routine. I can only remember snatches about "God is a woman. Whoa, man." Also "Shooting and killing is my bag, and I'm not a dude that would ever brag. I beat up the twenties, the thirties, the forties. Possessed by the Devil and . . . " something, something ending discordantly with "anti-Christ." There was a lot about nigger-Negro-black man, too, and more than a lot about a confused yearning that changed its shape so fast I couldn't follow.

"Aargh!" he shouted, abruptly doubling over and hiding his face in his hands. "I've offended you. Dis-gus-ted you. But no," he continued hurriedly, "don't apologize on my behalf—be half, get it?—I'm whole enough to pray for strength.

"Rest now," he whispered tenderly, leaning forward again and caressing me with his voice and eyes. "I will give you strength."

Aargh to you! I wanted to yell back at this enormous, quiv-ering man. Too much. Too fast. Get out from under my skin!

"Will you be able to help me?" he was now imploring, his face twisted in such anguish that I thought one of us was going to cry. "Are you strong enough, lovely lady—lady lovely? Will you follow me?"

"I will learn what you teach me," I answered warily.

There was a pause, short as pauses go in my experience, and then he leaned farther forward still.

"You *will* be mine."

The next time I saw Chuck he had just had "a pisser of a fight" with his grandmother and had become so upset by this "wormy little creature" that he had taken a Valium. ["Chuck and I had our differences like everyone else, but I was never afraid of him."] Thus he arrived at my office considerably calmer than before—calm enough to be looked at. This time I noticed that Chuck Willet was a generous six foot three and had a strikingly handsome face topped with straight black hair, which he parted slightly off center along a three-inch scar. His features were beautifully proportioned—square jaw, wide mouth, straight nose, high cheekbones—and the expressions that leapt from his light brown eyes were echoed and exaggerated by dark eyebrows, which met in the middle as boys' eyebrows often do. Of course he dressed with the perfect degree of cool. His white T-shirt had the right stuff on it—although I cannot remember now exactly what it said—and his long, narrow jeans accentuated the enormity of his still anxiously tapping Air Jordans. A new watch with a wide blue band hid the latest scars. Except for a slightly pale, indoor look about him, he was a model of the all-American boy.

"I've been manly since I was four years old," he commented, apparently reading my mind. "I'm an intense, fighting man." ["Chuck was the sweet one. So kind to everyone. So sensitive."]

I began gathering some background information from Chuck, both to learn how he would phrase and punctuate the story of his life and to compare his version of it with the versions I had encountered in the four or five hospital records that had been mailed to the clinic. Although Chuck had been hospitalized roughly twice a year since the age of fifteen, each time for several weeks, his records contained surprisingly little that was new or useful. Three obvious points were made over and over again. First, he scared people. ["This young Caucasian male has a history of aggressive and threatening behavior. He is noncompliant."] Second, he was suicidal. ["I'm going to walk into a phone booth and explode," he told his doctors. Or, "I'm making myself a lye sandwich."] And third, no one had a firm grip on the nature of his illness. Each of three hospitals and one clinic had given him a different diagnosis and had medicated him accordingly. Most recently, he had been labeled schizo-affective, a relatively new diagnosis that combines the hallucinations and thought disorder of schizophrenia with the extreme moodiness and depression of "affective" or mood disorders. Not surprisingly, schizo-affectives are given the medications used for both disturbances, and Chuck was taking hefty doses of antipsychotics, a lithium substitute, cogentin to control side effects, and Valium, which he compared favorably to burn ointment. "Doctor, I *have* to have it." ["He told me once that it made him feel almost normal."]

I did not quarrel with Chuck's diagnosis, but neither did I find in it much guidance or consolation. "Schizo-affective" gave me few clues as to why his brain or his psyche had swerved off the track so violently at age fifteen and was now propelling him at full speed down the side of a mountain. The man came without a map, and our job at the Hillsdale Clinic was to slow the slide, break the destructive cycle, and at the same time control the Valium so that drug addiction did not get added to his list of problems.

"Sharks are the mindless drones of hell," began the calmer Chuck Willet in answer to a general question about his family's background. He was sprawled in a large wooden chair in the corner of my office, and the late afternoon sun that lay on the linoleum floor was just about to reach his size 13 feet. "Also, Doctor, I am not used to Yankees." ["We moved from the West Coast when the family broke up. Chuck was very upset. His brother stayed behind."]

Chuck continued to describe his family in a fragmented, lethargic way and made it clear that this topic was not uppermost in his mind.

"Dad is a hell of a man and an asshole," he stated flatly. "The fighting Irish. The doubter. I'm a pessimist like him, but I get my niceness from Mom. Now she's the wimp. But my brother, Steven . . ." and here his voice changed as he drew the name out ecstatically, "I *miss* Steven. The pain of having him, but not being able to eat him up." ["No one in the family understands Chuck. I'm the only one he trusts."]

According to these snatches of history, Chuck had been born at full speed and had continued to accelerate. He showed me scars to prove it. In first grade he had stepped on a rake and gotten bashed in the head. In second grade he had tackled his cousin only to embrace the sharp edge of a picnic table. In junior high he had fought with "street niggers," and white kids, and later he had taken on two men at a time outside a bar.

"I've had the reputation of being destructive since third grade," he said matter-of-factly. "I was unbelievably savage. . . . You know," he continued, slumping even more into his chair, "my whole family's paranoid. It runs in the blood. When anyone passes by my house, I run upstairs in fear unless I can see bare legs." ["We were broken into four times before we left L.A. Terrorized. The guy who did it—they finally found him—smeared grease on, well, in my bedroom. He did terrible things. Steven would hide in a closet. It got so we'd go to the bathroom together."]

The family had indeed been knocked around. During that second hour I learned that when Chuck was thirteen and living in the suburbs of Los Angeles, his mother had left his father and started working full time. Chuck maintained that his father was verbally abusive to him. For a year or so the division held, and as a handsome freshman, Chuck began to create quite a reputation for himself as a promising, charismatic student. He played school sports extremely well, and he loved to be watched. He wore nice clothes, which he stole from stores with sophisticated security systems. He attended most of his classes. He fought the toughest kids in school and rarely lost. In his mind, it was this last quality that attracted the attention of beautiful girls. By the end of ninth grade he was being actively courted by a savvy, good-looking sophomore, Barbara Bailey. Life looked good.

Sophomore year was something else again, however. Although the luscious Barbara Bailey had landed him as her Number One boyfriend, his mother got sick and was forced to return her two boys to their father. Chuck was enraged. Prodded by a violent temper that daily roared out of control, he fought with his father until forced to move out and live with a friend. At the same time he was trying to be a star on the high school teams and mold himself to Barbara's classy image of a so-fine guy. Although he wore the clothes she bought him, took her to the right places (at her expense), and soaked up the new pleasures and unexpected pain of sex, he was rapidly falling apart.

"I *loved* it, the whore . . . and it was bad—not wrong, I
don't mean that wrong shit. I mean . . . like it took my skin off.

"That's when it started," he continued, beginning now to
shift uncomfortably in his chair. "I would have these seizure-like
things, and my brain would feel like it was flipping kinda ass
over."

"During sex?"

"Of course not," he replied, frowning. "I was tripping on
acid and foaming at the mouth. Flunking out. Falling apart. One
morning I went down to the kitchen and I heard—well, it wasn't
like hearing a voice. It was like feeling a presence, real strong
and angry. 'Getcha, Chuck. Gonna getcha, Chuck.' Shit, I was
scared!" ["He called me at work, terrified. He'd gone into the
kitchen and heard voices outside saying 'Getcha, Chuck. Gonna
getcha, Chuck.' He was fifteen."]

During the next two years, in spite of a savage resolve to
hold himself together, Chuck started to come apart at the seams.
Moving from school to school didn't help, but his mother, having reclaimed one of her two children, wanted to leave her memories of violence and break-ins and start fresh in a new community. With Chuck, she moved first to Columbus, Ohio, and then
to New England. Chuck moved from being uncontrollably
angry to inconsolably sad.

"I couldn't pull it together. I didn't know what was going on."

One thing he remembered, however, and told me about in
that second hour of therapy was flying back to California for a
visit at Barbara's request.

"She paid my way, the whore, then didn't want to see me. 'I
can't see you now. I have to go out with my girlfriend now,'" he
recounted in a silly falsetto. "So she came over, fucked me, and
then went out with someone else. I flew back east and cut my
wrists. Mom and Grams never knew." ["She was a sweet girl.
She loved him to death."] ["Once some girl hurt Chuck's feelings and he held his hand over the stove. Burned it real bad."]

Nothing went well for Chuck in New England. Several trips
to the hospital in handcuffs punctuated a whirling blur of fights
and betrayals. Another Barbara came into his life: "My summer

sex. She was no good for me." ["She was a steady girl, a good influence.] He barely managed to graduate from high school, held and lost four or five jobs, then retreated to a room he'd fixed for himself over his mother's garage. Increasingly, he devoted himself to a personal investigation of hell.

That second hour was probably the calmest I ever spent with Chuck Willet in the short time I knew him, not that he didn't hop around a bit when he recalled his fights or scowl blackly while testing my tolerance for descriptions of pain. And pain was what he really wanted to talk about. I learned in the following weeks that mental anguish was his new arena, and although he hadn't chosen it and was often terrified by it, he waded into the unfathomable dangers of psychosis with a heartbreaking bravado.

All discussions of pain began with his guardian angel Kasheen, who ordinarily attacked at dawn. Chuck would wake from a broken and often dream-filled sleep with the weight of a woman pressed against his chest and the pressure of a strong hand on his genitals.

"Fuck me!" Kasheen whispered urgently inside his head. "No one else! Do it now!"

Sitting in the corner chair opposite mine, Chuck let his head roll back on his shoulders. "Fuck me," he repeated slowly as his heavy black hair fell back from his face, strand by strand. "Doctor," he said, gazing at the ceiling, "she explained the mystery of Xanadu to me last night, and it was magic, wonderful." Chuck straightened up and I could see that his eyes sparkled with a melodic happiness. "She wants me to die and be with her."

"And what do you want?" I asked cautiously, surprised by the sudden turn that rapture had taken.

He was silent, and then, in the time that it took him to shift backward then forward in his chair, he became terrified.

"Doctor, I saw disembodied eyes last night." He shuddered violently. "Glowing. Right in front of my face. Alive. What I fear *the most* is turning off the TV and going to bed. They start with me then, Doctor," he said, his young voice breaking. "Can you understand that? Can you hear me? Satan lures me with a little bullshit of love. Doctor, my head is so bad." His voice was still rising. "The voices are so believable, unresistible. . . . I know they're coming back for me.

"How about a little more hell, Chuckie?" he now asked, mimicking sweet, dark-haired Kasheen with the "subtle curves." "She gives me such pain."

"And promises you such bliss?"

"She tells me to commit suicide, and she means it. The way hell wants me, Doctor. . . . I'd hang myself if it was more pleasurable, but I'm not into life for the anguish. Besides, Grandmother would hear me stringing up the wire. I'll use two guns on the day I turn nineteen. Like this. See?" And here he held his forefingers to his temples. "Two pistols. No pain."

["We all thought he'd do it when he was nineteen. He was very convincing."]

The light in the office on that windy December afternoon was dimming and brightening in a distracting manner as clouds tore themselves across the sun and went wavering down the sky.

"What do you say to Kasheen when she tells you to kill yourself?" I asked.

"*Wait*!" he pleaded so loudly that I jumped. "You'll fucking have to wait!"

"And yet you took the sleeping pills when she told you to fall into her arms."

"She was just testing me then," Chuck answered quickly. A growing excitement had displaced the terror of a moment before. "She told me to take thirty-five thousand milligrams—guided my shaking hands—and I did it for her. *I hit it out for you, Kasheen*!" he boomed in the "luminous voice" that he believed he got from lifting weights, and as he raised his hands above his head in a wide sign of victory, I could imagine him back in high school running the bases and gathering the smiles of girls. "Count on me, Kasheen!

"So then she appeared in a dream and told me to go into my mother's room. Doctor," he whispered, "*she saved my life*."

["He walked into my room and threw up. Green stuff was coming out of his mouth."]

The light darkened again in the office, giving Chuck's face a grayish pallor. He sprang from his chair and in a single step was standing over me.

"Doctor, I'm being electrocuted at night," he began, raising his fists over my head against an unseen attacker. "Wired and plugged into an outlet. I can see the blue sparks." He paused. "I'm being fried. Like a pork chop, Doctor. Fried."

"Is it getting worse?" I asked, shoving my chair out from under his towering form.

"It's always getting worse," he snapped, dropping his arms and starting to pace. "I've always been unhappy."

"Does your family know what you're going through?"

Chuck shrieked with laughter. "No, no, no, no, no. With Mom and Grandmother, I'm Mr. Sweetness. I bite up their ass. I smile. I eat them up. And what do I get? Grandmother, the dream-killer, works me up into a lather. 'What pain, Chuck?' she whines. 'What pain? You have a headache? Is that it?' She doesn't know *shit* about hell. ["He'd carry on about the pain, and I'd tell him to take a Tylenol."] I'm the only man who has seen the blue blazes." He pointed to his chest, tapping it hard with his forefinger. "Purgatory is my bed."

"Have you read Dante's *Inferno*?" I asked.

Chuck was taken aback, but only for a moment. "Some Latino, right? I knew him, and I beat his ass."

And so it went for a month, as a psychiatrist and I cautiously adjusted his medication. We wished to reduce his Valium little by little, replacing it with a less addictive medication. There were two reasons for this. First, the drug tends to disinhibit or unleash whatever passions are present—in Chuck's case, a great deal of rage—and we certainly did not want to prescribe the increased doses of Valium he would need to remain at his present level of equilibrium and watch his anger escalate. Second, the drug invites a kind of blackmail that can be difficult to handle. Because it is standard practice to discontinue Valium slowly to avoid seizures, gastrointestinal complaints, sudden mood swings, and other problems that abrupt withdrawal can trigger, Chuck knew that we would not yank the drug away from him suddenly. If he chose to take a two-week supply of Valium in five days, he could be quite sure we would refill his prescription rather than risk the complications of withdrawal. To avoid both the rage and the power struggle, we tried other medications until we found a beta-blocker to supplement the Valium. Together, they produced roughly three-quarters of the calming effect he was used to—not as good as straight burn ointment, but, as he put it, "about enough to chill out."

By the fifth week Chuck reported feeling better—or at least a little safer. I did not. Although the two of us were establishing a fairly firm relationship, and he clearly found relief in meeting with someone willing to share the desperation, I felt that Chuck was inflating my influence in a dangerous way. As he walked to my office from the parking lot, I now noticed that he scanned my window. When he sat in the waiting room, sprawled gorgeously across the flowered couch, he listened for my footsteps and sprang to meet me. In my office, his references to eating me up or carrying me away in his head to nibble on as needed increased. I felt he had turned me into a Valium tablet.

Other times I felt he had turned me into a fantasy so vivid, so personal, so ultimately powerless that he would not notice if I never spoke. He would look over my head and talk of a yearning that was as long and thick as a snapping turtle's neck. He would take my eyes in his with such intensity that I sometimes looked away. He showed me—in my face—that his most recent scars were exactly the color of his tongue.

Kasheen was also swinging from one extreme to the other "like a black silk whore on a sizzling trapeze." This week she had risen into heaven where she had no power to speak of, and Jesus-Lord had returned and assumed his rightful reign. Although Chuck was still tormented by nightmares, he was now somewhat comforted by Kasheen's watchfulness.

"She watches my nightmares, you know. I can feel her dreaming along with me. I love that feeling. You know, I'd like to drown myself in you, Doctor. I'd like to take you away in my head."

With this slightly calmer Chuck I was finally able to ask about the kinds of family relationships he enjoyed, rather than merely ride the roller coaster with him up and down through his pain. He described an agreement that he and his mother had come to concerning hospitalizations. Rather than trick him, as she had the last time, telling him he needed stitches in his wrist then driving him to a psychiatric hospital, she would be up front. When he "started acting strange," she was supposed to say, "Chuck, time to chill out." He hated being hospitalized, he told me. He desperately wanted his family to give him a chance, but a chance to do what was never clearly or realistically explained.

"I'll be tough!" he would shout in his good moods. "And cool," he added, preening delightfully and flashing me a cocky, ready-for-anything smile from his three best angles. "I've seen *Lethal Weapon* thirty times, Doctor. I've got it all figured out."

At the opposite extreme of his fantasies stood the silent threat of life as a mental patient. He almost never acknowledged it, but once, at the sound of my footsteps coming down the hall, he had burst out of the waiting room to tell me he had just seen six or eight elderly chronic patients stumble out of a van.

"Those poor, pathetic people!" he cried in great distress. "Those brainless *scum*. I'll die first. Doctor, death is my option. When you give up," he added, "the buzzards come down for you just like out there."

"Do you see yourself in those people?" I asked.

"There's nothing here for me in the future," he answered, which I took to mean yes. "A cheating wife. No money. Old age. I think hell is a lot like life.

"And I think women are the *greatest* thing," he continued, shaking off his pessimism abruptly. "My mom is the hardest worker in the world. We fight, but I'll always give her a second chance. We saw *Cats* together, and she drank it up and got cool."

"What does your mother hope for you?"

Chuck was silent for a moment. "Sometimes," he began uncertainly, then dropped whatever answer he had formulated, "but she's too loving to get the picture. She can't see that we're surrounded by spirits, that the dreams are on our backs. She can't see evil." ["He said that blue is the color of hell—Satan's color. I told him the sky is blue and God made the sky. Blue can't be the devil. He said there are souls all around us trying to hurt us. We're packed in souls. I told him, 'No, Chuck. That's not the way it is.'"]

Curiously, Mrs. Willet's inability to see the devil was a comfort as well as a frustration to Chuck. He leaned very hard on his brother Steven to sample the pain firsthand by burning himself or cutting, and he leaned on his mother to see evil. ["He'd tell me about hell and the devil, and I'd try to listen until my head sort of wobbled around, but I couldn't take it."] But he was glad that his mother remained for the most part outside the circle of his torment. He seemed to realize that just as she could not see the evil that existed in life, neither would she ever be able to see evil in him.

"She was the impatient, loving one," he explained. "It was her nature."

Other times, of course, Chuck would lump his mother, grandmother and girlfriends into a single wad of hysterical bitchiness and toss them to hell. Down they would all go, Chuck driving them relentlessly in his imagination, then up they would come again a minute or two later, whipped back onto the narrow staging of his life by a chance memory or, more often, by his need to eat his way into someone for a moment of dubious safety.

When it came to his father, Chuck, like the rest of his family, had little to say. Although he had lived with him until age thirteen and briefly a year later, his father's ideas or opinions did not figure largely in Chuck's thinking. "Dad was a tyrant," he would say. "We were glad to break up with the asshole." Or another time, "Steven is like Dad. He has a big nose." Once, however, I asked Chuck for his earliest memories and was surprised when a jumble of pleasant recollections came tumbling out.

"Jungle gym, pet rocks, and . . . making stuff for my dad. You know, once I stayed home from school sick, and Dad came in and put his hand on my head."

But that small window of happiness had apparently closed a long time ago. Now it was just his brother with whom Chuck felt close, which was almost more than Steven could stand on the rare occasions when he came east for a visit.

"Doctor!" Chuck shouted happily as he danced into my office towing after him "a great gift of a man.

"Didn't I tell you he was handsome? And look at his build. He's a hell of a lifter, Doctor. I was sure he'd outpress me, but hey, Steven," and here Chuck embarrassed his smaller, younger, and altogether ordinary-looking brother with a dramatically affectionate hug. "You couldn't beat me, could you. Doctor, we had a *terrible* fight. I can't get him to feel the pain."

It was a tricky hour. Steven was exhausted from riding Chuck's moods up and down for nearly a week, and he desperately needed to explain to his brother that there were points beyond which he would not go in the name of empathy. He would not burn holes in his hands with cigarettes, for example, to glimpse the edges of Chuck's hell. And he could not get nearly as excited as Chuck by the fights they watched together on television. Chuck saw in these hesitations both cowardice and rejection and did not hesitate to say so in threatening ways. Fifteen-year-old Steven responded by backing and filling manfully in an attempt to hold on to both his sanity and his role as the only truly understanding person in his brother's life. ["No one liked talking with Chuck. He scared them and tired them out."] Chuck, of course, further compounded the confusion by setting Steven up as superior in strength, intelligence, and loyalty, then demonstrating how he fell short in each of these areas.

"You alone have the power to save me," Chuck all but said to his younger brother, "but you don't love me enough to do it." ["Steven was simply furious when he heard the news. I don't understand it. Simply furious at everyone."]

The following week, Chuck was in a black mood. Usually I would find him sprawled on the couch in the waiting room, his head peering over the back, ready to spring for the hall that led down to my office, but on this particular afternoon he was slumped in a chair, hair over his eyes.

"My brother has betrayed me," he said dramatically as he entered the office. "I asked him to give me back the Special Forces shirt. He doesn't deserve it. I don't know how many times I showed him my wrists," he continued, obviously running over in his mind the occasions of his brother's failings. "I tried to explain to him about the pain. The daydream-nightmare witches. The voices. They don't leave me a way back."

Chuck went on to describe how much he had been counting on his brother and how let down he felt because the two had disagreed—had fought, in fact. It was the old pain of having Steven with him but not feeling close—not being able to eat him up. ["He sobbed when Steven got on the train."]

Chuck's wildly fluctuating evaluations of his family were tame, however, compared to those he projected heavenward and transposed into religious terms. Loading onto the shoulders of the Almighty all the impotent goodness, mixed messages, and confusion that he had encountered in his short life, he regarded Jesus-Lord, even more than his mother or brother, as both his last hope and his ultimate disappointment.

"A Section 8 from Christ," Chuck once shouted, thumping his fist into his other hand as if it were a baseball mitt. "A pink commitment slip from heaven." And before I could ask him whether Christ was asking for suicide or hospitalization, he drove on to assert that "God is behind the scenes and can't do much. He loses his power for me. Maybe he abused his magic. He's a cockroach. Who would want to be God even if he could? Tell me that, Doctor."

"Hold on a minute, Chuck," I said slowly, hoping to stem the tide before it swept us both away. "What do you think the Lord wants—"

"Me!" he shouted, interrupting my attempt to go back to God's plans. "He loves me. The Holy Spirit dwells in me intensely, Doctor. Intensely. I talk to Him all the time."

Suddenly Chuck was on his feet again, shouting, "I'll knock it out for you, *God*! Count on me as your bodyguard!" He began punching viciously at the air in front of him, his hair flying back and forth across his face like the brushes in a carwash.

"Or His hitman," I thought, staring in fascination as Chuck turned on the charm for God.

"God loves me *so much*," he was saying with a quick and winning glance, "that he plays with me as a child." He ran both hands through his slippery black hair. "Lord?" he called, glancing coyly heavenward. "Lord?"

Chuck had smoothly exchanged his bodyguard snarl for his "luminous voice."

"Marbles, Doctor . . . marbles," said this strikingly handsome man, spreading his arms wide and pronouncing the word with obscene exactness. His eyes flickered heavenward again, and my son's handsome young smile frolicked across his face. "The galaxies, get it, Doctor? The stars and the planets? They're like mmmarbles to him."

Chuck was crouching on the floor now like a kid, inviting God to a game of marbles. Flexing, posing, freezing, smiling, he trampled charmingly back and forth across the usual boundaries of reality, time, manners, and space. One minute he was earnest and, I believed, on target: "God knows that I'm a doubter, a real pessimist like my father. Doubt, doubt, doubt." And the next instant he was soaring among grandiose expectations like a comet through the black night sky.

"God tells me the rapture will happen," he said, flicking an imaginary solar system across the bare linoleum floor and gazing after it contentedly. "He loves me so much. . . ."

As always, or so it seemed to me, an excess of happiness opened the door to fear, and within a period of several seconds Chuck was sitting in his chair again needing to "drink up" my voice and play with my name to keep Satan off his back.

"What's your first name, Doctor?" he suddenly asked. "Or does everyone just call you Doctor?"

"Susan," I answered, rising to leave.

Chuck, too, rose fom his seat, suddenly towering over me. He casually stepped between me and the door. "What do you like to be called? Susan? Sue? *Susie-Q*!" He lit up at his own cleverness. "Susie-Q," he repeated and, arms akimbo, actively blocked my passage.

"Don't get wise with me, kid," I said, with a casualness I did not feel as I looked up at the six and a quarter feet of tense, muscled male in the doorway. I stepped toward him as if to pass.

"Hey!" Chuck shouted sharply, putting up his dukes in mock fright and dancing in place like a boxer. "We have a contender for the title."

"Not so," I said quickly, and my mind raced over alternative plan—all for escape. I stepped to the side. Chuck moved closer. I stepped back several steps, but he bobbed forward, now scarcely eighteen inches away from my face. He was staring intently, and I thought he was going to tell me again that he wanted to crawl in my mouth. Crap. Should I get angry? A memory of Chuck screaming at the psychiatrist jumped into my mind. Should I appease him and play for time? I remembered him raging at cowards.

As I was about to try to distract him by looking in my appointment book, Chuck abruptly landed a gentle punch on my shoulder and, laughing, twirled away across the room. Giddy with relief, and with a memory from high school suddenly coming to mind of the mock fights that were the breathlessly exciting beginnings of a crush, I stamped my foot in what I hoped was a teenage sign of good-natured impatience.

"I gotta go to my locker and get my gym clothes—now," I said firmly.

"Sure, Doc," he replied, smiling broadly. "See you in study hall."

In spite of these intense exchanges, which Chuck fed on and which blurred the usual distinctions between past and present, him and others, or rather *because* of these visceral exchanges, I had already gathered that the essential lines of battle inside this young man's head were drawn between incorporation and rejection—eating and spitting out. Sin and salvation, like macho manliness and insipid wimpishness, represented other tensions, but these were not as intense as his need to take in and be taken in by another person—and his fear of *both* these hungry, invasive maneuvers. This led me to suspect that Chuck's troubles reached far, far back into his past, and that, in addition to being schizo-affective, he was also what is usually called a borderline personality. In the local jargon, he was a "kiss, kiss, bang, bang." To me, however, he felt like a window-screen person.

I have found that certain intensely baffling behavior can best be understood by the metaphorical idea that for some individuals skin seems to have been replaced with some frail and permeable netting that can neither hold anything in nor keep anything out. Such a person is in constant jeopardy of either leaking all energy and ideas out and shriveling into a husk or being swamped by the energy and ideas of others to the point of drowning. Chuck was one of these people who seemed to lack the membrane that both establishes the boundaries of his being and regulates the common give and take, or rather the "take in" and "hold off," that goes on whenever two people interact. Without skin, he was in danger of being drained or over-whelmed, and depending on which of these terrors was striking him at the moment, he would either try to dive down someone's throat or spit them out—preferably off a high bridge. ["I can't listen to him when he's upset. Nothing I say is right."] He was a difficult person to help.

Chuck's difficulties in regulating his fragile, porous self made life tense at home. When voices threatened him with or tempted him toward violence, he sought to escape by taking medications, by shocking himself out of his misery through physical pain, or by losing himself in a passionate exchange with another person.

Not surprisingly, the more desperate Chuck became in his pursuit of relief, the more resolutely did his family retreat to the high ground of common sense. Chuck's insistent plea to share his pain was met more and more frequently with advice along the lines of "You need to budget your money." Or "Exercise would do you a world of good." The mutual frustration grew. Chuck became increasingly isolated. There was no place, it seemed, where he fit in.

After meeting with Chuck weekly and only for two months, I took ten days off to travel on business, and as I crossed the country by air, I sketched out a rough plan for his treatment. His nineteenth birthday was approaching, and I wanted to step up the pace of therapy. My first objective—to form an alliance with Chuck without being seen as the family's agent—was com-pleted, and I surmised that I could now bring his mother into our sessions occasionally without making Chuck feel I was diluting my allegiance to him. The immediate task was to help Chuck survive beyond March 26, less than two months away. As I played with a cup of bad coffee and stared out over a wing at the banks of pearly morning clouds, I realized that the greater challenge was to help Chuck and his family realize that the plans for his future they had all drawn up in their minds needed drastic revision. The goal was not how to convince Chuck to budget money, get motivated, and go on with the old life, but, far more dismally, it was how to grieve for all his lost opportunities, temper the lethal fantasies that both threatened and sustained him, get a job at McDonald's, and attend a support group for the mentally ill.

It was a shame, I thought, that he was so tall and good-looking. It would make his adjustment much, much more difficult.

When I got home, I discovered that the accounts of Chuck Willet that I had left behind—his own, his family's, the psychiatrist's, the casual observances of my colleagues—had burst like a fireworks display into a dozen new renditions. Two days before my return, and one month and twenty-two days before turning nineteen, Chuck Willet had hanged himself in the family garage.

The common reactions to unexpected loss are simple and irrational.

"*No,*" I'm sure I said after hanging up the phone, the words of the psychiatrist still stuck somewhere between my ear and the part of my brain that would not accept the call, "not Chuck." ["Chuck Willet hung himself in the garage."] "Not such a big, handsome boy. Not a man of such intensity." ["I'd hang myself if it was more pleasurable, but I'm not into life for the anguish."] ". . . couldn't kill a man that size with a piece of string. Maybe years ago," I thought irrationally, "maybe on his birthday, but not today . . . can't be dead today." ["On the day I turn nineteen. Like this. See?"]

"Dead now? All dead? Fucking, goddamned son-of-a-bitch dead forever?"

I reached the clinic later that morning. There is something about a brain that cannot tolerate abrupt endings and, like an exhausted runner kept going beyond the finish line by his supporters, Chuck Willet was still being carried forward in everyone's mind.

"I lost him," I acknowledged, as a therapist put his arm around my shoulders.

"He did the decent thing," he replied. "He found the thera-peutic dose that finally stopped the pain."

"Had he fought with his family?" asked another, reminding me that Freud explained suicide as anger turned 180 degrees—homicide turned against the Self.

"I lost him," I repeated, picturing against my will that huge, vibrant boy—that two-hundred-pound body that could not pos-sibly be dead.

"It's so hard for people to understand an individual like Chuck who is in so much pain," said a particularly kind woman. "These individuals say, 'I can't go on with this life. I have to move on. Whatever lies ahead is better than this.'"

"Poor prognosis with that illness," suggested another, as I continued to struggle with Chuck's after-image. "At that age sui-cide is the third leading cause of death."

"We don't know why he killed himself," the psychiatrist had said firmly on the phone. "The compulsion to tell *any* story, rather than no story at all," he added, "is the bane of clini-cians."

In spite of his reasonable warning, each of us comforted our-selves by offering an explanation for Chuck's death that estab-lished, if only for the time it took to tell it, a version of his life that was dominated by his last act. To lay him down in our minds, to try on the idea that he might really be dead, we made up stories about an angry life, a painful life, a sick life, even a supremely smart life. ["My neighbor said it was his finest moment. He was totally sane. I didn't agree at first, but now I think she may be right."]

But the death is not the life and, like the universe collapsing in upon itself eons after the big bang, like the roller coaster finally sinking into the hollow of its cradle, the fragments of Chuck's life that had been broken loose by illness, misadventure, and finally death came flying back to coalesce into the family's final account.

["I had the strongest thought as I was driving to work that day. I said to myself, 'You'll always remember this day—the sky so blue, the frozen fields so clean and hard, the sunlight so clear.' I had a feeling of absolute peace then, and I thought, 'I must notice these fields more often.' In the afternoon, I went to my second job. 'Call home,' they said. My mother had found him."]

["So peaceful. Just looked so peaceful. His toes touched the floor."]

["The first thing you think of if you're Catholic—in the back of my mind, I mean. . . . What if he goes to hell? But I don't think God would send him to hell. He'll have compassion."]

["We all thought it would be March, after his birthday. He wasn't impulsive about this."]

["God will have compassion for Chuck. He'll have the highest place in heaven. I wish I'd hugged him more. I believe that God granted him his wish to tell those he loved that he's all right. And I prayed. I said, 'Chuck, don't scare your brother, but do something for him.' That night Steven had a dream about him resting in one of those cool, blue winter fields. Steven told me his brother didn't look sick anymore."]

["We sorted through his writings after that and threw away the psychotic stuff. We deleted the weapons—the worst stuff. We'll remember the old Chuck."]

And so within a week following his death, the desperate years of Chuck Willet's life were rolled back into an addendum. The dramatic ups and downs of his fiery moods were replaced by memories of hard-won lacrosse games and exhilarating tournaments. A photo of Chuck in third grade—sweet, anxious, vulnerable—was placed on the mantel. ["You should have known him in grade school. You would have loved him."] The nine hours I had known him dwindled to a thin sheaf of progress notes documenting a case of mistaken identity. Chuck's own stories of a blue, electrified hell, of Kasheen and Jesus-Lord, of "*terrible* fights" he could neither explain nor avoid, of sex and violence—all these tumultuous, poorly understood metaphors gave way before an account of a sensitive boy who had always been stumbling toward heaven.

Did this hasty resurrection of the old Chuck feel like a mistake to me? Was I sorry that the nearly incoherent Chucks I had known disappeared both from life and then from memory as well?

One of the hardest tasks that a person changed by accident or illness faces is to convince others, as well as himself, that he will not ever be his old self again. The sea has breached the dunes, new inlets and outlets are formed, and the very circulation of the system is changed. Neither Chuck nor his family had gotten very far in the painful process of accepting such deep changes, and because they had not, neither could they fully appreciate the subtle forms of bravery that are required of the ill and which can be added to a man's story without shame.

On the one hand, it is unfortunate that his last years were not appreciated enough to be included in his brief biography— for the omissions shorten the life and narrow the picture of a vibrant and exceptional human being. At the same time, it is a wise thing that the Willets have set aside the confusing portions of Chuck that do not fit within their scheme of things. In doing so they have brought him back to the fold. The old Chuck fits solidly into the family once again, his life paralleling theirs, his journey pointing to the same distant goal. And this is a great and necessary comfort: among those of us lucky enough to have loved another person, who could tolerate the thought of separate eternities?

2

NARRATIVE TRUTH AND HISTORICAL TRUTH

> *To say that all human thinking is essentially of two kinds—reasoning on the one hand, and narrative, descriptive, contemplative thinking on the other—is to say only what every reader's experience will corroborate.*
>
> WILLIAM JAMES

"I'M AN INTENSE FIGHTING MAN," CHUCK WILLET TOLD ME THE second time I met him. Manly since the age of four, destructive since third grade, at eighteen he described himself as a lethal weapon, as the toughest of the tough.

"Chuck was the sweet one," his mother had explained to me when we finally met several weeks after his death. "So kind to everyone. So sensitive."

Even allowing for the probability that Chuck exaggerated his toughness and that his mother overemphasized his sensitivity (as mothers will), how can both accounts purport to describe the real and abiding Chuck? Did it make any difference to anyone that the two descriptions were so far apart? And does it make any sense now to try to figure out which one is true? "Yes" is the answer many social and cognitive psychologists would give to both questions, but they would also ask, "Which kind of 'true' are you talking about?"

In the late 1970s and early 1980s the idea that there were two distinct kinds of truth that we deal with every day blossomed into one of the most fascinating and productive discussions held in a long time by philosophers, historians, linguists, and psychologists. In simplest terms, social scientists posited that historical or empirical truth concerns the facts of a matter, whereas narrative truth carries its meaning. Historical truth, they agreed, is judged by logical, scientific criteria and is expected to be verified and supported by other evidence. Its language is constrained by the requirements of consistency and noncontradiction, and its goals are facts and laws of nature. That Chuck Willet was born in Los Angeles on March 26, 1972, is a historical fact. Narrative truth, on the other hand, does not mirror a fact or set of facts but is used to construct a coherent, inclusive story that explains events and feelings by finding the links that might connect life's separate occurrences. It is laden with our concern for the human condition. It makes a good story. A simple example is often used to illustrate the two truths: "The king died and then the queen died," is a fact. "The king died, and the queen died of a broken heart," is a narrative.

In his book *Narrative Truth and Historical Truth*, psychoanalyst Donald Spence investigated what this double accounting system means to analysts and their patients.[1] He challenged the metaphor, popular since Freud, that the analyst unearths hidden (historical) truths from a patient's memory the way an archaeologist might unearth artifacts from Pompeii. Instead, Spence asserted, with the help of the analyst, the patient both revises and reselects his memories in order to come up with a new version of his own history. If this new story has more narrative truth than the old account—that is to say, if it makes better sense of the patient's troubles by explaining where they came from, how they have imprisoned the patient, and how they may be modified—then the new autobiography is more useful,

---

1. Donald Spence, *Narrative Truth and Historical Truth: Meaning and Interpretation in Psychoanalysis* (New York: W. W. Norton, 1984).

regardless of how well it fits the historical facts. It is important to note that narrative truth is malleable not primarily because our memory is unreliable or because our skill in telling stories is uneven, but because the meaning of any event changes over time as we ourselves grow and change.

For Spence, then, Chuck Willet's job in therapy was to construct a narrative account of his life that fit his *present* circumstances better than any of the old accounts had managed to do. He needed a story that included as much of his life as possible, rather than an account with a narrow focus, and he needed an account that made sense to other people, not one that made him seem alien.

Another analyst, Roy Schafer, observed how these new narratives are actually constructed in therapy.[2] He noted that the analyst guides the patient in formulating new questions, not only about life in general but about the presence or memory of significant others. An example is the common progression from questions directed outward—Why does Grandmother torment me? What have I done to deserve this?—to questions that are increasingly directed inward: What am I doing that sets her off? How can I help myself feel better? The new way of looking at life, engendered by the new questions, gradually spreads—not just forward through current endeavors, but backward through memory as well. An individual's whole life is thus recalculated from a new perspective. The goal, Schafer maintains, is to retell the story of a person's life in a way that allows him or her to understand the origins and significance of present difficulties, and to do so in a way that makes change seem possible.[3] This taxing process of revision matters, he says, because we act on our explanations. We live the stories that we tell, meaning that the identity we give ourselves, whether of a hard worker, a lethal weapon, or a helplessly ill person, shapes how we will see things, how we will feel, how we will act, and how we will move into the future.

One more aspect of narrative truth needs to be mentioned—

2. Roy Schafer, "Narration in the Psychoanalytic Dialogue." *Critical Inquiry* 7 (Autumn 1980): 29–53.

3. Schafer, "Narration in the Psychoanalytic Dialogue," p. 38.

namely the degree to which others participate in prompting or obstructing the process of revision, which, of course, takes place throughout all lives both in and out of therapy. The continual revision of a life story is always made in relation to a listener, even if there is no person present and even if the self seems to be talking only to some other part of its being. Stories are justifications intended for listeners, and research has shown that the feedback received when explaining who you are or how you feel is a remarkably powerful agent of stability and a much less powerful agent of change.[4] In other words, the evidence that confirms is a lot more powerful than the comment, glance, yawn, or sigh that contradicts. Not surprisingly, people elect to spend most of their time with people who confirm and further stabilize their own view of themselves. The tendency is to consider these agreeable companions reliable judges of character and, perhaps more important, the tendency is to forget, distort, or discredit the feedback that comes from persons whose opinions contradict our own. Quite a number of factors influence whose words we will take to heart, but one of the essentials in this endeavor is the establishment of an area of agreement or at least of understanding.

Returning to the dissimilar stories that Chuck and his mother tell, we see that there is really no quarrel between them in terms of historical truth, but each has selected such a different set of facts and memories that two different stories of Chuck have emerged. Their narrative truths contradict. Mrs. Willet's story suggests that her boy's unusual sensitivity was the main reason why he succumbed so completely to the stresses in his life—his father's alcoholism, divorce, break-ins, moving, access to drugs, and so forth. Being more than usually affected by these upheavals, Chuck finally snapped and retreated both from the real world and from his real personality to a fantasy land where he was so tough that he no longer feared disturbances and displacements. The hope this story held out was that medication and an absence of stress would restore Chuck to his former way

4. William B. Swann and Steven C. Predmore, "Intimates as Agents of Social Support: Sources of Consolation or Despair?" *Journal of Personality and Social Psychology* 49: 1609–17.

of being, although Mrs. Willet admitted that over the years her hope had almost disappeared.

Chuck, however, had put together an altogether different story which, he claimed, antedated his illness by many years. In his version, he was a fighter, and whether he was mixing it up on a soccer field, behind the school gym with a troublemaker, in a department store with a store detective, or in his bedroom late at night with demons, the two things he did well were to fight hard and take punishment. No one, he believed, could take the bruising, burning, and bullying, as well as he could. No one got the thrill he did from throwing himself recklessly into any maelstrom he could find. Years of mental anguish had apparently pounded his story into pretty simple terms: fight and endure.

When we hold these two stories of Chuck's life up to the criteria set for adequate narratives—credibility, coherence, inclusiveness, and what might be called vitality or a lively openness to alternatives—we see that both accounts fall short. Chuck's account of being fought over by God and the Devil did a fine job of expressing the extreme mental torture he endured. Although he expressed himself in dramatic metaphors that most people would label delusional and discount as incredible, no one would argue that Chuck's account of being tormented by horrifyingly sadistic and duplicitous spirits was not a nightmare. Dramatic as it was and incomplete as it was, the story explained how Chuck felt.

But Chuck's story was not a useful one. It was not believable enough to allow him to share his problems with family or friends, and it was not inclusive enough to create a map of life with more than one road through it. His account left out hospitalizations, hours and months of apparent lassitude, social isolation, financial dependency, and the diagnosis of mental illness. Because all these parts of his experience were missing, his story suggested no alternatives. From Oedipus Rex to Goldilocks and the Three Bears, a good story always points, albeit ambiguously, to the future. It is open to multiple interpretations, each of which suggests a slightly different way to proceed. There is a lesson of sorts to learn and a new approach to try. Chuck's story gave him no help in this respect. Endure, it said simply, for as long as you can. Hold out.

Mrs. Willet's account was much better than Chuck's in terms of credibility and social acceptance. She could talk over her version of her son's troubles with almost anyone and expect them to understand and sympathize. There were no disembodied eyes, demented angels, blue flames, or flirtations with God in her account to drive other people off. But credibility was her account's only asset. Her concept of Chuck's sensitivity to stress did not begin to explain the pain he felt—it made no sense of his present situation. Her account also skirted around her son's fascination with violence and his intensely ambivalent feelings about sex. In addition, because her story conceptualized mental illness as a roadblock rather than an alien countryside, it suggested no ways of being mentally ill but only ways of waiting for the obstacle to go away. This is not the real you, her story said, and there is nothing you can do about it except wait and hope to resume your journey when sanity returns.

When two relatively narrow versions of a life grow far enough apart, the usual business of negotiating a common understanding is gradually replaced by mutual distrust and defensiveness. The facts of the matter may not be disputed, but what each fact means will be so different that the platform of agreement and understanding on which social negotiations proceed collapses and conversation comes to an end. The pain that signifies a headache cannot talk to the pain that signifies a trip through hell.

And what the handsome Chuck Willet desperately needed, and what finally failed, was conversation. Whether he was shaking up his family at dinnertime with accounts of hell or explaining the sensation of electrocution from the corner chair in my office, what needed to take place was the kind of endless conversation—call it confiding, call it making sense of things—that can very gradually and stubbornly revise a life. It wasn't that anyone's explanation of what was happening needed to be thrown out. It was, instead, that we all needed to guide each other in putting together a much broader story that encompassed and respected all the narrower versions, and that offered just enough hope, enough room to change, to warrant Chuck's continued desire to live. In such a story of Chuck Willet's life there would be room for stress and sensitivity, for laziness and a reluctance to help himself, for a chemical imbalance in need of redress, for the need to love and to fight. Most of all there would be room for his own brave epic of endurance and his mother's story of love. The facts of Chuck's life do not change, but the narrative truth—the story—might have been reshaped by the patient exchange of words. But this business of negotiating stories—the give and take among competing versions of reality—takes time and trust, and in some lives such luxuries are unobtainable.

3

THE LAST HAPPY TIME

There is no story without a listener.

CHARLIE ISABELLA, MIDDLE-AGED SON OF AN OLIVE IMPORTER, spent the first sixty years of his life trying to get someone to take care of him. Naturally, he began with his parents—the short, successful Enrico Isabella who commuted back and forth between a home in Providence, Rhode Island, and the olive districts of central Italy, and the taller Ellen Isabella, his American wife. After his parents (and grandparents) expressed a chronic disinterest in caring for him, Charlie tried teachers, employers, a lover, a wife, four dogs, two children, the Department of Welfare, Catholic Charities, and finally the planet Earth in the guise of the then-popular American Indian god, Kehtean or Great Spirit. Kehtean did far and away the best job of caring, only Charlie Isabella had to follow the Great Spirit very closely to reap the benefits of his generosity. He had to sweat just to keep up with him, and he had to concentrate feverishly to match exactly the spirit's cadence.

"It was like drafting God in a bicycle race," he explained.

I first met Mr. Isabella when he was fifty-nine, and he did not look as if he had ever ridden a bicycle much less been in a bicycle race. A thin man of average height, he had about him a doubly disjointed quality. For one thing, he appeared to be uncoordinated, with arms, legs, cane, feet all going their separate ways; for another, his head was too large for his body and his features too large for his head. Heavy eyebrows crawled across his forehead like caterpillars, and a wide mouth floated beneath his prominent nose. His skin had been scarred by acne. The gray-haired Mr. Isabella limped on a cane into my office at Hillsdale wearing a badly wrinkled suit. He positioned himself over a chair, then let himself fall backwards into it with a rattling sigh. His features bounced for a second before recomposing themselves into their bland and apparently habitual arrangement.

"Whoof!" he sighed and took a deep, rasping breath. "Whoof . . . whoof . . . whoof."

It was then that I noticed the flicker in Mr. Isabella's eyes. Contradicted by his awkward shape and contemptuously careless dress, and all but hidden beneath his brows, were a pair of lively, pale blue eyes. It was not their color that arrested, nor the shape, although each was a graceful, downward-curving crescent, but rather his eyes attended. They stretched toward. They inquired. And it was a good thing they did, because except for his eyes and his somewhat labored breathing, there were no other signs of life.

Mr. Isabella was preceded by his record, and from it I had already learned that he had recently moved from Rhode Island to Hillsdale to live with his cousin Theresa. Several years earlier he had been hospitalized twice for attempting to kill himself— once in an imaginative and once in a conventional way—but no one could agree on a name for his problem. He was variously labeled depressed, bipolar (manic depressive), schizophrenic, and just plain psychotic "NOS"—Not Otherwise Specified. Nevertheless, his discharge summaries were unanimous in their descriptions of a frustration so intense that it bordered on hatred. For one thing, the patient was incurably sad for no good reason, and for another, he was contrary. He was slow, although his early history indicated he'd been fast, and he was relentlessly silent, although the usual indicators such as intelligence and education indicated he ought to be articulate. What did the man want? And why wouldn't he bestir himself to get it? His cousin Theresa didn't know, and when, upon his arrival, Charlie Isabella stayed in bed for three silent days smoking tiparillos and sipping ginger ale, she sent him to the clinic to talk.

Thus, when I met Mr. Isabella on a warm and windy day in May, I was prepared for silence but surprised by his willingness to talk. On and on he went about various aspects of his life, and his voice seemed to waver and sway in rhythm with the shadows that rippled in across my windowsill and went sliding up and down his rumpled side.

Among many other things, Mr. Isabella told me that he and his older brother, Enrico Jr., had been born in Trenton, New Jersey, into a large, well-to-do family of Italian businessmen. When he was five, the family, including paternal grandparents, moved to Providence to be near still more Isabellas. The six of them settled into a grand three-story house just down the hill from Brown University. The family expected Enrico Jr. to take over the family business, and Charlie, with his artistic bent, to follow his Uncle Carlo into the jewelry trade. As a child he may have had an artistic bent, Mr. Isabella now conceded with a shrug. He had liked to draw. He entered the art contests in school, and one summer he and his cousin Jimmy made an entire circus out of wire, probably, I thought, without knowing that Alexander Calder had once done the same.

After high school, Charlie enrolled in the Rhode Island School of Design. He did well enough, he stated, and even sold a couple of his designs for jewelry early on. In his senior year he surprised his family by dropping out and moving in with Charetta.

"She was a dancer," he told me matter-of-factly. "My family disowned me."

For five years Charlie and Charetta lived like bohemians on the edge of the South Providence slums. I did not get a clear picture of his partner during our first hour (never did, for that matter), but I remember being intrigued by the couple's decision to name their two sons after cities—Stamford and Compton. During those years Charlie worked occasionally as a jewelry designer. Most of the time, however, he did not work. He preferred spending his afternoons at Narragansett Park watching the horses or at Raynham watching the dogs.

Life did not go smoothly for him, however, and one winter, after he had left Charetta and the two young boys, he suffered a relentless bout of bronchitis. In fear of contracting pneumonia, he moved from an unheated apartment to a shelter and shortly afterward went on general relief.

"I had my troubles then," he said, referring to what I imagined were bouts of depression as well as ill-health and unemployment, "but I got by. I still smoke."

Some ten years later, Mr. Isabella's life took a dramatic swing in a direction that most people would call favorable. At forty he married "a settled woman" and together they lived a life free from plastic, red meat, aerosols, processed foods, pesticides, and town water. In fact, they became devoted and respectful students of ecology and tried to guide their negotiations with the planet by the rituals and teachings of American Indians.

"I was very effective in that movement," Mr. Isabella said, expressing pride in himself for the first time. "I went on retreats, and several times I have had mystical experiences. My life was clear. I was useful, and I was happy."

But not forever. For reasons he did not choose to reveal just then, Mr. Isabella recounted that after a decade he became tired and gave up. For the past ten years he had lived as I saw him now.

"I cough. I sleep too much. I smoke," he said in his low, pleasant voice. "Lately I have become inexplicably difficult to talk to."

And that, apparently, was all that Charlie Isabella felt I needed to know about his life. As his cousin requested, he had talked, and now he was finished. Having given me this glimpse of what he insisted was the unremarkable life of an unremarkable man, it was now up to me to . . . to what? I wondered.

"Well, at some point I'll need the secrets," I said, looking into the blue eyes that peered at me now with no hint of emotion.

Mr. Isabella was silent.

"Can you wade?" I asked.

"I suppose."

"Fine. I'll meet you next week at the boathouse on Silver Pond. Same time. We'll wade."

Perhaps it was the day. The same warm wind that had blown shadows across Mr. Isabella when we first met was now tossing honeysuckle and blueberry into waves of greenery that rolled to the edge of Silver Pond. Redwing blackbirds conversed in the rushes that crowded either side of a modest dock on a narrow beach, and a late afternoon sun skipped and darted across the ruffled water. The ungainly Mr. Isabella propped himself against the multiple trunks of a swamp maple, shook off his shoes, and rolled up his pants. Together we advanced upon the shallows of Silver Pond.

"I think I have always been afraid of life," Mr. Isabella began with remarkable openness, as we waded some dozen feet from shore to a point where the hurrying wavelets splashed against our kneecaps. "And afraid of people." There was a long pause. "Looking back, I can see that it started as early as ninth grade. I was sent to the academy then. My cousin Jimmy wasn't. I hated being away from the family, and the more I resented the dislocation, the more I resented the family that sent me away. I got no support.

"So I learned to do without my family and to concentrate instead on drawing and making things," he said, rocking slightly. "I hid away."

Charlie Isabella proceeded to tell me about the hours he spent alone each weekend in the little workshop he had built for himself above the family's carriage house.

"I copied flowers from *The American Flora*," he said, "and soon I could reproduce them perfectly. Later I copied Martin Johnson Heade." He was rocking in earnest now. "I used his orchids and passionflowers."

As I grew increasingly dizzy watching the waves slip by and Mr. Isabella sway, he returned in his mind to his solitary perch above the garage where he fashioned flowers out of wire, drew them into designs for jewelry, taught himself to solder, and immersed himself in the pleasures of imagination.

"It was a happy time," he said sadly.

And productive. By the time he went to RISD (or "Risdee," as everyone in Rhode Island calls the School of Design), he had developed a style of his own that was both sensuous and organic. From his description, his earrings and brooches had a pendulous, almost decadent quality about them, like ripe fruit that dreams of dropping off the vine. I suspected that Charetta shared something of this vine-ripened quality, because Mr. Isabella would invariably go from discussing jewelry to describing his life with her. I gathered that she had "attractions"—not the least of which was the horrendous effect she had on his family. (I did not know yet that Charetta was black, but I did understand that she was not welcomed by his family and also that she alone nurtured Charlie's fierce, resentful hope for "uncomplicated happiness.")

It was at this point, apparently, that Mr. Isabella began to pretend he was ordinary, the better to steal up on life's simple pleasures. He worked as a finish carpenter, although he was always too slow, rebuilt carburetors and alternators at a big greasy garage, and even tried driving a newspaper truck at four in the morning. Mostly, however, he did not work, he told me again, this time explaining that there were times when it was all he could do merely to hang on.

"Hang on?" I echoed.

"Literally."

He paused for several minutes as if changing reels on an old projector. "When the boys were little there were days I was so depressed I couldn't walk, couldn't move. I don't know where it came from, this blackness, but it was in me." He paused again. "Charetta worked late, and it was my job to get the boys off to school. I remember crawling—actually crawling—into their room. I would focus on getting to the blue-painted footboard and then I'd pull myself up on the bed." (Here I found myself picturing the elderly, barefoot Mr. Isabella in his rumpled suit crawling across a dingy bedroom floor.) "I would hang on at the end of the bed and fight off . . . fight the . . . ah . . ."

"Voices?"

"No . . . not exactly. More like waves of bad news, waves of inevitability. Each time one hit, I *knew* I was supposed to give up. I *knew* it was hopeless. There was such dread, too, such crushing certainty of damnation.

"Of course, some days I couldn't get out of bed at all," he said, pulling himself up a bit self-consciously, "but it's hard to remember now. I suppose you'd say I was crazy."

"That doesn't explain much," I countered, dodging an important question with a standard psychological maneuver, "what would you call it?"

"Worse than dead."

"Was it during these times that you tried to kill yourself?" I asked, although I already knew the answer.

"No, that was later," he said with some embarrassment. "I thought about it then, but I didn't have anything to lose."

Mr. Isabella was still for a minute as if pondering his curious answer, and then, having climbed up from those sad South Providence memories, he moved ahead from what I imagined was depression to the other extreme in his life, a time of voracious living. Rocking again, he told me of his passionate affair with the land. It had begun simply with the adoption of his new wife's commitment to recycling, retreats, and powwows, and it had proceeded quickly with his own interest in reforestation and nature conservancy. As I listened to him go on, quite beautifully, about seedlings and saplings, drumming and Indians, phone campaigns and fund raisers, I thought I sensed a driven, possibly manic quality underlying his dedication, but this he emphatically denied. He had not been extreme, he argued. One got used to recycling, and it became second nature. He also claimed that it was easy for him to make whatever he needed (from a toothbrush holder to a sweat lodge), and that he enjoyed immersing himself in Indian lore. He listened to Slow Turtle, visited the ceremonial sites of the Nauset and Narragansett Wampanoags, grew his own herbs, and ate pokeweed and fiddleheads.

Even when I questioned his intense attraction to the Indians themselves, and to one woman whom he mentioned with particular reverence, he saw nothing unusual in his devotion. And yet when he spoke of the dusty, barefoot dancing or the late-night games of fireball with blackened Indians kicking a flaming, kerosene-soaked ball back and forth across a dark field, there was a vibrancy in his voice that set my mind to wondering. Not only were the scenes he painted exciting in themselves, but there was, beyond the obvious, a buzzing cloud of mysteries. Had he experienced an unusually long and muted manic episode during the happy years, as his records, if benignly interpreted, suggested? Or was there something about ecology and Indians that had allowed this man who usually drew back from life to throw himself headlong into an active, communal existence? The depression at either end of Mr. Isabella's life seemed real enough to me, but the glorious eight- or ten-year interlude—the period that he insisted upon calling "the last happy time"—was out of focus. And the more I learned about it, the more bizarre it seemed to be.

For six or seven years after redirecting his life, Mr. Isabella told me, he had spiraled upward into an ever busier and more productive life. He supported Indian affairs and raised four wolflike dogs who became his constant companions and became, I imagined, a familiar sight to those he referred to as "the fruit and berry motorcycle gang." (Later he showed me a photo of himself in a VW beetle festooned with smiling, raggedy kids and panting dogs.) At the same time, he was active in a nature conservancy project and was personally reforesting an abandoned ski slope.

That all this activity drove an ever-widening wedge between him and his wife, he did not mind, he said. He was living at last within the demanding security of Kehtean's embrace, and although the work was hard, the choices were clear and easy to make. Having taken the Great Spirit as his guide, his only job was to keep the channel open between them so that he knew how best to help. It was during one of those first open times that he received the gift of reading shadows.

"It began in the evening of a day not unlike today," he told me, his quiet voice drifting out across the now less agitated water. "I had been out on a retreat for several days and had returned curiously unsatisfied. I had not slept much, eaten less, and I was more than usually irritable. My wife and I had taken separate rooms by then, and I was relieved to be able to retire without fuss or explanation."

Here Charlie Isabella paused, and for a second I thought that this generally inexpressive man was going to smile. "I remember lying down in my bed and noticing that the evening sun coming through the windows cast the shadows of trees on the opposite wall. I began watching them, and it was like a movie—a movie with a divided screen made by the mullions of the windows. In each of the squares was a gently waving shadow that moved like . . . well, like a dancer performing some ritual. Billowing shadows parted and came back together, moved and lay still, and gradually I sensed not that the shapes were shifting across the wall as the sun set, but that the earth was turning. Lying on my bed I could actually *feel* the earth turning as it whirled through space.

"I knew then that the Great Spirit was with me, really with me, and he was showing *me* all the harmonies of his world."

After a pause, Mr. Isabella continued: "I think I watched the shadows until the sun went down, but in any case I remember thinking as they rolled across the bedroom wall that they were pointing, very quietly, to what is important. It's hard to explain, but I became literate then in an entirely new way." His voice dropped lower. "I could read those shadows with my heart."

"And now?" I ventured as the sun dipped behind a tall tree and we headed unsteadily back toward shore.

"It's over. I no longer notice shadows at all. I became lazy, even greedy, you see. I stopped trying, and I was rejected. Now," he said, shrugging, "it's a matter of drifting back to the bottom."

"Because you lost the enchantment?"

"Exactly," he answered in surprise.

"Then why come to me?"

"It's part of admitting defeat," he said without apparent rancor. "You can't give me back what I lost, but you can witness the decline."

"Terrific," I said as we scuffed on our shoes. "I'll be your ah—"

"Undertaker," he supplied.

≈   ≈   ≈

In spite of this unusual beginning, Charlie Isabella and I settled cautiously into what appeared to be a conventional therapeutic alliance complete with trials of antidepressant medication, which curiously had no effect on his heavy heart. For my
part, I was more interested in the flashes of enthusiasm he
showed for the happy years, and whether they were simply good
years, a manic high, or a complete fabrication threaded into his
past to explain his present feelings of loss, I could tell that his
heart was still devoted to that time. In more scientific terms, I
wanted to know whether Mr. Isabella had enjoyed a remission
from his depression during "the last happy time," suffered a
long manic episode, or had succumbed to a curious psychotic
interlude. In addition, I wanted to draw out this talented, eccentric man. I wanted to hear more of his quietly animated stories
of luscious jewelry and dancing shadows. On his part, Charlie
Isabella continued to come to the clinic both because therapy
was supposed to document his decline and because he was
slightly intrigued by my own enthusiasm, which reflected the
continued existence of some small part of the happy Isabella—
or so I thought.

After meeting for several months, I had a clearer picture of
Mr. Isabella's history, although the personalities of those closest
to him remained so remarkably flat that I never got a real feel
for what had gone on in the big house in Providence a half-century earlier. Without feelings, I discovered, I could gather facts
but almost no information. Nevertheless, I gradually formed a
picture of a man who had felt either insecure or angry most of
his life. In each of many situations—family, school, and marriage—Mr. Isabella felt set up for inevitable failure by being
forced to meet spectacularly rigid expectations with no understanding and little support. This disagreeable combination was
first encountered within the bosom of his ambitious family.
Apparently his parents—as attractive as they were singlemind-
edly devoted to their own preoccupations—expected their two
sons to enhance the family's status by succeeding in grand and
unambiguous ways. Enrico Jr. played along as best he could,
although his health broke down at inopportune times; whereas

Charlie, admitting to a more rebellious nature, learned to throw himself off the right track more actively. His pattern was to succeed marvelously at whatever he turned his hand to, just long enough for parents and later for employers, wife, and even therapists to understand that he was a man of talent. Then, presumably fearing that he would fail to live up to the promise he'd seductively displayed, he abruptly walked away from the job-at-hand leaving volcanoes of rage rumbling behind him. Initially, this pattern of pulling back was an innocent reaction, in the sense that it was triggered by a desire to avoid his family's unfailing criticism. For example, when I asked him for his earliest memory, a technique some psychologists use to elicit the important themes that run through a person's life, he told me that when he was five he had been working on a picture puzzle his Uncle Carlo sent from Italy showing a girl sitting under a tree.

"I remember that I couldn't finish it," he said, his mind drifting back to the black and white tiled kitchen of the family's opulent east side home, "so I hid it in a basket of potatoes."

"And then what happened?" I asked.

"I don't know, but I'm sure my grandmother screamed at me. She always screamed at me. My grandfather had to translate."

Later in life, merely the possibility of being criticized for not completing a task was enough to send Mr. Isabella scurrying for cover—a maneuver he called "being rejected for good reasons" but that others wrathfully called "copping out" for no reason at all. The words he used to describe his rupture with Kehtean—"I stopped trying, and I was rejected"—came straight from his childhood and had not been modified by the understanding that ideally comes with age. At fifty-nine, he remained as perpetually ready to be disappointed and to disappoint as if he still lived with his handsome, smiling family in Providence.

To confirm my growing suspicion that Mr. Isabella's life had progressed in a series of cycles that began with social acceptance—perhaps while he was showing off his talents—and proceeded through times of escalating demands and resentments to the inevitable withdrawal and depression, I asked him to describe how the good times in his life had begun. He tried to comply. He told me a little about his boys, a little about a friend at RISD who dyed his hair blue, but it became clear that the seasons he had spent in the company of Indians had vitalized him in a way that nothing else ever had. At the core of this experience swayed the mysterious figure of Cassandra Sousa, a sixty-year-old doyenne who had passed her moons, as the Indians would say, and had time to guide. It was she who befriended Charlie Isabella and connected him to the Wampanoag community.

It was hard to know where the "truth" of Mr. Isabella's stories about Cassandra Sousa lay and where loneliness or even illness had added lush detail. At first he spoke of this mythical woman only in abstractions:

"I recognized her immediately as my guide," he would say. Or, "I sensed that she knew all the rituals and remedies." But gradually he recalled seeing her dressed in buckskin dancing behind a trailer at the edge of the fairgrounds or watching dust rise from her moccasined feet as she pounded rhythms into the hard New England soil, scenes that gave her a real presence. Just five feet tall and possessed of remarkable grace, Cassandra wore her hair in a single gray braid that hung to her waist and swung when she danced. Mr. Isabella encountered her, and her husband, at almost every powwow on the Northeast circuit, he told me. He particularly recalled that she could draw the incense stick around and across each person who stood in a prayer circle more beautifully than anyone he had ever seen. She had drawn it around him one hot, humming night, and as she held it before him so that he could sweep the smoke of sage and cedar and old wisdom into his inelastic lungs, he knew that she, too, had the gift of reading shadows.

He confronted her with this intuition at the next powwow, and it came as no surprise to him when she not only acknowledged the ability but called it the mark of a mystic. There followed two years, or rather two summers and two golden falls, of wonderful communion. When they were together, head to head over lemon balm tea or palm to wrinkled palm over an offering of rose water, Mr. Isabella felt himself appreciated as never before. And when they were apart, connected only by their habit of reading shadows, it became clearer still that she accepted his silent and unusual gifts.

"Shadows connected us in a special way," Mr. Isabella said, and I thought his eyes were daring me to call this mental illness. "I would think of her while watching the shadows merge and spread on the bedroom wall, and we would send each other"—he paused—"messages of love."

"Were you physically attracted to Cassandra?" I asked, bringing the conversation back to earth with a thump.

"Yes."

"Did you become her lover?"

"Not exactly."

"Not exactly," I echoed.

"No. Not exactly.

"Besides," he added a minute later, "Cassandra guided others."

"At the same time?"

"No, later."

"She left you for another."

"The time was right," he said dispassionately, then added, possibly for the first time in his life, "I was hurt.

"It was my fault," he added quickly. "I was distracted by my divorce. But yes, it hurt."

That was not quite the end of Mr. Isabella's shadowy affairs. At the same time that he was joyously exploring a mystical portion of the world with Cassandra Sousa, he was also reforesting an ordinary ski slope. In this arena it was he who led, and among his helpers the most devoted were identical twin girls, about eighteen years old, who had grown up in what used to be called reform schools and are now, with late-twentieth-century delicacy referred to as "residential placements." For these tough young women, he served as a spiritual companion—which he again claimed meant deep understanding, physical attraction, but no sex. He spoke of trusting them, of "tolerating their bad character," whatever that meant, and of passing along to them "some of the things they had missed in childhood." And that was it. I have a picture of the three of them eating spaghetti in

Mr. Isabella's kitchen after a long day planting seedlings, but it is largely composed of my own imaginings. And I have another image of a certain pleasant tension pervading the room as one or the other of the girls glanced up to find Charlie looking at her intently, but this, too, is based on innuendo. In any event, after Cassandra Sousa went on to guide someone else, Mr. Isabella briefly threw himself into his role as leader with renewed zeal. His hope, he told me, was to teach the twins to read the rolling shadows. "They had potential," he said. But not enough. Within a year he dropped everything he'd been doing for a decade, sold his VW, and gave away the four dogs.

Once Mr. Isabella had filled me in on the last happy time, I was convinced that these years were not figments of his imagination, but I was still unable to decide whether they represented a time of mental imbalance or, instead, an interlude when he was far enough removed from Isabella values and interactions to sustain a good life. The shadow business sounded awfully bizarre, but the Indians sounded like a foster family who gave him a degree of acceptance he had never experienced, and his work sounded as reasonable as the straightforward telling of his tales.

In hopes of getting a different perspective, I invited his cousin Theresa to join us. The two cousins were still squabbling over Mr. Isabella's reclusive habits, and he told me that he handled their differences by not speaking—at all.

"She sometimes catches my eye when I'm at the table," he had told me. "'So?' she'll say as I look at her. 'Still nothing? Nothing at all?'"

Cousin Theresa arrived at the clinic on a late summer afternoon when the air conditioner was broken and the air outside throbbed with the dry gratings of insects. She was a short, black-haired woman in her late forties who moved with the brusque assertiveness of a person who is accustomed to being contradicted. She sat near the door.

"What's it like to live with Cousin Charlie?" I asked her.

"He doesn't speak, so what's to tell?" she shot back, pulling her large black purse close over her stomach.

"Must be frustrating to live with someone who won't speak," I offered sympathetically.

"Hey, I'm not the boss of his mouth."

"And the smoking in bed?" I continued a few minutes later, pushing to see how far she, like her cousin, would go to deny the discord that stretched like tight elastic bands between them.

"It's only my house. If he wants to burn it down with me inside . . . ?" Cousin Theresa folded her hands with finality.

When I quizzed Theresa on the last happy time, she was a little less sure of her answers. She had not lived in the same household then, she explained, but pointed out realistically that Charlie had gotten divorced during those years and that his then teenage sons, feeling no kinship with either their father or Indians, refused to visit, much less attend powwows.

"So how happy is happy with no family?" she asked rhetorically.

"Well, he had the Indians during those years, didn't he?"

"Had them for what? Does my cousin look like an Indian to you?"

It was hard not to like Cousin Theresa.

"Did your cousin ever tell you about Cassandra Sousa?" I continued.

"Yes, yes," she answered, waving back the heat that shimmered through the casement windows. "Carlo tried to tell me funny stories, and I told him they should stay in his head, not mine."

"So you don't believe his stories?"

Cousin Theresa pursed her lips and gave an exaggerated shrug. "He should take stronger medicine."

Later in the hour I asked her if she had ever thought of her cousin as a passionate man.

Cousin Theresa looked genuinely surprised. "Well," she said after a pause, "my mother used to say that Carlo had a risky smile . . . the risky smile of a passionate man. Maybe he did."

Cousin Theresa's testimony as well as her relentlessly adversarial style answered some of my questions. Her account suggested that the last happy time was neither as simple nor as idyllic as her cousin insisted, and the mutually expressed yet unacknowledged animosity between them further suggested that Mr. Isabella's problems in sticking with anything or anyone stemmed more from old anger and abuse than from a chemically unbalanced brain. In addition, their mutual distrust of communication, which Mr. Isabella had told me was characteristic of his entire family, made it easier to understand why the last happy time remained for others "a funny story," a mythical interlude with no power to move.

"I still lie in bed and go over it in my mind—good parts and bad parts," he had once said. "But I don't talk about it."

"How can anyone understand your unhappiness if you won't discuss what you've lost?" I had asked, but, as with Cousin Theresa, he was adamant in his preference for silence over discussion, which he was sure would lead to misunderstanding. What Mr. Isabella called "meditation" I guessed was endless rumination.

With Cousin Theresa's contributions in hand, I was finally willing to bet that during the last happy time Mr. Isabella had honestly, if a bit naively, prospered. He had been supported by a well-structured movement that was so different from his upbringing that his old, destructive habits had less grist for their disagreeable mills. Later when his wife divorced him, his boys ceased visiting on weekends, the twins disappeared, and Cassandra left to guide someone else, the old passive-aggressive patterns reasserted themselves, triggering a resentful withdrawal and depression.

Having formulated this hypothesis, I now had a plan. I would help Mr. Isabella feel the old hurt that stemmed from his demanding yet neglectful parents and encourage him to express more directly and accurately the anger that those years of hurt had fostered. I expected his therapy to gain momentum.

Mr. Isabella did not. As the early autumn days began to cool, so, it seemed, did he. There were missed appointments. There were invitations to stop therapy. "Don't you think we're talked out?" he would ask. There were longer silences. When he did speak there was a slipperiness to his pronouncements that slid our conversations off the track and into a ditch. Once he called me twenty minutes after the hour had begun and announced that he was still in bed. At the beginning of this decline, Mr. Isabella and I would unconsciously take turns in rescuing therapy from the doldrums. For my part, I would charge resolutely into his past and, if I had enough momentum, I could usually jump into a pocket of interesting memories about Enrico Sr.—for example, he was so handsome that once a woman fainted at his feet—or about his sons Stamford and Compton, who had given Mr. Isabella gray hair by running drugs between South Providence and the affluent East Side. For his part, Mr. Isabella learned to reel me back from discouragement by telling me more about the Indians or, once, by smiling.

I remember the gray October afternoon when I first saw Mr. Isabella's risky smile. He had announced again that therapy was over, and, naturally, he was not about to tell me what was really on his mind. Instead, he offered me generalities.

"You won't be able to change me," he began.

"Perhaps," I replied, "but you're still too much of a mystery to let go. I haven't caught your rhythm."

"It wastes taxpayers' money," he said.

"Time will tell."

"You must be bored," he insisted.

Abruptly I burst out laughing. "You're much too smart to believe that," I said, tossing my pencil on the desk and leaning back in my chair. "I love it when you come here. I love it because you're so smart and because you're so *damned* difficult."

"You do?" he asked.

"Yes, I do," I answered.

There came across Mr. Isabella's heavy, disorganized face a look of utter astonishment. And then, for the first time since I'd known him, he smiled. Trembling briefly, his ponderous features rose in chorus and lifted themselves into a triumphant hallelujah while his sad, slightly milky blue eyes crinkled into an expression of great sweetness. Dumbfounded, I stared. I gawked. And finally my thoughts began to spin. What was it in this complicitous, all-or-nothing smile that drew me in as, in the past, it had drawn in and enchanted women, children, dogs, and gods? What was there in this quick, private smile, that felt so open for a second that it could have been a pact? My mind rose to meet this man in his eyes. I caught the rhythm.

There then ensued ten minutes, or some blissfully interminable period of time, of that cerebral cavorting that is the genuine and unique reward of my profession. My mind charged back over everything I had learned about Charlie Isabella and slammed the information into the present tense. My attention hovered, herded, ran after, pulled back. I took in his words with their hidden whispers of emotion, and I took in his tone of voice, smell, movement of lips, and tilt of head. For the moment at least, they all seemed clues of the utmost importance. I juggled his associations in one hand and with the other I collected my own ideas about everything he said. I formulated at least two questions for every sentence he spoke and tested each line of thought against what I knew about him and about the world. And when he fell silent—fell into one of those long Isabella pauses, then I really got down to work.

The minute hand on my clock, having reached the top of the hour, was now slipping past four P.M.

"See you next week," I said, handing him an appointment card.

Mr. Isabella smiled shyly. "You don't give up, do you?"

"Is that good or bad?" I asked in reply.

He shrugged.

Only days later did I ask myself what had actually happened in the ten minutes after Charlie Isabella smiled. I had not gathered any new or remarkable facts, and I had merely confirmed rather than reorganized my ideas about him. But I had seen firsthand the shy, sweet unfolding of the happy Isabella. As I sat in my office, recalling his smile, I suddenly remembered a trip I had taken to a long-forgotten garden when I was eight or nine years old. It was nearly nightfall and I remember that lightning bugs flashed through clumps of flowers that were now only darker and lighter shades of greenish gray. Someone bent over me and pointed to a viny plant that, I believe, hung down from a planter. An enormous gray blossom swung at eye level, and what I remember being told was that this great mythical blossom unfolded only one night in a hundred years. I and all who stood by me would long be dead before it bloomed again. I had not thought of that garden (nor of my mixing up a century plant and a night-blooming cereus) until I saw Charlie Isabella smile.

It occurred to me then that I had caught a glimpse not only of the last happy time but of the prize that people close to Mr. Isabella kept hoping to win away from his depression. What a powerful contradiction his smile mounted against his persistent assertions of hopelessness. What incentive it provided to those who would throw him a line and pull him back to shore.

And how angry the memory of that smile made me feel the following week when he sat before me, silent and unresponsive. As Thanksgiving approached, Mr. Isabella grew increasingly uncooperative and his dress—haphazard at best—became aggressively sloppy. I could actually feel him breaking the connections we had built together. He would arrive like a black cloud of anger, sullenly scuffling into my office, smelling of tiparillos and unwashed clothes. He no longer bothered to wear a tie or fasten his pants or tie his shoes, and when he dropped himself into the corner chair, waves of body odor radiated through the office. He was at war, all right, and the part of this fuck-you dressing that made the biggest impression on me was a deepening yellow stain that hung like a small bib beneath the collar of his shirt.

"He sleeps in that shirt," I would tell myself. "He intends to wear it until one of us dies."

For most of each hour Mr. Isabella played with his cane. After asking him three or four questions, to which he gave no reply, I, too, would fall silent. I would watch as he turned the simple ivory knob in his hands for minutes on end. I would look at the yellow stain. Sometimes I kept up a hovering attentiveness, an empty readiness to listen, but just as often I fiddled, too. I counted the rate at which Mr. Isabella turned his cane. I noted the patterns of perspiration on his shirt, pretended I could deduce his diet from spots on his jacket, and watched a reddish, trapezoidal birthmark blush and fade just above the collar of his shirt. Intermittently I asked for dreams, drawings, and whatever else I could think of to rekindle the dialogue, but his only response was a pleasant "I have nothing to say" or a bland "I'm

not thinking about anything." The old cycle had turned, and not
only was he not trying anymore, he was treating me like an
enemy he intended to starve out. He had slapped an embargo on
our commerce.

There were other problems as well. After a brief period of
panic, Mr. Isabella was finally persuaded to try yet another
antidepressant medication. Surprisingly, he reported almost
immediate improvement. Not surprisingly, he stopped taking the
pills. It was at this juncture that he admitted "cheeking" all the
previous antidepressants (storing the pills in his cheek until he
could spit them out unobserved). This explained why earlier trials had not helped and raised strong doubts about the course of
therapy.

There was also a rather lackadaisical suicide gesture that
consisted of ordering a black-handled stiletto from Italy, then
leaving it on the kitchen table for Theresa to find and confiscate.
This briefly reopened the subject of suicide, and Mr. Isabella
described for me the two attempts he had made on his life some
eight years before. The first was a straightforward overdose of
antidepressant medication mixed with alcohol. He had fallen
into a deep coma, but was inadvertently rescued some twenty-
four hours later by a neighbor. By this time his sons had moved
to California and could not (or would not) return to see their
father through the crisis.

"What was their reaction?" I asked.

"Annoyance, I guess. They gave up on me years ago. They're
Charetta's sons, not mine."

The second attempt was quite different. Despondent and
enraged at the loss of the shadows, he decided to teach Kehtean
a lesson he could not misinterpret by killing himself with the
very shadows he so cherished. Carrying only a pint of whiskey,
Mr. Isabella had driven north and picked up the Appalachian
Trail in the dead of winter. His plan was to hike up the western
face of a mountain, watch his own shadow waver, elongate, and
fade in the setting sun and die of exposure when night settled on
the mountain. Less than three hours into the plan, however, he
was intercepted by backpackers who saw at a glance that he was
dangerously underdressed and unprepared. They insisted on

escorting him back to a base camp and furthermore turned him over to the safety patrol. Mr. Isabella spent three weeks in an overheated psychiatric ward.

Except for such curiously unexciting recollections, we sat in silence as winter settled quietly over Hillsdale. Occasionally Mr. Isabella expressed annoyance at "people's" unwillingness to recognize that he had permanently, one might say terminally, changed for the worse. And occasionally I felt, but did not express, a mounting sense of frustration. In Mr. Isabella's chart I had seen remarks that expressed with unusual candor his former therapists' explosive reactions to this same letdown. I was not going to follow in their footsteps.

"Client is persistently negative and pessimistic." "Client admits he does not want therapy." "Client's self-hate and hostile silence *taunt* his therapists. He defies our every attempt to improve his outlook."

Although determined not to join these disappointed "parents," I, too, felt betrayed. I had not taken the easy route with Charlie Isabella, which would have been to build an explanation of his life and troubles around a diagnosis of lunacy. Had I done so, I could have dismissed every dancing shadow and swaying Indian as delusional. I could have juggled only those few common facts that were documented—divorced, unemployed, uninvolved as a father, self-destructive—and I could have built on that constricted armature a pitiful figure indeed. Instead, I had included in my account of his life many of his own interpretations and much of his mysteriousness. I had acted on the understanding that for a portion of his life he had embraced a system of beliefs upon which reason cannot significantly comment. And at first my willingness to respect an unusual life had paid off. As Mr. Isabella talked, his fascinating story made more and more sense to me, and he, too, had begun to revise his rigid belief in absolute and perpetual rejection to include the more common ingredients of changing affections and hurt feelings. Now, however, as he retreated, trampling over the trust I thought we had established and breaking the connections I thought we had built, the story we had begun to put together of his life seemed to curl out of shape like plastic near a flame.

I did not know immediately just why Mr. Isabella's withholding bothered me so much. After all, I knew it was part of his characteristic cycle, and I had expected each period of joining to be followed by some form of divorce. Even his profound conviction of damnation—his cosmic disappointment—was ordinary enough among the depressed. But whereas most depressed people wait sadly or numbly or noisily for some relief, even death, Mr. Isabella was elaborately determined to remain miserable. Here was the problem: he didn't want to feel better. Where was the ambivalence and anxiety, I wanted to know, that colors even deep depression? Where was the yearning that gives to hopelessness its poignant and human quality?

"I am worse than cedar rust in the orchard," he once said. "Worse than the maggot. I'm a spoiler."

"And what does that mean?"

"It means I am too lazy and stupid to do what's right, even when it's laid out for me, stuck under my long nose."

"And?"

"And I damage what others create, then suffer the punishment. Nothing will change this."

"Nothing will change you?"

"That's right."

Therapy limped along through the winter and nothing ever did change Charlie Isabella's determination to remain inconsolable, nor did anything change my determination to rekindle some portion of his old enthusiasm. And yet, some peculiar shiftings and sortings were going on beneath our apparent deadlock.

This became clear one lovely day in April, when a slightly more contained Mr. Isabella sat down in the chair opposite mine. He wore a new gray silk tie, which contrasted oddly with his wrinkled suit, and for the first time since I had known him he had snugged the knot up tight against his collar. His shirt was washed, too, and his shoes tied. Nevertheless, trying to pick up our usual themes was useless that afternoon, and the session lurched off in all the wrong directions. Five minutes before he was to leave, however, Mr. Isabella cleared his throat and announced that he and Cousin Theresa were returning to Providence to live with her ailing sister. I was taken totally by surprise.

"No!" I wanted to say. "You can't leave now. I want to know if you're going to start living again or if you're going to continue your breath-holding contest with the Great Spirit."

"I can't afford this anymore," Mr. Isabella was saying, waving his cane in a gesture that seemed to encompass me, the clinic, and Hillsdale. "We're moving to Providence. Cousin Jimmy is moving us down in two weeks."

"*Two weeks?*" I spluttered. "And you wait until the end of *this* hour to tell me? Don't you think that's cowardly, leaving us just one more hour to . . . I mean it's the old Isabella now-you-see-me-now-you-don't maneuver."

Mr. Isabella looked me straight in the eye. His heavy eyebrows lifted slightly and he began to smile.

"I *am* the old Isabella," he said, to my surprise.

It was my turn to gaze sadly across the plain office at the indomitably miserable and gently smiling Mr. Isabella. Sharp shadows from the windows divided him into shifting parallelograms that, I found myself recalling, proved that the earth still turned. My mind went back to the afternoon we had waded in Silver Pond. "I think I have always been afraid of life" he had said then, and I imagined an old home movie run alternately forward then backward, in which Mr. Isabella constantly waded into the water and backed out, waded in and backed out.

"I had hoped that you would want to live again," I said slowly. "You know, put down roots and—"

"Kehtean was my roots, my trunk, my leaves," he broke in, continuing the metaphor. "I have never been able to do these things on my own. I was given a happy time in exchange for obedience, and I am not a good or an obedient person."

"Children talk like that."

"And so do adults who have never learned to love. We are incomplete. Unreachable."

A breeze had begun to move the budding branches outside the office window and thin wisps of shadows were beginning to stroke Mr. Isabella's old suit. Charlie Isabella rose slowly from his chair.

"I think I am unreachable because I have no love in me, nothing to connect to," he said seriously. "I've been trying to tell you that."

"But you reach me," I replied, looking up at the strange, unruly man who was stalled in the middle of my office. "If you are such a terrible, sealed-off person, why do you tell me beautiful stories? Why do you smile?"

Charlie Isabella rested on his cane. His shaggy eyebrows crept down over his wrinkled eyes in a deep frown. "I am surprised by how much I have told you about my life," he said, nodding slightly but still looking at the floor. "You might say we've gone on a journey through . . . well, into parts of my life. Not one I trust," he added quickly, glancing at me. "I mean the punishment still lies ahead. But a journey."

I gave Mr. Isabella his last appointment card, and we shook hands solemnly. His flickering blue eyes met mine briefly and expressed again the distant, bemused curiosity I had first noticed nearly two years before. I heard him walk down the hall, and moments later I heard a car leave the lot. Crossing the office, I sat down in his chair, held my hands the way he did, bent my head as he had done, and watched the attenuated reminders of branches ripple in across the floor. I felt beaten and strangely pleased. Whatever conditions had convinced Charlie Isabella so many years before that obedient dependence and stubborn rebellion were his only choices in life had eluded me, or rather, us. I did not think we had seriously embarked upon that journey of discovery and change. Yet we had not merely held each other off, either. He had enchanted me with shadows and with a smile as rare as a century plant. He had stubbornly urged me out of the usual precincts of psychology into a broader and more difficult terrain. He had convinced me he had experienced that last happy time, which, quite possibly, was the one great gift he felt he still possessed. Struggling through the seasons with the disheveled Mr. Isabella, I had not managed to give him what I thought he needed, but neither had I been his undertaker as he'd originally planned. Together we had taken a detour on the way to his anticipated hell.

"It has become more difficult for me to leave life," he had said during the stiletto incident. "I keep trying, but not very hard."

"A detour," I thought to myself as I continued to watch the late afternoon shadows from Mr. Isabella's point of view, "a detour in a trip I cannot follow any longer."

And although I am old enough to understand that I will not be able to read to the end of all the stories I have started, I do not accept such natural disappointments gracefully. Like a planter of bulbs faced with a winter move, hopeful and unsatisfied, I am left with the budding shadows of branches that remind me of a story that Charlie Isabella and I had just begun to tell.

4

THE PSYCHOLOGY OF CONFIDING

However much we are affected by the things of the world, however deeply they may stir and stimulate us, they become human for us only when we can discuss them with our fellows. . . . We humanize what is going on in the world and in ourselves only by speaking of it, and in the course of speaking of it we learn to be human.

HANNAH ARENDT

CHARLIE ISABELLA WAS NEARLY THREE TIMES THE AGE OF CHUCK Willet when he spent those two years at the Hillsdale Clinic renegotiating and humanizing the story of his life with me. During our weekly visits, he did what Chuck could not manage. He began to talk to me about his life in terms that I could understand and comment on. He began to tell the rambling, private kind of story we call *confiding*. Some psychologists now argue that in so doing, a patient such as Mr. Isabella was not only changing his outlook on the very events he described but also giving himself a measure of protection against his chronic bronchitis. Confiding, these investigators maintain, affects an individual's physical as well as mental health.

Much of the work on confiding has grown out of studies of misfortune and, especially over the past fifteen years, the ordinary person's reactions—both public and private—to the death of a spouse or a child, the onset of a serious illness, sexual abuse, and the like have been investigated in an attempt to understand the normal processes of grief and adaptation. In general, psychologists have found that these unexpected reversals shatter a person's perception of living in a just and orderly world and compromise his or her sense of being secure and in control. For at least a year after the misfortune—much longer periods are suggested by recent studies—the shaken individual is also likely to be depressed, anxious, distracted, prone to accidents, and more than usually vulnerable to physical breakdowns, which range from colds to cancer.[1]

During the years of active grieving, the majority of mourners report that they ruminate about the event, not only reviewing or reliving it in their minds but asking again and again some common questions: "What if I'd done something different?" "Why me or my child?" "Why did this happen?" "What is to blame?" "What now?" In other words, the survivors of misfortune struggle through a period of emotional and constitutional disability, speaking as if they needed to make sense of their misfortune before recommitting their full energies to living. Psychologists who investigate how these people go about the rebuilding of their worlds and themselves suspect that "making sense," or as we might say, "getting at the narrative truth of the experience," is a key part of the remodeling process that must take place before the world again seems manageable and the self secure. As the storyteller Isak Dinesen is supposed to have said, anything can be tolerated if you can turn it into a story.

Recently it has become apparent that some people go public in this quest for meaning—they like to confide—and some do not. By talking to close friends, joining a self-help group, finding a therapist, or confessing their guilt and fears to a religious per-

1. Darrin Lehman, Camille Wortman, and Allan Williams, "Long-term Effects of Losing a Spouse or Child in a Motor Vehicle Crash," *Journal of Personality and Social Psychology* 52 (1987): 218–31.

son, the former try to assimilate the difficult event into their lives in the presence of others. More private individuals hold the pain in their hearts and deal with it alone.

That confiding assuages distress more quickly than silence is no new discovery.

"The best way for ease is to impart our misery to some friend, not to smother it up in our own breast," Robert Burton reminded readers of the *Anatomy of Melancholy*, which, although published in 1621, drew on the wisdom of classical scholars who had thought about the effects of confiding long before. "A friend's counsel is a charm like mandrake wine, *curas sopit* [it assuages our care]; and as a bull that is tied to a fig tree becomes gentle on a sudden, so is a savage, obdurate heart mollified by fair speeches. 'All adversity finds ease in complaining . . . '"[2]

Freud agreed, although for somewhat more complicated reasons. At the end of the nineteenth century, he and his colleague Josef Breuer developed the cathartic method, which emphasized the importance of remembering and talking about traumatic experiences, especially in the relief of hysterical symptoms. A half-century later, it was noted that certain psychosomatic problems such as asthma, ulcers, or high blood pressure could be relieved by encouraging the patient to confess repressed desires. Still later it was noted that talking with others or even writing about one's problems could do the same. Recent experiments have found that when therapy begins, use of medical facilities drops.[3] Today investigators study in detail the particular ways in which confiding affects our physical resistance to disease and our mental defenses against anxiety and, especially, depression.

For over a decade, James Pennebaker, a psychologist at Southern Methodist University, has been conducting a series of investigations on the physiological correlates of confiding. One of the first observations he made, studying the effect confiding had on men and women who had recently lost their spouses

2. Robert Burton, *The Anatomy of Melancholy* (New York: Vintage Books, 1932), pp. ii, 107.

3. E. Mumford, H. J. Schlesinger, and G. V. Glass, "Reducing Medical Costs through Mental Health Treatment," in *Linking Health and Mental Health*, ed. A. Broskowski et al. (Beverly Hills, CA: Sage, 1981).

either by suicide or in accidents, was that the more his subjects talked about their feelings, the less they were likely to ruminate or worry. In addition, the more they confided, the fewer additional health problems they experienced in the year following their loss.[4] Pennebaker did not yet know exactly why this should be so, but he pointed out that the act of talking about the upsetting event could be useful for a number of reasons. First, there is the reminder that others have suffered similar losses—that one is not alone. There is also a sense of support as friends rally to provide food, comfort, information, and other services. And finally there is a subtler benefit that confiding bestows, which is that, as opposed to ruminating, actually talking about the sad event forces a person to organize the experience in a way that makes it understandable both to the listener and to the teller. A story of "how he died," "how I fell ill," or even of "how I found and lost the last happy time" are all attempts to explain what happened by the rules that our culture has agreed must be followed if an account is to make sense. This same movement from confusion toward the clarification of an account also occurs in writing, to which any diarist will attest and as we will see later in chapter 13.

On the other hand, Pennebaker pointed out, there are disadvantages to silence—at least for the body. Summarizing previous studies, he noted that nonconfiders have been found to have higher rates of disease, higher mortality rates from certain illnesses, and a more exaggerated response to stress. In his own studies, Pennebaker and his colleagues expanded upon these observations. In one investigation they asked college undergraduates (psychology's guinea pigs) to write about either the most traumatic and stressful event of their lives or about a trivial topic. Each of the students wrote about his or her selected event on four consecutive days. Some subjects were told to set down only facts, others were instructed to concentrate on feelings, and members of a third group were asked to describe both facts and feelings. The students who wrote out their feelings (or facts and

4. James Pennebaker and Robin O'Heeron, "Confiding in Others and Illness Rate Among Spouses of Suicide and Accidental-Death Victims," *Journal of Abnormal Psychology* 93 (1984): 473–76.

feelings) about stressful events reported feeling much more upset
than those who wrote on trivial topics or merely stated the facts
of their adversity. Blood pressure measurements rose among the
students who were actively remembering traumas, which included
such misfortunes as death of a sister, rape, or serious accidents.
A day or so later, however, these students felt calm and their
blood pressure had dropped, not just back to their baseline levels but to points below, as if getting troubles off their chests had
helped their insides relax. Six months later Pennebaker checked
records in the student health center and found that the emotionally expressive students had visited less often than other subjects. In addition, the students who had written out their feelings
reported fewer days of restricted activity and a general feeling of
better health. Pennebaker concluded that communicating traumatic events with feeling fostered health. He surmised that the
nonconfiders were unwittingly expending a great deal of energy
inhibiting their emotions and that these inhibitory processes—
expressed as muscle tension, raised blood pressure, and other
autonomic activity—might open the door to psychosomatic
problems. Indeed, his next experiments, in which he collected
blood samples from confiders and nonconfiders before and after
the writing exercise, showed that the inhibitory processes that
characteristically remained high in the nonconfiding students
were lowering their bodies' immune response. Stating Pennebaker's conclusion more positively, confiding reduced autonomic activity—reduced sweating, tensing, and higher blood
pressure that go along with nervousness—and, in taking these
burdens off the body, either preserved or actually enhanced its
capacity to fight off disease.[5] This model of confiding suggests
that therapy may have helped Mr. Isabella get through the winter without an attack of bronchitis, although we cannot know
for sure.

So much for confiding and physical health. What is it about
talking earnestly with another person that seems to preserve
mental health as well? Another way of asking approximately the

    5. James Pennebaker, J. Kiecott-Glaser, and R. Glaser, "Disclosure of
Trauma and Immune Function: Health Implications for Psychotherapy,"
Journal of Consulting and Clincial Psychology 56 (1988): 239–45.

same question is to try to ascertain what it is about putting grief, fear, or confusion into words that change the speaker's outlook on the very event he or she is relating. There are two parts to this: one is an examination of the difference between ruminating and recounting; the other is an investigation of what goes on when two people talk about themselves to each other.

First, worrying or ruminating. Of the several ways we have of organizing experience—thinking, telling stories, writing formulas, making graphs, and so forth—worrying is one of the most primitive and least controlled.[6] Unlike narrative accounts that require effort to organize, worrisome thoughts flow effortlessly through the heads of the anxious. Charlie Isabella, for example, spent hours every day troubled, in a flat sort of way, by fragmented fantasies that alerted him to the torment that lay ahead. Although he maintained that his dismal procession of ideas could not be put into words, he acknowledged that they were largely previews of impending disaster. One of the few scenes he managed to describe for me involved leading his family into the path of an avalanche where they perished, he last of all.

Research done on these bursts of negative thoughts and images suggests that they resemble fear reactions, except that worrying is triggered by ideas rather than actual events. Unfortunately, these ideas have a way of proliferating, and any topic that is drawn in or associated with the worrying then becomes a trigger for further rumination. Soon almost every topic, person, and situation that is encountered triggers a burst of fearful possibilities.

A second and more curious aspect of chronic worrying is that in some magical way it seems to protect worriers from still greater anxiety and is therefore subconsciously nurtured. One experimenter reported that many of his subjects realized intellectually that their worries were illogical. At the same time they all worried that if they did not worry, the events they feared would be more likely to happen.[7]

6. T. D. Borkovec, E. Robinson, T. Pruzinsky, and J. A. Depree, "Preliminary Exploration of Worry: Some Characteristics and Processes," *Behaviour Research and Therapy* 21 (1983): 9–16.

7. Borkovec et al., "Preliminary Exploration of Worry," p. 9.

Both in and out of the laboratory, worrying has been found to put people in a bad mood, disrupt their ability to concentrate, foster indecisiveness, and focus their thoughts far more on what may go wrong than on what can be done about it. Worrying tends to be an intensely private, self-perpetuating process that remains unresolved first because a thorough examination of the problem is not made and second because no action is taken.

Narrative accounts are different. Whether they are spoken or written, shared or kept private, as in a journal, stories take information and organize it in such a way that it is comprehensible to other people. Unlike worries, stories make sense of a situation by integrating the unexpected into the normal scheme of things, and this, in turn, suggests possible actions.

In simplest terms, a narrative is a succession of events that fit into a plot that is experienced by some feeling creature. It usually concerns people, it has a sequence of causes and effects that unfolds, and it links the out-of-the-ordinary to the ordinary in a way that makes the unusual event understandable. This last quality is of great importance, for the search for the extenuating circumstance that allows us to fit the unfamiliar experience back into the known world is the mechanism by which narration allows us to resolve the conflicts and contradictions that arise both among people and within an individual.[8] In short, language is our main tool for creating and then negotiating what we think of as "reality."

With Charlie Isabella, the path from worrying to confiding took a long time to negotiate, and thinking aloud with a trusted friend never became habitual. When, for example, he first broke off his relationship with Cassandra Sousa, he says he forgot about her by turning his mind to the reforestation project. However, he remembers one of the twins climbing wearily into the backseat of his VW at the end of a fourteen-hour day, saying, "Christ, Charlie, does your Indian god want us to work ourselves to death?" He had wondered, then, if he was running away from something, but he decided work was what Kehtean

8. Jerome Bruner, *Acts of Meaning* (Cambridge: Harvard University Press, 1990).

wanted him to do. Only when he swung from frantic activity to withdrawal a year or so later did Mr. Isabella begin to put his wordless worries and hurt into a crude story. Initially, he told himself that because he disappointed Cassandra, she rejected him. He said to himself that because he had let down Kehtean, the last happy time came to an end. These were the stories he brought to the clinic—abstract, unemotional, and incomplete—a poor antidote for worries. Thus when I first met Charlie Isabella, he had attempted to make some sense of the ups and downs in his life, but not in a way that satisfied anyone. He had left out too much of the information—the beautiful stories, the jewelry designs, the reforested ski slope, the smiles and sadness. In his first accounts to me, he had not satisfied any of the requirements of a good narrative, and his story was not coherent, believable, comprehensive, or livable. It was the kind of narrow, poorly formed story that results from excessive rumination and no discussion.[9]

When Charlie Isabella finally came to the clinic and tentatively began to confide in me, his story began to change. Many therapists would simply say that talking put Charlie in touch with his feelings. Others might point out that remembering aloud tends to enhance the narrative truth of private accounts. Bruno Bettelheim has said that therapy is the development of an intensely personal relationship that convinces the client of the value of other relationships.[10] But at least one artificial intelligence expert would claim that these good things happened because confiding gave Charlie a chance to listen to himself talk.

In his book *Tell Me a Story*, Roger Schank transposed the process of understanding into terms of storytelling in hopes of learning what it would take to build a machine that seems to understand what we tell it. He discovered that for a person (or a machine) understanding an account means mapping the story

9. In a study of the speech patterns of a large family, Jerome Bruner noted that the "bad-luck" boy used more mixed-up and incomplete sentences than the others. His narratives were less structured than those of his more successful siblings. *Acts of Meaning*, p. 130.

10. Bruno Bettelheim and Alvin A. Rosenfeld, *The Art of the Obvious: Developing Insight for Psychotherapy and Everyday Life* (New York: Alfred A. Knopf, 1993), p. 28.

being heard onto one's own fund of explanations and beliefs. In
other words, to convey understanding a speaker must find and
then relate a story from a personal fund of experience that captures the gist of what the speaker is talking about. Different listeners understand the same story in different ways because the
stories they know and tell back to the speaker are bound to be
different.[11]

Schank found that when he asked a student to "say something back" to a monologue from a movie, for example, as if the
student were having a conversation with the character, out came
a personal story. In the majority of cases the response was simple and could be subsumed under the heading, "the same thing
once happened to me." What that "same thing" was, however,
differed greatly from student to student and depended on what
each had experienced in his or her lifetime.

According to Schank, then, when Charlie Isabella told me
about the dancing shadows, he judged whether or not I understood him by the kind of story I told back. If it was "the same
thing once happened to me" kind of story he would feel understood. If it was "I've never heard of such a thing" or "the same
thing happened to one of my very sick patients," he would *feel*
that I had not understood him. Depending on my response, he
could also feel partially understood.

Although it appears from the foregoing that the goal in an
exchange of stories is for two people to gain a better understanding of each other, Schank noticed that a goal of equal
importance seemed to be the enhanced understanding an individual gains of himself from telling his own stories to different
people in different contexts. Schank would say, for example,
that as Charlie and I talked back and forth about shadows, families, and lovers, we expanded and elucidated those parts of our
own stories that were not yet entirely clear in our own minds. In
other words, we learned about ourselves by listening to our own
explanations. As Schank's college students had done in saying
something back to movie monologues, so Charlie and I filled in

11. Roger Schank, *Tell Me a Story* (New York: Charles Scribner's Sons,
1991).

gaps and finished off our own stories with insights that the other person's questions suggested.

For example, Charlie initially maintained that Cassandra's decision to leave him and guide another man on a spiritual quest did not bother him. Whatever emotions the event had actually stirred up had been energetically denied. Although this was neither an accurate nor a useful story, Charlie stood by it. Then in therapy—that rather lopsided example of confiding—I responded repeatedly to Charlie's "Cassandra story" by telling one that could be called "people get hurt when someone they love walks out." Eventually he incorporated this observation into his own account, where it took him by surprise and he changed his story.

"It hurt," he finally said, adding, much later, "I was surprised to hear myself say that. I don't know where it came from, but it fit."

Schank makes the same point again and again. We learn about ourselves—meaning we modify and complete our stories—less by listening to others than by talking to them. We learn by listening to what comes out of our own mouths. When it fits, we take it to heart.

So Charlie listened to himself tell of loving and losing and being lonely, and I listened to myself say that the last happy time existed and that it was not the product of a faulty mind. Both of our changes illustrate the process of confiding or, if you will, of constructing a negotiated narrative. His memories and my uncertainties were reworked, from stories so narrow and private that they could not be shared with each other or with a larger society, into accounts that began to connect us to each other and to alternate ways of seeing and doing things. For Charlie, putting experience into words for another person had in a small way transposed his private suffering into a story that could be taken up and acted upon. It returned him to the community—a little.

Some seven months after Charlie Isabella left Hillsdale, I received a hand-drawn card showing a winter oak forest in the rain—and I knew the Indians were back. The message was brief. "Apartment O.K. I help out Sats. at Narragansett Center. Best wishes."

I pictured Charlie Isabella in his rumpled suit, cane in hand, walking up the broad stone steps of the cultural center where dark-eyed children learn to pound the hard New England soil with their moccasined feet and bind herbs together with silky strands of red and yellow thread. At least for now, the detour around Hell that Mr. Isabella and I had built along a slender causeway of confiding was holding him within a kind of family.*

* A year later, Mr. Isabella began working half-time for the cultural center. He has bought his own home and invited his grandchildren to stay with him in the summer.

5

THE CLEANING-COMB WITCH

*Any idea, when firmly held, nurtured, and culti-
vated, will eventually create its own reality.*
                                        PAUL WATZLAWICK

ONE MORNING AT THE RESIDENTS' MEETING, WHICH IS HELD WEEKLY
in the living room of Reliance House, I found myself staring at a
woman I had not seen before and who had just been assigned to
my care. She was probably in her late forties, although she
looked older, and what first caught my attention were the skeins
of gray and bleached-blond hair that coiled over her head and
shoulders like water snakes. Through a narrow opening in this
tangle a dark eye peered out suspiciously at the circle of residents and staff around her and a set of crooked teeth were bared
in a rather frightening smile.

"I have tried to love him," she hissed angrily through her
hair as a discussion of chores and outings went on around her.
"But that's none of your business, is it?"

The woman continued to rock and whisper, and apparently
no one took much notice. Now and again she twisted her hair
tightly across her eyes then reopened her peephole—now
through gray, now through blond—and glared. Her horny fingernails had not been cut in months, nor, for that matter, had

her toenails, which I could see sawing their way through an old pair of slippers.

"Is that Angie Savalonis?" I whispered to the aide who sat beside me.

"Yup," came back the answer. "She's been here a long time, but she won't stay if she don't straighten out. Bad behavior. Bad time of life."

"Fall off da earth and go ta hell!" Miss Savalonis suddenly shouted in what I gathered was a Brooklyn accent, and as the patients around her got to their feet, she rose, inspected her chair, and shuffled off after them.

"Don't wobble, Miss America!" I could hear her say as she went out onto the wide front porch. "Wave ya panties out da window!"

When I followed Miss Savalonis outside that mild May morning, I found that she had already positioned herself at the far end of the porch—as far away from others as she could get. There she sat on a folding chair, gazing with an affectionately bemused expression into her lap. She had skewered her hair at the back of her head with a stick, revealing a tired and rather swarthy face. Her feet jiggled restlessly beneath a long cotton skirt of grays and dingy greens. As I approached, I could see that she was cleaning her fingernails with the sharp prongs of a teasing comb.

"Hello, Miss Savalonis," I began, drawing up a chair. "I'm—"

"I don't wanna talk about it," she interrupted, thrusting her hands into her skirt and pursing her lips in a straight line.

"I was hoping that—"

"I don't make you talk when you don't wanna, do I?"

We sat for several minutes without speaking. Her slippered feet tapped out an irregular rhythm that slowly faded. Soon only her toes were moving.

"Let's get a cup of tea," I suggested.

"No," she snapped, her legs jumping back into the dance. "You wanna do something for me? Then get me outta this prison." Miss Savalonis rolled her upper lip under and gave me a toothy, lipless smile. Her alert brown eyes darted over my face.

"Go on with your little life and leave me alone. Commit suicide."

With that she rattled to her feet and inspected her chair again, then scrambled back into the house, rudely shoving aside anyone who stood in her way. "Have a nice day, moron!" she called back over her shoulder, and with that the screen door banged, and she was gone.

I watched as an aide heaved himself reluctantly off the porch step and followed Miss Savalonis into the house and then heard: "LEAVE ME ALONE!"

Leaving Reliance House, I trudged uphill that warm morning toward Mountain Valley Hospital. I had some time before seeing my next patient, and I intended to review Miss Savalonis's record to see if I could discover how this wiry little woman had become so angry. Treating her was clearly going to be a challenge.

At Mountain Valley Hospital patients' records are kept in a low fieldstone building situated among towering rhododendrons near what is now the hospital's back gate. After signing in at the desk and going downstairs to the basement, I let myself into the cool and rather gloomy records room. Here on metal shelves that reach from floor to ceiling are piled the notes and records of every patient who has ever passed through this institution. In bulging manila folders of various design are crammed the hourly progress notes kept by nurses (written in on white paper), the doctors' orders prescribing medication (written on green paper), the blood tests required to monitor the medication, psychological testing, reports from consultants, and, most useful for my purposes, the standard admission and discharge notes with patients' histories, hopes, and inadvertent speculations.

I pulled four bulging folders from the "S" section, which together constituted Miss Savalonis's biography. As I had suspected, she was relatively young—only forty-six years old—and had, indeed, been raised in Brooklyn. She had been hospitalized intermittently since the age of twenty-one, and the record now spread before me documented twenty of those twenty-five years of mental turmoil. Her discharge summaries noted simply that she had been raised in a close family and had been a hardworking student at a community college until her second year. At that time she had begun to act on an imaginary love affair with a political science professor, and this made her feel so guilty that she became desperate. In ways that were not explained in the record, this chain of events led her to arrive at a hospital with her parents when she was twenty-one years old.

Initially, Miss Savalonis was diagnosed as suffering from a psychotic depression. She hardly spoke. She refused to eat. And, as was still common in the 1960s, she was labeled neurasthenic, which implied that unconscious conflicts were upsetting her digestion, sleep, and other functions in a typically feminine way. Consistent with the diagnosis of depression and neurasthenia, Miss Savalonis was given antidepressant medication and plenty of rest, which, surprisingly, made her worse. "Reacted violently" is all I learned from the record, but the fact that her diagnosis was then changed to schizophrenia, catatonic type, suggests that traces of chemicals found in all antidepressant medication that tip the chemical scale toward psychosis had precipitated a full-blown psychotic break. Immediately taken off antidepressants and put on antipsychotic medication, she did much better.

Over the next several years, Miss Savalonis went in and out of different hospitals. When her family moved to the country and she finally arrived in Mountain Valley Hospital, she was reclassified yet again as a paranoid schizophrenic. She told the admitting physician that "filthy words come to mind and I ought to be punished." (Included in the record is a touching letter from the local choir master attesting to the fact that Miss Savalonis had been turning around in her pew and mouthing lewd remarks to members of the choir as they tried to sing.)

Skimming through the rest of the record, I could see that nothing much had changed for Miss Savalonis over the past thirteen years either in terms of diagnosis, behavior, or living arrangements. Most of the time she had muttered and shuffled her way through various halfway houses except when "uncontrollable anger" sent her back to Mountain Valley. There she was treated with medications, or rather there she *had* been treated with these chemicals until she developed irreversible side effects that hampered her gait and movement. Now there was little anyone could do beyond briefly sedating her.

As I continued to leaf through the disheveled pages of this enormous record, I became increasingly bored. An illness was being described over and over again and the administration of a dozen different medications documented, but there was nothing written about Miss Savalonis's personality beyond frequent notations of noncompliance. Usually, it is intriguing to look through records to find at what point a patient manages to capture the interest of his caretakers. A couple of question marks on a typed page is a good sign; so is an interim summary or a handwritten note. Even speculations—"the patient may be rebelling against years of rigid control" or "the patient may be punishing her parents"—suggest that someone is still undecided, still thinking. But no one had been inspired to puzzle over Miss Savalonis's life. The entire chart, it seemed, discussed schizophrenia and drugs.

It was just before I left the records room that I came to an envelope in the back of Volume 4, crammed with notes written by the patient herself over a number of years.

"Oct. 1. I feel a little better today than yesterday. Mgs. [milligrams of some medication] dropped."

"I feel that it's like there's pressure way down deep on the base of my brain—like it pumps me to think thoughts."

"My mind seems to strain, which causes pain. Took the pill last night and had a good dream. Woke up feeling good."

"I go somewhere or do something and it's as if I'm left with nothing. Where did it go?"

"Nov. 3. I feel that it's like Fidel Castro out there with a machine of some sort that pumps feelings and emotions into my head."

"I think that I did a poor job in my typing courses and that someone's trying to get back at me. I want to cry all the time."

"June. I feel like I have black on my mind."

Such different concerns, I thought to myself as I left the building and headed back toward Hillsdale. In these notes of ten and twelve years ago, Miss Savalonis was actively asking questions. She, if not her doctors, was interested in why these terrible feelings had descended upon her. Were they her fault? A plot? The result of medication? I wondered which explanation she had settled on.

"*None of your business*!" she bellowed when I asked her the following week to tell me why she had fallen ill. "I don't pry into your life. Leave mine alone."

With that, Miss Savalonis pursed her lips and stared into her lap. Five minutes passed in silence, then ten, then twenty.

"Client declines to answer questions," I began writing.

"*Stop*!" shrieked Miss Savalonis. "Stop writing. You're hurting the pencil."

Subsequent meetings followed a similar pattern. As soon as I spoke, Miss Savalonis told me to shut up. Or, on those rare occasions when she was in the mood to talk, she endlessly repeated her need to be let out of prison.

"Listen!" she liked to shout in the clinic's crowded waiting room. "I live in da land of da free. So get me outta here!"

She was the bossiest client I had ever encountered.

As therapy crept along and Miss Savalonis expressed the beginnings of an alliance by calling me every week on the phone, her relationships with the residents at Reliance House grew worse. It was as if every step she made toward me had to be counterbalanced by some extra rudeness or willfulness at the house. She defiantly rummaged through trash cans, although this was against house rules. She obsessively collected bits of lint from the furniture even when other residents were sitting on the couch and chairs. And worst of all, she muttered incessantly whenever the television was on.

"Angie, shut up!" shouted a round little man who was always red in the face and damp with sweat. He was sitting on a brown plaid couch at one end of the living room trying to watch a game show. Miss Savalonis was cruising slowly around the room picking up tiny bits of lint and casually dropping them into the fish tank every time she passed.

"Mmm, mmm, dum dee dum," she mumbled to herself, gradually getting louder.

Flapping his arms at his tormentor as she passed, the round man rolled off the couch and shuffled across the room to the television set. With an angry twist of a knob, he turned up the volume. The game show host blared out the next question.

Miss Savalonis turned up her volume.

"MMMM, MMMMM!" she fairly shouted, sprinkling lint in the man's lap.

"Angie! I can't hear!"

"Turn off the TV," called an aide from the kitchen. "TOO LOUD."

And with that, Miss Savalonis was out the door and down the steps with a smile on her face—ready to roam the streets.

Everyone agreed that Miss Savalonis was becoming unmanageable. At the weekly residents' meeting a story began to be told that suggested she was too stubborn and self-centered to remain.

"She upsets us," one man told me, pointing insistently at the ceiling with a cigarette-stained finger. "She don't act reasonable. She gets into our skin."

"And into the Jell-O pudding," nodded another, referring to the time that Miss Savalonis had stuck her finger in all fifteen bowls of vanilla pudding. "Are you here to see me? Do you want to test my superpowers today?"

"No, not today," I replied, but the mention of superpowers reminded me of a taped interview I had made a few weeks before with a man who claimed he could detect witches no matter how cleverly they disguised themselves. Was he, too, describing Miss Savalonis?

"It's a gift," he had told me. "I was born very sensitive to that kind of stuff." He had already described for me a Caffeine-Ethyl Witch, a Hell Tracer, and a Razor-Ray Warlock, all of whom hung out around Hillsdale, and he now described for me another type, whom he believed was a cleaning-comb witch.

"So what's a cleaning-comb witch?" I asked in the interview.

"The pink plastic cleaning-comb witch," he began. "When I saw her, she was into electric spells, like she could generate static electricity that would pump spells right into your body. She's an old, gray-haired woman . . . and black," he said slowly, apparently bringing an image of this woman to mind. "But not really black. It was a kind of painted-on color that would come and go." He lowered his voice to a whisper. "I think they gave her a spell for the blackness.

"She talks funny, too," he continued, "like with a twisting and hissing of her words. She likes to sit on a bench and give off . . . Like she combs her long gray hair and gives off effortses and essences.

"She had this pink plastic brush, and she gave off essences from her . . . from her combs and all her different things. When she saw me watching her crackle her hair, she gave me this look like"—and here he scowled deeply, thrust his lips forward, and bobbled his head—"because she knew I didn't approve of her giving off effortses. She was set on her mission all right."

"And what was—"

"And one more thing. You won't believe this, but she took strands of hair, like off her sweater and things, and planted them right . . . back . . . in . . . her . . . head."

"No!"

"Swear-to-God-as-Jesus-is-my-Savior."

"Is there just one of them?" I asked.

"Witches have dozens of names," he answered obliquely. "They use any one they want. Something tricky."

"And where do you see her?"

"In and out. I think she was the one who wanted the hospital to burn down. She wanted Lucifer to rule so it would be full of witches, demons, and warlocks. Where people are sick," he explained, "it's easy for witches to take control. You could say that fear is their main ground.

"This is all pretty interesting for you," he surmised, "but they *scare* me."

If this was, indeed, a description of Angie Savalonis, it was a good one. It captured the unfortunate woman's rocking, pumping, and writhing movements, and it neatly focused attention both on her obsessive qualities and on the apparent seductiveness of her thinking. Earlier, the man who watched witches had described for me a Caffeine-Ethyl Witch—a big, wrinkled woman who moved "to the beat of caffeine" with a jerky pulsating rhythm and who had "a thumping quality about her" that I imagined was not unlike Miss Savalonis's incessant rocking. He had also told me about the Hell Tracer—"very stat-uesque, you know, square-looking"—who walked with the three middle fingers of each hand stretched rigidly toward hell and who also "moved her mouth funny, like a fish." Miss Savalonis complained of stiffness in her arms and legs—another result of years on medication—and she frequently worked her face as if shifting three or four sourballs around inside her mouth. My informant was sure that each of these eerie movements was a way of casting spells or, as he would put it, a witch's way of drumming evil ideas into her prey. Of course, doctors saw the same movements as the side effects of antipsychotic medication, and Miss Savalonis explained them either as the pumping of a thought machine or as "a good way to get people to leave me alone."

When it came to disturbing people, however, none of Miss Savalonis's mannerisms were as effective as her luscious, incom-prehensible whisperings. There was a subversive quality about these smiling monologues that set people on edge.

"I have asked the President of the United States to take away sex, but he won't," she said with bitterness as the two of us met on the porch of Reliance House. It was an early autumn after-noon, and Miss Savalonis had come down from the women's dorm dressed in a brown wrap-around skirt, a completely unbuttoned blouse, and several strings of beads that more or less kept her shirt in place. She was giggling to herself and her mouth was making involuntary sucking motions. They were the kind of small, constant movements that someone trying to bal-ance on one foot would make. She sat on a chair opposite mine, hiked her skirt up well over her knees, and gave me a complici-tous smile.

"What am I agreeing to, Angie?" I asked, as I smiled in return. She dipped her head coyly and giggled behind her hand. As was her way, she began to whisper to herself, smiling and chuckling all the while. I strained to hear but could only catch a word or two. So very softly I began to hum and, as I had hoped, Miss Savalonis whispered louder.

Now I caught snatches about "panties," "the rubbing hand," and names that included several presidents, Joe (McCarthy?), and one of her doctors. I hummed louder. Miss Savalonis whispered louder.

"The President wants me . . . yes, mmm, to have those feelings. [Something, something] can't get caught."

I hummed louder still—too loud, apparently—for Miss Savalonis began to hiss rather than whisper, but with a glowering frown.

"The United States of America . . . could get angry. Hit, hot, hurt . . . She could come to a bad end. [Mumble] could hurt her *very* badly."

I stopped mid-hum, and she shot me a sweet, victorious smile before resuming her chuckling, whispering fantasies.

"*Nice life!*" she suddenly shouted. "You've done it with a man. Well? Well, then?"

"Well, I'm lucky," I said, intending to agree with her indirect comparison of our lives.

"Oh, go kill yourself," she snapped and walked off the porch and into the street.

"We are *not* getting along very well," I said in frustration to her empty chair.

"No," I imagined her replying. "I'm not going to cooperate with the enemy. I don't want your help. I don't want to change my life. I don't want anything to do with your narrow, small-minded world. Can you believe that?"

"Yes," I continued, loudly. "Yes, I believe you, but my job—"

"Is not one I want any part of," I now imagined her saying tartly. "*Good-bye.*"

"*Then why have you started calling me?*" I shouted across the road after the retreating Miss Savalonis.

"I don't know," she called back without turning around.

For over two years I refused to believe that Miss Savalonis wanted to divorce herself completely from the rest of the world. We continued to meet, although, thank God, less frequently, and I continued to pry into her own explanations of her troubles. Most of my efforts were useless, although I did discover that she had lost her one serious high school boyfriend, Jimmy, in a motorcycle accident. She felt responsible for his death, possibly because they had been flirting and she had led him into, or more probably just toward, mortal sin. But these are only speculations. Miss Savalonis gave very little. She took less. Try as I might, I never convinced her that her abrasive demeanor bothered others or that her freedom would actually increase if she stopped breaking the rules.

"Do you scare people when you yell?" I once asked her.

"*I* scare people?! *I* scare people?!" she spluttered. "*I'm* the one who's scared and in danger. *I'm* the one with the hard life. Tell me, did Job scare people? Or was he scared by the Lord?"

"Both," I answered.

"What do you know?," she shot back. "I always vote for an easy life, so why do I have the hard life? You tell me. I must have done something horrible to be punished this way. When I was young," she continued without drawing a breath, "I had curly hair and my friends loved me. I was pretty and nice. Now I have a hard life and look at my hair." She paused to unknot her hair, the bottom twelve inches of which was bleached to a bright, dry yellow. "Doctor," she hissed, "it's ssstraight! You don't have ssstraight hair in a good life."

Miss Savalonis rose and bent over the step on which she had been sitting. Tight-fisted with physical as well as emotional information, she collected coffee cup, plastic spoon, napkin—and even, I finally noticed, several long gray and yellow strands of her hair.

"I used to have friends," she snarled from the bottom step, "but now they're better off without me. They're gone."

"I'm sorry to hear that," I said.

"*No, you're not!* If you were sorry, you would fix me. Put me back together again like Humpty-Dumpty. *You're* the doctor. *You* can get me out of here if you want."

"I can't bring back the happy times."

"*Yes, you can!*" she screamed, and with that she moved off down the street, trailing her familiar litany behind her. "I live in da land of da free. I want my civil rights in America. Let me outta here. Who will let—"

Suddenly she turned. "Jimmy Barber was the one I wanted," she shouted. "*I said*, Jimmy Barber was the one I wanted!"

~   ~   ~

It was boundless contrariness more than psychosis that finally evicted Miss Savalonis from Reliance House. Early one November, I was called to the house to witness her departure. She was being sent away against her will to a state hospital where she would have far less freedom than she did in Hillsdale. By the time I reached the house, the sun was low in the sky and the shadows of bare branches lay across the drive. I found Angie on the back steps, wrapped in a plaid jacket below which hung her blotchy gray and green skirt. Her spectacular hair was tied into granny knots all over her head, and the overall effect was of a soldier in full camouflage with leaves and sticks poking out of his helmet. It was guerrilla warfare, all right: Savalonis vs. the State. I joined her on the steps, and as we waited for the team of social workers to arrive, she threw up her old shield of complaints.

"There are citizens of the United States who liked me," she began angrily, hugging her jacket around her. "My friends said, 'We'll be there fa you. You can be our friend.' Jimmy Barber died in a tree. *Your* dog didn't die in a tree. You're a little goody-two-shoes doctor. America caught me and punished *me*, not you. The President said, 'You're a nothing no-good.' He gave me a hard life."

All the old phrases came back as if she were a tape that would play forever. "You wanna to do something for me?" she would ask rhetorically. "Then get me outta this prison. Go on with your little life and leave me alone."

On she went, sometimes rocking violently and looking upward with an angry frown, sometimes wrapping herself in her arms and scowling at me. The same old story of barely remembered sins and endless punishment poured from her unhappy heart. It wasn't fair, she said, and indeed it was not. As she rattled on, touching ever so lightly on the imminent move— "You're on your own in America, now. You're inalienable"— she slowly gathered speed. "Inalienable is more like it. Land of da free. All for da brave."

She rose from the steps and walked a few feet into the frozen yard. She halted, then suddenly said very clearly, "All men are endowed with certain inalienable rights, among them the rights to life, liberty and the pursuit of happiness.

"*You've* got those rights! *You've* done it with a man! WHEN IS IT MY TURN? *I* WANT HUGS AND KISSES—CIVIL RIGHTS AND KISSES!"

She stopped abruptly, and the late afternoon was quiet. Standing in the yard, she looked past me at Reliance House where she had lived for so many years then shifted her gaze to me.

"You know I'm hurt," she said softly.

I rose from the steps as she walked toward me. To my astonishment, we opened our arms together.

6

THE TYRANNICAL NATURE
OF EXPLANATIONS

*We do not first see, then define; we define first
and then see.*

WALTER LIPPMANN

WHILE I WAS GOING THROUGH THE MOTIONS OF TREATING ANGIE
Savalonis, I read Jerome Bruner's *Acts of Meaning* and was
struck by a simple experiment on storytelling he describes. Setting out to discover what kinds of things trigger storytelling, a
kindergarten teacher read two versions of a birthday party story
to her pupils and recorded the discussion that followed. In one
version there were no surprises. The birthday girl was happy,
the cake beautiful, the presents fine. Contented murmurs followed this story but not much comment. The alternate version
was full of surprises. The birthday girl was not happy. In fact,
she poured water on the candles. Ten times as much discussion
followed this version, and essentially all of it took the form of
stories. Perhaps the girl didn't know what day it was, one
kindergartener volunteered. Then she wouldn't have the right
dress, and if she didn't have the right dress, she wouldn't be
happy. Perhaps she was angry with her mother, began another,
and he, too, created a possible world in which the strange events

he had just heard about made sense. (When the experiment was informally repeated in rural Texas, a boy explained that surely a lizard had climbed onto the cake and had to be washed off.) The points the experimenter wished to make were that stories are generated in order to reconcile the unexpected and the confusing with the culturally expected, and that this process of imaginatively trying to fit the peculiar into the known is already well learned by the age of five.[1]

Hillsdale is a natural place for stories, as Angie Savalonis's presence inadvertently demonstrated. Her unconventional behavior elicited at least five distinct explanations—she was bizarre because she was schizophrenic, because she was self-centered and willful, because she was a witch, because she had sinned, or, as I came to believe, because she felt herself to be an outcast. It is not unusual for an action or a personality to elicit conflicting explanations: every family squabble involves such competitions. If the trash isn't dumped, Mother claims her daughter is self-centered and forgetful. The daughter claims she has too many things to do.[2] Nor is it unusual to discover that once an explanation is decided upon, it is extremely resistant to change.

The stories that purported to explain Miss Savalonis's behavior were neither integrated nor modified during the years I knew her. Part of the reason for this unfortunate impasse was that her own account of her troubles was too hard for others to understand and empathize with. But there are other reasons why explanations, once firmly set in mind, rarely change even when new and contradictory information is available. It is as if explanations have a life of their own, or as if explainers can't be bothered to expend the energy needed to reconsider their ideas.

Ever since a cognitive revolution occurred in psychology some twenty years ago and processes such as thinking, understanding, and believing came back into fashion as serious sub-

1. Jerome Bruner, *Acts of Meaning* (Cambridge: Harvard University Press, 1990), p. 81.

2. This kind of discrepancy in explanations is so common that it has been called the "actor-observer effect." Specifically, almost every actor or person doing something claims that she is prompted by the situation she finds herself in, whereas almost every observer watching the actor insists that the action is prompted by the actor's temperament.

jects of investigation, scientists have been asking themselves what happens when a person tries to understand someone like Angie Savalonis.[3] Actually they didn't start their research with the mentally ill, for good and obvious reasons, but began more simply by studying how we understand the characters we encounter in stories. A short soliloquy might be extracted from a popular book or movie, for example, and hundreds of students asked what the passage meant. Scores of experiments later, psychologists came up with the frankly alarming discovery that by and large we hear what we already know, believe what we already believe, and promptly drop confusing or contradictory information from our memories even when such information could correct our biased conclusions. There are exceptions, of course, but not nearly as many as an intelligent person would like to believe. Why, psychologists asked themselves, is this so? Why are the beliefs we hold about ourselves and others so difficult to change and so subtly but consistently biased? The answers lead us into a rapidly expanding area of cognitive psychology that is concerned with what is called "judgment under uncertainty" and examines how people come up with answers when they don't have all the facts.

First of all, it is obvious that our beliefs or "answers" are based on what we remember, not what we forget, and cognitive psychologists have increasingly discovered that our memories are not evenhanded or even very reasonable. A whole series of what are called egocentric and conservative biases have been discovered in memory that apparently help us maintain an unrealistically steady attitude about ourselves and about life in general.

One of the biases recently discovered is that material that is actively produced by an individual—say Miss Savalonis's tentative description of herself as a sinner—is recalled more easily and completely than material that is only passively read or

3. Psychology's cognitive revolution is part of—some say the leading part of—a larger movement that is in the process of replacing scientific reductionism, in which everything is determined from the cellular level up, with a system of reciprocal interaction in which, for example, what you believe is important affects your brain cells while your brain cells affect what you believe.

heard—say a doctor's description of Miss Savalonis as a schizophrenic. What you create, you remember. Another egocentric bias makes it much easier to recall material that pertains to oneself than material that pertains to anything or anyone else. What is associated with you, you remember.

The idea that certain information associated with the self or produced by the self has a privileged status in memory led to the suspicion that the pictures we carry around in our heads of ourselves and of others may be overly influenced by our own thinking. This would not be terribly detrimental if the concepts we created were accurate. But they are not, reported William Swann, who, using hundreds of students at the University of Texas at Austin as subjects, set about to discover how individuals enhance and maintain an always-too-stable picture of the self. In a long series of experiments on what he termed "self-verification," Swann showed repeatedly that not only do we selectively recall information that fits our picture of ourselves much better than we remember contradictory feedback, but that we actively look for confirmation and just as actively disregard, discredit, and distort almost everything else.[4]

In one experiment, Swann and a colleague gave students a list of adjectives that allowed them to draw a verbal picture of themselves. Students who were comfortable with themselves drew likable portraits, but others drew unlikable pictures of themselves. After several complicated manipulations, each subject was given evaluations that strangers had supposedly made of them based on a reading of the selected adjectives. As Swann predicted, likable students spent more time reading over evaluations they believed came from a stranger who thought they were likable than they did reading evaluations from a stranger who thought them unlikable. The uncomfortable students pondered the statements from strangers who supposedly already disliked them but spent less time considering the evaluation of strangers who thought them likable. Later, both groups recalled the feedback that fit their self-conceptions better than statements that

    4. William Swann Jr. and Stephen Read, "Self-Verification Processes: How We Sustain Our Self-Conceptions," *Journal of Experimental Social Psychology* 17 (1981): 351–72.

contradicted their own ideas. In other words, once students had
formulated a picture of themselves, they showed little interest in
redrawing or reinterpreting it.[5] As the artificial intelligence
expert, Roger Schank, said about narratives, "We rarely look to
understand a story in more than one way."[6]

The initial discovery, then, that the self and its activities are
preferentially held in memory, must be modified to reflect that
only the parts of an individual that the individual accepts will be
thus carefully preserved. No wonder Freud maintained that "the
weak spot in the security of our mental life [is] the untrustwor-
thiness of our memory."[7] Swann's work implies that we are all
staunch conservatives where social relations are concerned, and
that once we form an opinion of ourselves or of Miss Savalonis,
for example, we will only notice evidence that confirms our
views. As she, herself, loudly maintained, "I am not a sickness!
Everything I say and do now is used as proof that I'm insane."

In his classic study, "On Being Sane in Insane Places," David
Rosenhan dramatically showed how this can happen. Eight individuals posed as pseudopatients. A varied group, including a
graduate student, three psychologists, a pediatrician, a psychiatrist, a painter, and a housewife, they got themselves admitted to
a total of twelve psychiatric wards by claiming to hear voices
that said "empty," "hollow," and "thud." Beyond this fabrication and the use of pseudonyms and alternate occupations, however, everything they said and did during their weeks on the
wards reflected their true personalites. They did not impersonate
mental patients in any way. Although a sizable number of
patients on the wards caught on to the ruse immediately, the
staff in the various hospitals never discovered a single pseudopa-
tient. All were treated throughout their stay as schizophrenics
and all were discharged as insane persons who were temporarily

5. William Swann, Jr., "Self-Verification: Bringing Social Reality Into
Harmony with the Self," in *Social Psychological Perspectives on the Self, vol.
2,* ed. J. Suls and A. G. Greenwald (Hillsdale, N.J.: Erlbaum), pp. 33–66.

6. Roger Schank, *Tell Me a Story* (New York: Charles Scribner's Sons,
1991), p. 73.

7. Sigmund Freud, the Rat Man case, in *The Standard Edition of the
Complete Works of Sigmund Freud,* ed. and trans. J. Strachey (London: Ho-
garth, 1901).

"in remission." The label put on these people to explain one episode of hearing voices had created a new reality—a new life—for each. Even when one started conducting therapy sessions with his fellow patients and others wrote copious notes, all their actions were interpreted as insane. As one openly wrote down his observations, it was noted in his chart that "patient engages in writing behavior."[8]

This tendency to stick with our original explanation is not the only bias that psychologists have discovered. Another is that on occasions when we do change our minds, we usually forget the inconsistency and maintain that we have always believed what we believe right now. To demonstrate this, a psychologist had students rate their feelings on eight controversial issues, including bussing.[9] Later, the subjects in favor of bussing were joined by a confederate who argued persuasively against them. Those against bussing were given reasons why they should favor this method of school integration. Both groups were then asked to *duplicate* their pre-test assessment. As predicted, subjects distorted their initial stand on bussing, but not on the other issues, to bring it into line with their new and somewhat changed attitude. This unconscious tendency to revise our memories to fit our current outlook gives us the curious ability to change our opinions while simultaneously maintaining that we have been the same person all along. Revising personal memories also conceals the extent to which we are able to change, and this can be disadvantageous, as we will see.

Still another conservative bias does much the same kind of hat trick, but for people and events outside the self. It has been found that when an individual learns the outcome of an event that was once truly uncertain—will Richard Nixon travel to

8. David Rosenhan, "On Being Sane in Insane Places," *Science* 179 (1973): 250–58. In a later experiment, Rosenhan arranged for the entire staff in a hospital to rate nearly 200 admissions for possible sanity. He had told them that he would be sending them several pseudopatients over the next three months. Nineteen patients were identified as sane by a psychiatrist and one other staff member. No pseudopatients had been sent.

9. George Goethals and Richard Reckman, "The Perception of Consistency in Attitudes," *Journal of Experimental Social Psychology* 9 (1973): 491–501.

China or won't he?—he or she will thread the outcome back into memory in such a way as to minimize prior uncertainty and to foster the feeling that "I knew it all along." In one experiment, subjects were asked to estimate the likelihood of Nixon traveling to China. Some would say, for example, that there was a 60 percent chance that Nixon would go. Much later, after the trip had in fact occurred, the subjects were asked to remember their estimates. More than three-quarters of the subjects unconsciously revised their estimates upward and remembered that they had been pretty sure he would take the trip.[10] This unconscious assimilation of present information into an earlier, less certain outlook creates a coherent whole out of all that is known of the event and smooths out much of the unexpectedness that our lives contain. To some degree this bias, like the one mentioned earlier, is useful as well as comforting. It increases our sense of order and security and allows us to get on with life without remarking on how little we can accurately predict. The disadvantage, however, is that this conservative bias tends to trap us in the status quo. Because events apparently keep turning out the way we expected, we imagine that life proceeds now in the way it inevitably must. With no surprises, there is no need to explore or even note inconsistencies—no need to tell new stories. This delays our efforts to consider any beliefs other than those we already hold.

One final trick used by our inconstant memories to dissipate surprises needs to be exposed before we can see how biases and privileges combine to shut out the unexpected and the strange. In the 1920s Frederic Bartlett, an English psychologist, set himself the task of discovering "something about the common types of change introduced by normal individuals into remembered material with increasing lapses of time."[11] His most famous experiment involved a curious story about Indians who, in a

10. B. Fischoff and R. Beyth, "I Knew It All Along," *Organizational Behavior and Human Performance* 13 (1975): 1–6; and B. Fischoff, "Hindsight/Foresight: The Effect of Outcome Knowledge on Judgment Under Uncertainty," *Journal of Experimental Psychology: Human Perception and Performance* 1 (1975): 288–99.

11. Frederic Bartlett, *Remembering: A Study in Experimental and Social Psychology* (New York: Macmillan, 1932), p. 63.

roundabout and rather dreamlike way, were called upon to paddle upriver and fight other Indians. One was wounded and shortly after his return gave up his spirit. Bartlett had many students read this story, and over the following months and years he surprised them by asking them to recall it. The retellings were far different from the original. (In other experiments Bartlett found that changes were less dramatic when a familiar story was remembered. In these cases, however, the teller simply reverted to his general knowledge of the theme and created his own approximation of the original story.)

Bartlett discovered that big changes in the Indian story were made almost immediately and smaller revisions continued until the story was "set." The final versions either omitted or explained away all the confusing or unclear portions of the story, and the account became increasingly coherent and conventional. In many cases the story was even personalized and given a moral. Bartlett concluded that we do not copy events into our memories as some scientists had believed but rather remember general instances of familiar kinds of events. He called them *schema*. When required to remember a particular event or story, Bartlett maintained that we call forth the schema and "build up its characters afresh to aid whatever response the needs of the moment may demand."[12]

In short, our memory works in such a way as to hold the gist of familiar stories, events, or characters and dump the rest. Upon recall, the gist comes back, and our expectations or needs fill in the undetected gaps. A minor exception to this efficient process is the storing and recalling of an extremely unusual detail, especially one that comes at the beginning or end of a story. Thus, in the Indian story, Bartlett's subjects Anglicized the tale—for example, changing the eerie atmosphere to "a foggy afternoon"—but retained the last image, that of something black escaping from the mouth of the dying Indian.

Combining insights both from storytelling and from the biases of memory, we begin to see why it is so difficult to change someone's mind in any significant way. Take the doctors who

12. Bartlett, *Remembering*, p. 196.

have recorded their impressions of Angie Savalonis in her four-volume record, for example. Seeing and hearing only what already matches their firmly held beliefs about mental illness, then responding with questions that explore and confirm only these particular beliefs, the doctors interviewing Miss Savalonis are almost certain to ignore everything about her that is not classically schizophrenic. Writing out their reports will further commit this incomplete description of her to memory. Adding insult to injury, the doctors, *like all the rest of us*, will then mistake the explanations they have formulated in their heads for the reality that is "out there." They will create the very pattern they think they are discovering, and in so doing, the more extraneous material they manage to ignore—the more personal connections they fail to find between themselves and Miss Savalonis—the clearer and more persuasive the explanations will be. But without taking into account Angie Savalonis's curious childishness, without noting her rare and even more surprising expressions of appreciation, without, in short, the personal connections, Miss Savalonis cannot exist within the mental health community as a person. She becomes, instead, a stock character in a play, albeit one about the mentally ill or one about witches.

"Facts revenge themselves upon the man that denies their existence," Leslie Stephen wrote in his autobiography.[13] And here in Hillsdale it is the same. The certainty and stability we foster with our efficient but none-too-accurate memories is purchased at the price of an ability to see and act on alternatives. A broad range of observations collected from many perspectives—the doctors', the man-who-knew-witches', mine, the residents', and of course Miss Savalonis's—can wreck a lot of good stories. Facts about people don't fit together smoothly. But if we are to learn more than we already know and expect, and thereby gain a sense of the alternativeness or changeableness in a life, we need to work against the natural biases that tempt us toward premature conclusions. In addition, if we are to gain a necessary humility that comes with understanding how poorly we predict,

13. Leslie Stephen, *Hours in a Library III,* in A. O. J. Cocksheet, *The Art of Autobiography in 19th & 20th Century England* (New Haven: Yale University Press), p. 147.

we must pay attention to the facts that don't fit. And perhaps most important, if we are to strengthen our community by breaking down the narrow stereotypes we use to manage our own need for security, then we must traffic in the unexpected and the unclear. We must even risk seeing in Angie Savalonis's pain and confusion a reflection of our own experience.

Given what we have just reviewed about the stability of explanations and what we examined earlier concerning story-telling and its relationship to understanding, it is now easier to see why Miss Savalonis's monologues elicit apprehensive responses that address only what her listeners are familiar with. Doctors talk to her about chemicals and medications. Aides and family discuss shouting. Everyone else keeps out of the way. But what about therapists? Surely we are the ones who take into consideration the whole person, and our responses are supposed to reflect at least an earnest attempt to understand all aspects of her stories.

On the hunch that our replies to Miss Savalonis's baleful complaints might, like some busy psychiatrists' responses, be focused on the disease and the behavior and not on what it feels like to be a discarded, hallucinating woman, a psychiatrist and I designed an informal experiment modeled on Schank's work with movie scripts. Using the notes I'd found in her record, we compiled a monologue that we gave to several dozen therapists, mental patients, and outside individuals. We asked them to read these anonymous complaints and write out what they would think silently to themselves *and* what they would say back. The notes started with "I feel a little better today than yesterday, but I feel like there's pressure way down deep on the base of my brain—like it pumps me to think thoughts." They continued through some rather common complaints, including "I think I did a poor job in my typing courses" and her concern that "Fidel Castro is out there with a machine of some sort that pumps feelings and emotions into my head." The selection ended with her blaming herself for Jimmy's death and asking, "So why did I get a hard life?"

Although nothing was said in the brief introduction to the

notes to indicate that Miss Savalonis was mentally ill, every clinician responded with "doctor talk." As they read her notes they
must have thought, "What's her diagnosis?" "Sounds schizophrenic." "I think her illness has been exacerbated by a stressful
event." Out loud, they answered her complaints with invitations
to expand her own story rather than with personal stories of
their own. "You seem overwhelmed." "Would you like to tell
me about what went wrong in typing class?" In other words,
Miss Savalonis was defined as mentally ill, and to continue the
dialogue, clinicians reached into their fund of stories labeled
"other patients I have treated," not into stories labeled "sadness
and confusion I have personally experienced." This is not surprising, since clinicians are taught *not* to become personally
involved and *not* to talk about themselves. But if this objective
stance is maintained—and I don't believe that it always is—there
is certainly a risk that the *illness* will be what is understood—
and not the person.

Among Angie Savalonis's peers, who also recognized her as
mentally ill, the response to her monologue was both kinder and
tougher.

Each response began with sympathy: "Well, I'm sorry you're
having some pain," one man began.

"I would say to her that I care about her and she is a good
person and she should try to relax and remember all of her good
times when she was younger," wrote another, probably passing
on advice that had been given to him many times.

"It's OK to feel that way," began the most sophisticated,
referring to Miss Savalonis's pain and confusion. "We're all left
with nothing in the end." This writer then launched briskly into
a no-nonsense story about herself, which Schank asserts demon-
strates her understanding. "It was always airplanes that did it to
me. Landing at Dulles Airport with CIA agents who put trans-
mitters into my teeth. . . . You just saw Castro on TV," she continued, now explaining to Miss Savalonis how she thinks delusions work. "You're just psychic. You're picking up on *other*
people's shit and feeling like it's yours. You'll get used to it. We
all do."

This vigorous woman concluded her response with two more

personal stories, some bracing advice, namely, "Stop crying—GET MAD! FIGHT BACK!" and a first-rate insight into Miss Savalonis's sense of guilt over Jimmy's death. "You didn't have anything to do with that [accident]. You're mixing yourself up with him. Your feelings for him didn't kill him, ya know."

People outside the clinic had the hardest time responding to Angie Savalonis's notes. Most admitted that they didn't know what to say and were so uncomfortable that they thought they would want to walk away. Others said they would tell her to get help, and two responded as Schank's students had with personal stories of their own.

"It sounds like things are really hard for you right now," answered a liquor store owner. "I remember when I was going through a horrible time when things seemed overwhelming. I tried to sort them out, but I couldn't do it myself. I talked with friends. It took a long time for things to settle down in my life . . . but things get better. You have to have faith and hope."

Interestingly, this woman not only recapitulated the saner of Miss Savalonis's complaints but expanded upon her own story of sadness and confusion to include advice on how to cope—talk with friends—and an optimistic resolution. Not feeling competent to help with the "crazy" parts of the story, she urged Miss Savalonis to take those parts of her story elsewhere.

Not surprisingly, the only person outside the field who dared to understand personally the most bizarre aspects of the story was a musician, who was himself familiar with depression.

"A lot of what you're saying could apply to myself," he began. "I get confused, too. Why do I think the way I do about things? Why can't I go out and get a job and live a so-called normal existence? Maybe I can realize that life is kinda crazy. You work. You suffer. You worry. You have a good time thrown in here and there—somebody bakes you a cake—but basically it's kinda crazy."

He went on to explain that he takes his imagination very seriously and understands that "a few more tough times could make me really believe my imagination the way you do. . . . It carries us to places that are fantasies—likable places—and at times it carries us to the deep, dark unknown. There may be some truth to the idea that artists are unbalanced. That could be true. I'd ask her what she thinks about that."

This sample of responses left me with a decidedly uneasy feeling. Again using Schank's idea that understanding is indicated by the telling of a story that captures the gist of the dilemma posed by the speaker, it sounds as if my colleagues and I are preoccupied with the illness whereas others either try to understand the person or, if overwhelmed by the foreignness of the encounter, flee. What disturbs me in all this is the mismatch between what clinicians think they are doing—sympathetically listening to the mentally ill in order to understand them better than anyone else—and what this study suggests they are actually doing—at least with delusional patients. Although this survey is admittedly crude, it does suggest that clinicians responded to the illness and not to Miss Savalonis, and that our understanding in such cases is based on our funds of "doctor stories" and not on personal stories. If true, or rather, when true, the implications are far-reaching. Schank would argue that whenever Miss Savalonis is not understood on a personal level, she will not be listened to for long, will not be remembered accurately, and will not be taken seriously. *Perceived as having nothing useful to give her listeners, she will become an outcast.*

I believe that the amelioration of this unfortunate and increasingly divisive situation lies in us all. If we hope to expand our evaluation of Angie Savalonis, or of anyone else for that matter—both for their benefit and for our own sense of well-being and security—at least three conditions need to be present. Some uncertainty must exist in every listener (and this, we have seen, is not often the case); a large enough fund of stories must be present in our minds so that some will match parts of almost everyone else's experience; and enough clarity must be forthcoming from everyone, including the Miss Savalonises of the world, to create an initial story that contains recognizable feelings and beliefs. All parts of this equation must be attended to and, as we will see, each part circles back and interacts with the other two. Ideally, the requirements for productive dialogue and the sense of community it engenders fit together in such a way that when one is enhanced—say breadth of experience—the other two are boosted as well. Unfortunately, the circle can turn in a negative direction as well. As the beleaguered twin mothers demonstrate in chapter 11, the interaction among the ingredients for good dialogue are so closely bound together that a false story can distort and eventually change experience itself, not just for three weeks as it did for Rosenhan's pseudopatients, but for generations. Given the way our minds and memories work, it is as true to say that the story makes the life as it is to say that life makes the story.

THE DREAMING BRAIN

Dreams are rough copies of the waking soul
Yet uncorrected of the higher will,
So that men sometimes in their dreams confess
An unsuspected, or forgotten, self.
                    PEDRO CALDERON DE LA BARCA

ROY SCHAFER, THE ARTICULATE PSYCHOANALYST WHO STUDIED THE process by which analyst and analysand interweave their story-telling ways and in so doing modulate one, and possibly two, identities, claims that the best case history proceeds as follows: the patient's story is recorded as initially narrated. The doctor then records the transformations he himself is moved to make—toning down a guilt-ridden explanation in favor of a more rational one, perhaps, or shifting the patient beyond "I was angry" by suggesting "you probably felt hurt and disappointed as well." Finally the doctor listens for and records the patient's response to the modifications he has suggested. Do this, Schafer says, several thousand times, and you will have a true picture of the way a person changes not only in therapy but in ordinary life. Put more simply, true dialogue produces change, but silence, like inaction, leaves secrets disturbingly undisturbed.[1]

1. Roy Schafer, "Narration in the Psychoanalytic Dialogue," *Critical Inquiry* 7 (1980): 29–53.

When I first met Lloyd Bartlett, he was so full of secrets that he was afraid to open his mouth. A thin and unusually white-skinned man of about fifty, Mr. Bartlett stood out from those around him by dint of his intense vigilance and the air of intelligence that his questioning gray eyes conveyed. I liked him immediately. Although loath to join in conversation, which I soon learned would reveal the extent to which an absolutely fantastic world of his own construction dominated his thinking, he seemed fairly bursting with a frustrated need to explain himself. He read. He wrote. He brought an old leather briefcase bulging with notes with him to therapy every week. He seemed ready to take off and travel with a clearer eye through the extraordinary landscape of his life.

During the first six or seven months of therapy, my attention was divided between recording Mr. Bartlett's story "as initially narrated" and watching him reenter the ordinary world for the fifteenth or sixteenth time after a long hospitalization. The recording was more difficult than I had anticipated, both because there was an ordinary as well as an imaginary life to document, and because neither one of us could tell exactly which memories belonged in each. Despite this, the reentry process was going smoothly. Mr. Bartlett was settling into a small apartment, and was applying for a part-time job.

Typically, Mr. Bartlett would arrive at the clinic every Tuesday morning at nine A.M., dressed as if strolling onto a college campus to teach a class. He was a neat man, and although an income from Social Security disability insurance precluded him from dressing with style, he took pains with his attire. He wore khakis with a brown sweater or gray slacks with a blue sweater. The knot of a red tie poked above the neckline of both outfits, and in winter he wore old-fashioned galoshes over his shoes.

Once in the waiting room, Mr. Bartlett would stow his beat-up leather briefcase at his feet, settle into a wing chair and disappear behind a book. Sometimes he read about anthropology, I noticed, but just as often his taste ranged broadly over natural history, sociology, and linguistics. "I am comforted by order," he would say. Invited into my office, he would sit down and immediately steer the conversation away from himself.

"I have read the most wonderful article on dreaming," he would say, leaning forward with enthusiasm, whereupon he would launch into a long and curiously pointless discussion on the possible uses of dreams. Shakespeare, Freud, Seneca, and Lloyd Bartlett, all would rub shoulders in this discussion—all offer their comments in a single, unbroken, and quite uninterruptible monologue.

When corralled back into his own life, Mr. Bartlett became unhappy, a state of mind that by and large I deduced from his tone of voice. He was one of those unusual people who says more with the quality of his voice than with the words he selects or the expressions that he allows to cross his face. In fact, he seemed to have a flat, ordinary voice for ordinary topics and a deeper, richer voice for matters of importance.

"I have met my landlady," he would say in his ordinary voice. Or, "I dropped into the library yesterday and got a borrower's card."

"And?" I would ask.

"And I am not eager to associate with the people in either place. I make a strong impression, I know, and I think it is my apparent confidence which people find annoying. . . . Of course, I expect to be criticized."

"Why is that?"

"Well, I feel that my father rejected me—horribly—and my mother was powerless to do much about it," he would explain, hugging the safety of abstractions. "I stood up for her, but she was too disappointed to respond. They each oppressed me in their separate ways."

"And you were often criticized?" I asked, still shouldering Mr. Bartlett toward the particular.

"You could say they made it hard on me," he responded, shifting in his seat and fingering the knot of his tie.

"Could you give me an example of your father making life hard on you?"

This kind of question made Mr. Bartlett exceedingly uncomfortable. He stared at the floor and tapped one finger on the arm of the chair.

"Well . . . he tried to kill me by cutting through the steering cables on my car," he finally blurted out. "That's making life hard. If you want to hear about it."

I was silent.

"I know perfectly well *they* don't want me to talk about it," he continued with irritation, referring no doubt to a dozen hospital policies that discouraged the discussion of delusions. "It's all a delusion. Nothing of all I remember has ever happened, and everyone who has merely looked upon my countenance knows the truth of my life better than I do. It is best I remain silent."

Week after week we went through this same routine, I hoping he would show me where his heart lived; he anxious to tell me of his fantastic adventures but afraid I would reject them with an animosity usually reserved for lies. Gradually, however, he realized that I did not consider any parts of his life irrelevant, and we settled down to consider an outrageously adventurous life disguised as the wanderings of a shy eccentric.

The gist of Mr. Bartlett's ordinary life is easy to convey. The younger of two children, he was born in a small New England town to a mother he described as disappointed and a father who was manly, silent, and alcoholic. A domineering older sister overshadowed Mr. Bartlett throughout his childhood, and he did not break free of what he recalls as a triple tyranny until he left to study anthropology in college. After graduating, he moved to Michigan to work on a collection of Algonquin relics, and it was there, among the bones and baskets, that he had his first psychotic break. Diagnosed as a paranoid schizophrenic, he embarked upon what is not, alas, an atypical "career" as a chronic mental patient. For a year or two he would get a job and stay out of trouble—sometimes on medication, sometimes not— but then the delusions would intensify and he would be picked up along a river running away from invisible pursuers or arrested for trying to tear "his" fishing trophy off the wall of a tackle shop. Back into the hospital he would go for several months or even a year, at which point the cycle would begin anew.

Mr. Bartlett's other life was something else again. His troubles began shortly after birth, and he claimed that in one way or another, they all stemmed from a superabundance of mental abilities. He was an abnormally precocious child, he told me, who learned to walk and run at six months of age, talk at seven months, and read a few weeks later. At that point, his surly father caught him dragging copies of *Treasure Island* and *The Swiss Family Robinson* around behind him on a baby blanket and decided that the child could not be his. The elder Mr. Bartlett set out to destroy Lloyd, and he would have succeeded had not Mrs. Bartlett sent her son away in the care of an overweight Indian named Bobby Two-Ton Eagle.

For two and a half years young Master Bartlett lived in a basket strapped to the back of this great black-haired, hooknosed man whose job it was to protect his charge from the elder Mr. Bartlett and from other misguided characters, such as Benny Eiso (alias Medicine Man), Rollo Nomel, Rhea Bendix, the Ring of 100 Points, and the well-meaning but utterly demoniacal Marvel Red-Bone. There were a dozen or more of these curiously named characters in Lloyd Bartlett's world, each of whom possessed startling abilities such as superhuman strength, X-ray vision, a compendious knowledge of poisons, or the persistence to track the vulnerable Mr. Bartlett to the ends of the earth. Each of these personae was either hideously hurtful or, like Bobby Two-Ton Eagle and Armand LaCherry, helpful but somewhat inept. From my point of view, I believed that, good or bad, all of these fabulous characters would undergo a slow and magnificently intricate metamorphosis as therapy proceeded and the changes that Schafer outlined got under way. I was only sort of right.

Of course, when Mr. Bartlett walked into my office at nine and sat down with his briefcase between his feet, he did not tell me which of his two lives he was prepared to discuss.

"For many years I was afraid to walk to school," he might begin, ordinarily enough. "We lived in a farmhouse—rented, as I remember—and the quickest way to school was to cut across the pastures that lay behind our house. The fields were full of cows then, bulls, too, or so my sister impressed upon me, and I was very much afraid of being gored. Luckily, the Council saw the danger. I don't think I was supposed to notice ... but I knew I had escorts."

Typically, what sounded like a common childhood memory would slip sideways under Mr. Bartlett's reexamination and drop—slowly or quickly—into another world. From my perspective, it sounded as if he learned to cross the fields by telling himself stories of protection, but Mr. Bartlett did not intend to be metaphorical.

Once the Indians left him a pebble, which he pocketed and then stubbornly presented to his class as an arrowhead.

"Teachers resent anyone who knows more than they do," he said simply. "I was sent home because I would not cover up for their ignorance."

In this instance it seemed clear that the Indians were imaginary, but the pastures, cows, and pebble all part of his experience. In a somewhat similar fashion, Medicine Man's plans to kill Mr. Bartlett by dropping him on a glacier in Alaska or by throwing him off a fire tower were also clearly delusional, even though ordinary accounts of getting lost or of falling out of a tree house shadowed these adventures like faintly visible Indians. One morning, for example, I listened to another episode in the walking-to-school-with-Indians series, followed by an account of being teased by his sister and pushed out of a tree house on his head when he was nine-and-a-half. Unlike the Indian stories, the tree house account included both specific details—"I was nine-and-a-half"— and consequences such as, "Every time I tried to sit up, I'd get dizzy and throw up." These were missing to a remarkable extent from the other adventures, and soon I tended to consider any story real that was both plausible and described in detail.

But just as I was accepting the tree house episode as real according to these criteria, Medicine Man jumped into the scene and repeatedly urged his victim to sit up and vomit. Mrs. Bartlett then entered the story in a disembodied way to say, "You shouldn't have hit him on the head, now he won't grow any taller." These were particularly confusing complications, for schizophrenic delusions had no business invading a nine-year-old's world: in theory they are rarely in evidence before adolescence. It was possible, of course, that Mr. Bartlett had gone back over his childhood memories after he had become delusional and embellished them almost beyond recognition, as I had seen others do. In any case, he did not have two, clearly separable lives but a tapestry promiscuously woven out of everything at hand.

There were holes as well as unexpected repetitions in this baroque tapestry that made understanding its construction and its meaning more difficult still.

"They blew smoke up my nose to make me forget." Or "They drugged me till I passed out," were common themes in his accounts, as they are, indeed, for many schizophrenics. "I'd wake up and something would happen," Mr. Bartlett would say. "Then blank, I'd go to sleep. Then I'd wake up and something else would happen. It's a kind of brainwashing that keeps you from getting the story straight."

Regardless of origin, some of these holes seemed to be simple absences and others seemed more like shuttered windows behind which, I imagined, lay hurtful recollections. He referred to "pieces of my past breaking off" and blamed the phenomenon—again, as many schizophrenics do—on drugs and chemicals.

The repetitions were as strange as the holes. If he fell on his head at nine-and-a-half, then he seemed fated to fall on his head for the rest of his life—off fire towers, out of tall buildings, off bridges. And if he was tormented by some nasty little kid at school, he was dogged for the rest of his days by sadistic dwarfs like Rollo Nomel. Memories tagged along after Mr. Bartlett like pull toys, and nothing that happened to him was ever permanently laid to rest.

After covering his childhood adventures in this fragmented and confusing way, Mr. Bartlett moved on to his college years. He did well, enjoyed dating in groups, and was in love with a girl named Nancy when he graduated. Landing a job in a small museum, he rented an apartment with two friends, Donald and the four-foot-six-inch Rollo Nomel (whose name, I noticed, was "lemon" spelled backwards). Nancy was invited to join more and more of their activities, and gradually Rollo became interested in Lloyd's girl. Rollo, who had gone through college on his winnings from quoits and horseshoes, began leaving Mr. Bartlett suggestive messages with his quoits, and the young curator became convinced that Nancy was cheating on him. Possibly, he thought, Rollo was attracted to them both. Daily becoming more paranoid and rude, Mr. Bartlett soon kicked his room-mates out, tearfully broke up with Nancy, and was summoned to Small Claims Court for unpaid rent.

"Losing Nancy was the turning point," he said many times. "Before that, I had a high regard for—not just my abilities—but for my . . . my . . . "

"Deportment?"

"Thank you. Yes, my deportment. I prided myself on a lot of qualities—loyalty, reasoning, humor, a formidable wit. Many people were jealous of me. But I lost my confidence in all these areas after she left. Nothing has gone right for very long since Michigan."

Mr. Bartlett continued the story of his young adulthood, still halfheartedly trying to separate fact from fancy. It seemed that Rollo Nomel had been sodomized by a chief of police in his for-mative years, "which I *think* really happened and which could explain why he became such a spoiler." The dwarf came back into the picture when Mr. Bartlett began courting the sophisti-cated Natalia, a senior curator who worked at the same museum.

"I was led to believe that Natalia was everything I wanted." She was beautiful, he explained, outrageously intelligent, recog-nized and respected—she had graduate degrees in anthropology, psychology, physics, and law. She was also rich, oversexed, and attracted to him.

"I definitely remember that we challenged each other with crossword puzzles we made up ourselves. We joked around, too, but the best were our conversations. We talked to each other endlessly—I do remember that. We'd use a special channel and talk all night. 'In a dark time,'" he quoted in his rich voice, "'the eye begins to see.'"

It was at night, talking over the channel, that Natalia explained to Mr. Bartlett that she had years of work to complete before considering marriage, but that in the meantime her sexual appetites forced her toward some rather extreme solutions, which she would share with him when the time was right.

"That's about the time I was eased out of my job, no question about that. I returned to New England."

Hardly was he back east, however, when Rollo Nomel, who was now ejaculating on the hour in a frenzy of hostility, got Rhea Bendix to go after Mr. Bartlett while Rollo took care of Natalia. The tall, asexual Bendix, as she was called, was a vindictive man-hater who, I noted, used many of the same tricks that Medicine Man kept up his sleeve. Catching Mr. Bartlett in his rented room one evening, she knocked him out with smoke. (The story staggered here as it changed focus and Bendix was, perhaps suddenly, given a history that linked her to Mr. Bartlett for decades.) When the helpless Mr. Bartlett woke up, Bendix told him pointedly that she had not raped him with a dildo, but that Natalia may not have been so lucky. Mr. Bartlett frantically called his former love in Michigan only to hear "what I'm quite sure was a simulation of Natalia's voice telling me that she was all right and didn't need my help."

Believing that this was a trick rather than a rejection, he threw himself on the first bus he could find and set off westward.

"I don't think I'd slept for days," he recounted, "and the warm rumbling of the bus drugged me. I remember the conductor shaking me, maybe in Detroit . . . at night. I had to get off the bus. I'd lost my wallet, so I think I hitchhiked." He paused a long time. "I don't think it was a delusion, but I don't remember the rest."

Another one of those shuttered windows, I thought, and surmised that splinters of painful reality—in this case, an outright rejection by Natalia—lay behind it.

At the same time that Mr. Bartlett was giving me spotty accounts of his two lives, he was also embarking upon a third. He had found himself a part-time job as a cataloger in the local library. Although winter was approaching, he added a three-mile walk and a trip to Edna's Coffee Shop for chili to his daily regime.

All this progress in the community made Mr. Bartlett increasingly miserable. It seemed that the more contact he had with what might be called ordinary life, the more he realized how unacceptable his ideas were and how little he desired to fit into the social slots available to a chronic mental patient.

"I see now that my thinking has all gone to hell," he said one morning in great agitation. "I have nothing to talk about except delusions, I'm old, marginally employed, and totally unappreciated. My chances for a good life are nonexistent."

"Did something happen at work?" I asked.

"No, nothing ever happens at work or at 'home,' either." He leaned on the word *home* sarcastically. "People don't have room for me the way I am."

"What do they have room for?"

"The dull, stupid part," he shot back. "The mind spinning in neutral, unconnected, without love or imagination or invention. A boring, depressing nothing of a person."

There was very little encouragement that I could honestly give to Mr. Bartlett when he complained, as he increasingly did, of having a life that degraded his natural abilities. As he himself occasionally understood, he was caught in a vicious circle that made friendships almost impossible to develop. Afraid of ridicule, he was so guarded in his conversations that no one learned enough about him to feel comfortable in his presence. His acquaintances remained cool, and this made Mr. Bartlett even more wary. If on the other hand he dropped his guard, the results were equally unsatisfactory. If he attended a meeting of the Travelers Club at the library, for example, and found himself sitting next to an attractive woman interested in Alaska, he might casually tell her of being left to die as a child on the Mendenhall Glacier. Whether Mr. Bartlett remained aloof with his acquaintances or tried to draw them in, the result was the same. He was held at arm's length by the rest of the world.

The more Mr. Bartlett felt confused and unappreciated, the more he turned to his imagination, not exactly to comfort himself with make-believe, but more precisely to give himself the illusion of being connected to the rest of the world. After one particularly disastrous misunderstanding with a woman in the library, which Mr. Bartlett "mended" with elaborate delusions, he said, "I have imagined many things in order to comprehend what happens to me and what I feel. It's my attempt to understand what's going on."

To make sense of the scrambled messages sent by your brain and the pejorative ones sent by society, I thought to myself.

"You might say there is such a thing as a necessary illusion," he continued thoughtfully. "There are times in my life when the illusion of love is necessary for my stability."

Nowhere was this more evident than in his stories of Bobby Two-Ton Eagle. Although he had good things to say about Armand LaCherry, Minister of Indian Affairs, who "was behind every good thing that ever happened to me," the memories that gave Mr. Bartlett the most solid sense of connection revolved around his dearest companion, Bobby Two-Ton Eagle, "the man who could not fly."

One early December Mr. Bartlett arrived in my office looking noticeably sadder than before. His shoulders slumped forward and he carried his briefcase as if filled with stone. He told me in a rather lackadaisical manner about being tracked by Rollo Nomel and his Ring of 100 Points, whose goal it was to bring down anyone of superior intelligence. He told of hiding out in the woods with Bobby Two-Ton Eagle, of falling into a chasm, and of having the bodies of dead deer catapulted at them from trees. He told me again of his concern for Natalia, and how he must have gotten to central Michigan somehow to make sure she had survived Rollo's attack. But wherever the story went, it kept circling back to Bobby Two-Ton Eagle. "He never betrayed me," he would interject. "He risked his life forty-four times for me."

"What brings Bobby to mind so much today, Mr. Bartlett?" I finally asked.

An expression of pure anguish snatched at his usually well-composed features.

"It's his birthday," he said, and I thought he was going to cry.

"His birthday," I echoed in surprise. "And you're wishing . . ."

"I just want to know he's all right," he replied in his deeper, fuller voice. "Forty-four times. I wish I could see him again.

"You know, I could feel him as a kid," he went on after a pause. "I could feel his voice." He paused again. "Bobby would always tell me the truth. No tricks. No games. The man was the yardstick for my reality."

What I found most astounding in this period of deep sadness that lasted through the holidays and on into a new year was not that delusions could seem more real than ordinary experience, but that Mr. Bartlett expressed such moments of real concern for his creations. Delusions are generally such self-centered affairs that even when their theme is altruistic, every bit of the action travels inward, as if along the spokes of a wheel toward the mind at its hub. Yet here was Mr. Bartlett hoping that one of the most purely delusional of his companions, Bobby Two-Ton Eagle, was "all right" on his birthday. My dreams of fully understanding his delusions melted away as easily as I imagined Mr. Bartlett's enormous Indian could disappear into a morning mist.

On into the new year, Mr. Bartlett mourned the loss both of the men and women he remembered loving most and of the opportunities he'd had in middle age to build a satisfying life. As powdery snows fell upon powdery snows, he waded into reality with his galoshes on and admitted to being delusional "part of the time." But even part of the time meant losing large chunks of his past, losses he had to endure uncomforted by his meager and uncertain future. He noticed he was sleeping more. I noticed he was losing weight.

"There was a time when I knew how to cry," he said to me one wintry day. Or another time, sitting stiff and reserved in his wool sweater and khakis, "I can tolerate almost anything—the torture, the loneliness, even the hospitalizations—as long as I have someone to love."

It was a sad time, but one of real gains. For several months I had heard almost nothing of his great accomplishments—his prize-winning books on anthropology, which described rites of passage among the Algonquins, or his exhibits at the World's Fair where he demonstrated the life-saving technique of "melting" (through walls), which sounded like the disappearing acts I yearned to accomplish myself in childhood nightmares. More significantly, certain people like Rollo Nomel and Natalia were changing, as Roy Schafer had predicted the major players in a person's life would. In the case of Natalia, the metamorphosis from passionate (but unconsummated) love object to "not such a big deal, I was probably still thinking of Nancy," seemed a familiar progression and one that I gently encouraged. Long ago he had turned a desperate crush into the promise of Paradise and now, in retrospect, he found that he had overreacted. He was, simply, embarrassed. The change in his point of view moved him a step closer to "reality," one might say, but the important result was that I thought he could tell this disappointed-in-love story to others, whereas he could not share his magic-lover account with anyone except, sometimes, a therapist.

With Rollo Nomel, the change proceeded differently. Personally, I expected the man to grow a foot taller and lose his malevolence. Instead, he seemed to split into two beings, a plausible, abstract entity and a well-remembered, fleshed-out delusion.

"I *may* have been delusional at that time," Mr. Bartlett would say seriously. "I may have embellished. Still, I heard his voice coming through my pillow, night after night. *His* voice. And I'm sure I saw his quoits, the way he arranged them. I can picture them now. I can draw you a diagram."

"So what are you left with?" I asked.

"The wrong set of memories," he answered. "Logically, I can guess at what probably happened, but the actual memories I have in my head are of a miserable little man who was after my girl." He shook his head. "It is extremely disconcerting to doubt the contents of your own mind."

This, then, was Lloyd Bartlett at his best—reasonable and depressed. His hopes for an interesting life were realistically minimal, but he was doing his best to say good-bye to the florid phases of his illness when, as he had told me, "I was *alive*. Ideas flowed. I had momentum. Even if all the exchanges were with myself, I had momentum."

And this, then, was perhaps me at my best as well—reasonable and confident. My hopes were that Lloyd Bartlett would gradually adjust to a life in Hillsdale. I pictured him living alone for the rest of his life, an accepted, even respected fixture at the

Hillsdale library—a person like my Latin teacher in high school, who quietly commuted between the present and Caesar's Rome. Frankly, I hoped that Mr. Bartlett would never again become *"alive"* in that irrational, hard-driving way that invariably led to terror, restraints, medication, and more of those blank spots in his memory. Instead, I hoped he would perfect the trick he'd already started to use when tripped up by a real-life companion. "Excuse me," he had learned to say. "I got that mixed up with a book I'm reading."

As winter overstayed its welcome and wood smoke continued to spiral into a lead-colored sky, Mr. Bartlett seemed to divide himself in two, much like Rollo Nomel. On the one hand there was a cautious Mr. Bartlett who added four more hours a week to his job at the library and asked for more medication when he caught himself "starting to create things again." On the other hand, there was a newly ardent Mr. Bartlett who smiled and looked me in the eye when he spoke. This one was becoming more and more interested in re-remembering Natalia.

"'What lips my lips have kissed and where and why,'" he began on one occasion, quoting Edna St. Vincent Millay and giving me a wink. "You have to understand," he continued as, to my surprise, he leaned back languorously in his chair, hands folded behind his head, "that when I think of Natalia, it brings back other memories as well. I went home for lunch yesterday and napped until three."

"You thought of Natalia till three?"

"I am gradually piecing my life back together," he continued, sweeping grandly around my question, as he increasingly did, "and memories seem to come back when I sit in the rocking chair and smoke. I pull the blinds, and just let my mind wander. I had forgotten Natalia's passion for pistachios."

As I watched, Mr. Bartlett deftly slipped his mooring and drifted away.

"I had forgotten Natalia promised to train me as a masseur," he was saying in his strong voice. "Natalia used to tell me that when she had finished her work she would take me on a cruise with her. She had a license to navigate ships of any size—you see, her uncle was an admiral in the navy. We would spend hours at night planning our trip—I had been given a complete world atlas by the *National Geographic* for some work I had done for them—and we would dream along together until she had to go. ... " Here he interrupted himself with a private chuckle. "She explained to me about . . . well, about her sexual appetite. Pro-digious. She had arrangements, you know, but I couldn't be included in them quite yet. You see, she had made a pact with someone whose name I forget, but it was through a branch of the Council on Indian Affairs directed by Armand LaCherry, to remain unmarried—but hardly celibate—until her work on the Algonquins was finished. She was studying tribal rites of passage—she had a degree—and it was important that she not contaminate her views with a Western-style marriage. So in the meantime we, ah, we enjoyed ourselves."

Propelled by the twin streams of memory and imagination, Mr. Bartlett's rudderless craft swept onward through a fabulous countryside of pacts, arrangements, possibilities, and dreams. His resonant voice pitched and rolled over waves of words as he described, more for himself than for me, the sights he encountered. Unlike other travelers who are content to leave what they see behind them, Mr. Bartlett had a compulsion to acquire everything he laid his eyes on—everything that crossed his mind. Thus, as he went bobbing through his own imagination, he took on board as personal cargo pedigreed livestock, plots of movies, plans, arguments, Indians, knockout drops, perversions, and hundreds of love songs. With explanations as logical as they were implausible, he lashed cows, couples, and castles to his raft. As he pulled a scheme for steam-cleaning the Grand Canyon aboard with his other creations, Mr. Bartlett himself disappeared from sight.

"I had forgotten so much," he concluded, emerging at last with a satisfied smile. "*Dear* Natalia."

As spring arrived, Mr. Bartlett continued to feel and look better. He walked longer distances, he worked harder, and for the first time since I'd known him he came to sessions in shirt sleeves. He explained that the "brainwashing" of some thirty years was finally wearing off and he was thrilled to be reunited with so many parts of his past.

There was a freshness, too, in his views on delusions.

"I can tell the difference now," he maintained, noting that his former confusion had resulted from going over and over his adventures so many times that they had become real for him. And he had a theory as to why such stories had developed in the first place: "I think they were a substitute for a boring life, a kind of antidote for failure. I needed to give my life significance."

In spite of these insights, it was clear that Mr. Bartlett was becoming increasingly delusional. Fantasy infused his recollections as naturally as green returned to grass. His stories sounded less and less real, while a personal happiness that seemed genuine in every respect mounted visibly from week to week.

So when he strode into my office, tossed his jacket over the back of his chair, and announced that he finally remembered what had happened in Michigan, I was not sure what to expect.

"Do you remember when I was worried about Natalia?"

I nodded.

"When I sensed that Bendix was after me and Rollo Nomel was threatening Natalia?"

I nodded again.

"Well, I'd forgotten a crucial fact. While I was riding toward Detroit on the bus, I finally remembered that the Ring of 100 Points had installed a transmitter in my briefcase. *All the rest came back.* I remembered overhearing their communications and realizing they were closing in on Natalia. It sounded as if they had surrounded her apartment and had the drugs and creams hidden in a postal truck out front. When I got to Detroit, I realized that the Ring knew I was coming and had stolen my wallet in hopes of stopping me. I had to hitchhike out of the city at night—got two rides in jalopies with black hoodlums, I finally remembered—and ended up in one of those huge truck stops with diners and rigs and diesel pumps spread over acres."

Mr. Bartlett paused slightly here, as if suddenly uncertain which way to go, and I had time to note the surprise I felt in finding a forgotten delusion rather than a sad memory emerging from one of his "blanks."

"There was a fence," he continued, peering back into the past. "Yes. There was a fence. I was pretty scared at that point."

"Scared of what?"

"Scared of the thugs who were chasing me, of course. I had gone into a men's room . . . somewhere . . . and I think the guys I'd been riding with followed me. They may have been Ring members, but in any case I ran and they chased me with their pants open. That's when I went over the fence and lost the rest of my stuff. But I still heard the broadcasts," he continued rapidly, recovering his former confidence. "And I knew that they'd gotten Natalia. They were damaging her with the, uh, well with the ring of hypnotic masturbation. . . ." He shook his head sadly.

"I told you that there was a time when I felt things intensely, when I knew how to cry," he continued, his voice full of concern. "I cried then."

We sat in silence for a minute or so.

"Were you able to help Natalia?" I asked.

"No, not really. I had to run for it for days. You know, I had also forgotten that when I was dating Nancy. . . ."

Mr. Bartlett then launched briskly into an unrelated account and was annoyed when I brought his attention back to Michigan.

"The police picked me up and put me in a hospital for protection," he concluded, "and that was that."

"Did you visit Natalia when you got out?"

"Yes, but by that time the danger was over and we didn't have much to say."

Mr. Bartlett fell silent, and I was left again with my sense of surprise. I had believed the trip to Michigan to be a classic example of one of those missing pieces or shuttered windows that gave Mr. Bartlett's autobiography such a decidedly fragmented style. I had expected that a real scene with a stern and rejecting Natalia lay behind the shutters, and that its restoration would improve the coherence, if not the happiness, of Mr. Bartlett's account. Instead, a further set of delusions was being revealed. He had finally remembered the original delusions he had experienced on the trip. I thought then of the concept of "state-dependent memory," which suggests that memories formed in one context—say as an inebriated person at a bar or as a delusional person in a rocking chair—will be more easily recalled in a similar context than they will in a different place or during a different state of mind. Apparently, as Mr. Bartlett got deeper into his delusions, memories of old delusions became easier to remember and came flooding back. I was also beginning to understand that Mr. Bartlett was usually forced into a hospital just as the great barge-loads of delusional material he accumulated were overflowing, and because he was then medicated and discouraged from discussing his adventures, he did not have the opportunity to fix the newest adventures in his mind by thinking and talking about them. Understandably, the dramatic denouements that took place several days or several hours before being sedated were the most difficult, in later years, to remember.

I was also beginning to realize that Mr. Bartlett's stories, regardless of their mixture of experience, misinterpreted experience, and pure fantasy, had a curiously inconclusive quality about them. Not only did they repeat themselves with minor variations, but they never ended, never got to the point. Initially I had believed he was not telling me his stories' conclusions because they were too outlandish or risqué, and I had tried to finish off the loose ends by asking him directly how a story ended or by trying on a resolution borrowed from other patients' experiences. Neither method worked. The hypnotic ring of masturbation, for example, was a topic Mr. Bartlett brushed aside as being beneath both our dignities, and the descriptions of masturbation under "hypnosis" I received from two middle-aged women gave me only marginally useful insights. One of these women, a charming redhead, said that one night in the hospital her memory had been tampered with, and a dream had gotten mixed up with a happening. She explained this disconcerting feeling by surmising that doctors had crept into the rooms and hypnotized the patients.

"Next," she said, "they had us get out of bed and stand in

the hallway in a line and masturbate. The staff watched us and then I think we watched them. Something happened, and we were used."

This sounded like a memory or a reliving of childhood sexual abuse, complete with the common feelings of distance and numbness. The second woman's description of a "hypnotic" state sounded much the same. She told me she had turned into an inert, doll-like being who was laid out on a marble pedestal while men masturbated around her. She was then forced to witness drooling, blank-eyed women in barrels having intercourse with donkeys and was finally handed over to a necrophiliac who mistook her for a corpse.

Like Mr. Bartlett's stories, both accounts described a confused, dreamlike state in which one was powerless to avoid sexual acts that I sensed were both abhorrent and intriguing. Also like his accounts, there was no action that produced results, not even imaginary results.

"One thing is certain," my red-haired patient told me, "there's no way to find out the truth when you're trapped halfway between the dream and the world."

Spring at last began to appear, and as the blunt spikes of daffodils paraded around the clinic's cement foundation, Mr. Bartlett announced that he was no longer in need of medication.

"We've been given the go-ahead," he proclaimed by way of explanation, "and I'm going to need all the energy and quick thinking I can muster. Marvel Red-Bone is on the scene"—he rubbed his hands—"and it's my belief that things will start to move pretty fast now."

Mr. Bartlett was in fine form that morning. Handsome, confident, witty, charming, and finally "feeling like *me!*" he whisked me into a scheme that, although not yet on the front page of the *New York Times*, was putting a gleam into ten thousand pairs of Indian eyes. It seemed that the Cleveland-educated, half-Navaho engineer Marvel Red-Bone had returned from designing a desalinization plant that would use pulverized ice from Antarctica to water Australia and ultimately solve the world's hunger problems. Now, in search of some fun, he was assembling Indians from 302 tribes to clean the Grand Canyon.

It was going to be an enormous, noisy, month-long party, and Mr. Bartlett would be at its center.

Over the next six weeks Mr. Bartlett rollicked and swaggered among the crème de la crème, the bluebloods, the giants of the earth. And "no," he did not need extra medication, "thank you." Every week he strode into my office so full of news that his briefcase hadn't touched the floor before I learned that at his prompting, Marvel Red-Bone had convinced the Sikorski Aircraft Company to donate helicopters. At his suggestion, Marvel Red-Bone had made a deal with the Yosemite Vacuum Company to build enormous steam cleaners. And acting on Mr. Bartlett's inspiration, Marvel Red-Bone had convinced the United States Geological Survey to offer $4 million for a before and after photographic study. Mr. Bartlett himself was in charge of cultural affairs and was organizing a powwow of heroic proportions. He would launch into a long discussion on the customs and contributions from the different tribes, and while thus engaged, no question could deflect his imagination and no challenge undermine his city of dreams.

I am willing to wager that the memory I have of the great spring-cleaning plan is very different than the account that Mr. Bartlett carries in his head, and in these differences lies a clue to one of the essential problems of delusions. As Mr. Bartlett would describe the project, I pictured the helicopters—tribal symbols emblazoned on their sides—that were scheduled to drop over the rim of the canyon at daybreak as deep purple shadows gave way to startling shades of orange, red, and gold. I imagined the steam jets carried aboard the helicopters turned on with a sound like distant explosions. Foaming columns of steam and water burst onto the canyon walls. As Mr. Bartlett outlined the tricky parts—many involving aerial acrobatics performed by the dauntless Marvel Red-Bone—the accumulated grime from millions of auto exhausts was scoured away, and I could see the colors brightening until, beneath a hundred sparkling sheets of dripping water, the true glory of ancient rocks returned.

Not so for him. Although he would tell me that the details of each adventure were "altogether too vivid to be imaginary," I found quite the opposite to be true.

"Marvel Red-Bone will clean the intricate areas," he would say, then veer off into a description of who was supplying what equipment to whom. "Marvel Red-Bone will receive acrobatic training from the famous Provazza family in Italy," but he would not describe a single swing or leap. Mr. Bartlett clearly preferred the abstract possibility over the concrete occurrence, and when a delusion came entirely from his imagination, or from what he referred to as his "channels," then abstraction was dominant. By contrast, when a delusion came from the mis-interpretation of an actual event—the finding of a piece of pink paper in his wire wastebasket, for example, from which he deduced that his office had been searched—then telltale adjectives and adverbs enlivened the story. In these instances, he was left with a mental picture that was complete with ordinary details. But Mr. Bartlett distrusted even the few props that were stolen from reality because, I was beginning to see, particulars pushed his stories toward action whereas abstractions did not. Here was a problem.

All stories sustain themselves by progressing along a winding path of particulars, and so do lives. Real actions are undertaken by specific individuals who suffer the results of their deeds, and this creates the plot of a story and the life of a person. It works in this rather haphazard but particular way on every level, from sentence to story, and from cell to soul. Descartes to the contrary notwithstanding, we do not think ourselves into existence. In a well-known experiment, rats who were allowed no activity other than watching other rats live a normal, ratty life failed to develop the kind of brain cells needed for fast and complicated process-ing. We do not live by thinking nor by watching. We must do, and even our fictions reflect this essential habit of action.[2]

2. Another way of saying that a schizophrenic can't fully identify with his own experience has been proposed by Louis Sass in *Madness and Modernism*. Sass makes the astute observation that an individual such as Mr. Bartlett *simultaneously* feels himself to be both the author of his fantasies and the object—a helpless pawn caught in someone else's story. To adopt this impossible, unstable position of being both master and slave at the same time is, in Sass's opinion, a caricature of modern thinking. Louis Sass, *Madness and Modernism: Insanity in the Light of Modern Art, Literature, and Thought* (New York: Basic Books, 1992.)

Thus, as I listened to Marvel Red-Bone's endless prepara-
tions for an act that would never be attempted, I realized that
Mr. Bartlett's delusions did not represent true stories, any more
than our conversations about these adventures represented true
dialogue. Marvel sprinted endlessly toward a hurdle that
retreated just as fast as he approached, and we talked for hours
about people we could not possibly engage and possibilities we
could not realize. The essential problem with Mr. Bartlett's delusions was not that he loved fantasy and internal dialogue, which
represented, as they do for all of us, his need to rehearse many
kinds of negotiations in private, to take a break from ordinary
frustrations, or to supply himself with admirers when no real
ones were at hand. Instead, the problem was that he was both
afraid *and incapable* of moving from mental rehearsal to performance.

Mr. Bartlett had often told me that he had no desire to deal
with people because they were not willing to accept his stories
or to respect his qualities of intelligence, wit, and fairness, which
he erroneously believed were only and best illustrated by his
adventures. I think, however, that his deeper fear of acting-in-
the-world sprang from a subconscious understanding that his
brain, with its unpredictable misinterpretations, exposed him to
unacceptable dangers. On some level he realized that when he
dated Nancy, took a bus to Michigan, or struck up a conversation, he exposed his wavering perceptions of reality to other
people and that hurtful misunderstandings were bound to occur.
So pervasive was the danger of *doing* that it had pervaded his
delusions as well. When a reincarnation of Rollo Nomel named
Razor Rinaldo started confusing the complicated exchanges on
which the cleaning project depended, it became clear that such
dangerous misunderstandings were about to begin.

Just as Rollo Nomel and Medicine Man had done for forty
years, Razor sliced his way into Mr. Bartlett's happy plans with
frightening speed. One week Razor was slipping along the edge
of Mr. Bartlett's delusion; by the next he was breaking into the
channels at night with threats of torture. Shortly thereafter he
sent the sinister black giantess, Mama Louis, to torment Mr.
Bartlett as Rhea Bendix had done before.

In May Mr. Bartlett quit his job, and by June he had all but dropped out of therapy. The hours he gained were spent rocking in his living room or lying in his bed with the curtains drawn. He walked only in the evenings. He became shy and agitated.

"If all this business about the Grand Canyon is delusional," he snapped at me one mild spring morning, "then I sure as hell would make my stories have a happy ending. I am being given the runaround again and used as a pawn. I was *assured* that Razor Rinaldo was dead, out of the picture, gone. So who comes breaking into the channel again last night, or whenever it was, but the Gang of Eight. Dr. Baur, this is a serious turn of events. I am not safe any longer and *no one* is helping me. No one believes what I say, and the Razor *knows how to exploit that*. His threats are cleverly ambiguous. I called the police last night—911, that recorded line. I explained quite calmly at first that my landlady's house had been broken into. I saw an old leather glove of mine lying just inside the door—it was stolen out of my coat two months ago—lying behind the door, and I knew that Razor was telling me that he can walk into my apartment any time he pleases. I am not safe. I do not want to be sliced."

"And the police?"

"They took their time as if *nothing* was going on. Finally some fat buffoon came by and suggested I put a dead-bolt on my door. A dead-bolt! Dr. Baur, these men are trained better than Green Berets. There is no lock they can't pick. You can't stop them."

"This has happened to you before?" I asked.

"Oh, indeed," he answered, slumping back in his chair as if quitting the fight. "There must be a law of nature that says, 'Lloyd Bartlett shall not prevail.' I try so hard, and I get stopped so often."

It was three weeks before I saw Mr. Bartlett again. I learned later that he had gone straight home and shut himself in his room. He would not answer his landlady. He would not leave the house for food. He would not run water or walk on bare floor. When the landlady's brother-in-law finally broke down the door a week later to see if the the tenant had died, Mr.

Bartlett jumped from his second-floor window and disappeared into the woods.

I found out later that for several days Mr. Bartlett hitchhiked toward Phoenix with no money and a broken foot. Everyone who picked him up was initially a rescuer, but as soon as Mr. Bartlett told the driver about Razor Rinaldo, he was let out. In similar fashion everything he saw offered a false promise of safety. Traffic lights that were green turned red as he approached. Filling stations that had an even number of pumps were, on closer inspection, found to have a diesel pump out back that made them dangerous, odd-numbered places. Radios that normally played music now carried only the snarling crackle of Rinaldo's sadistic threats.

Driven by hunger, the distraught Mr. Bartlett finally swiped a chocolate bar from a convenience store just as a cruiser pulled up to the pumps outside. The proprietor yelled, Mr. Bartlett hobbled painfully out the back door, and without hesitation dropped into a swamp at the back of the property where, to his amazement (and mine), he noticed a perfectly formed jack in the pulpit growing at the base of a moss-covered stump. Almost immediately, he was immobilized by a weapon that could not be seen or heard. It was at this point that two policemen, guns drawn, ran toward him, shouting angrily in a language he could not understand. One carried a radio device over which the Razor's crazed threats continued to hiss and croak, but the other wore the silver sign of the rising sun. It was to him that Mr. Bartlett surrendered with a feeling of profound relief. As usual, the police put Mr. Bartlett in the one place the gang would not go—a mental hospital. A week later, a heavily sedated Mr. Bartlett was shipped back to New England like a sack of potatoes.

Several days after his extradition, I met Mr. Bartlett on the ward. I was a stranger in this particular hospital and I noticed as only a stranger would the shine on the clean linoleum floors, the emptiness of the corridors, the poignance of the muffled chuckles and murmurs emanating from the nursing station. I was accompanied courteously to an oddly low-ceilinged game room, and there, in a corner behind a pool table, sat a miserable

Mr. Bartlett. He was huddled beneath a beige blanket, and his bandaged foot stuck out of a pair of baggy trousers that had probably been left behind by someone else. He was staring at the floor and frowning.

"Mr. Bartlett?"

Raising his head in alarm, Mr. Bartlett's white and terrified face looked at me in horror.

"They won't turn off the radio," he whispered in a shaky voice as I approached.

"Voices?"

He nodded. "They follow me right into my sleep."

I sat down in the chair next to his, and he told me of his ordeal. From time to time he would stop, and I got the impression that he was listening to messages that played through his head. One silence continued for three or four minutes, broken abruptly by what sounded like stifled whimpers.

"Mmm . . . nnh. Mn-mn."

I glanced sideways as unobtrusively as I could and saw his throat and face working to pronounce words without opening his mouth. "Non, non, mn," he continued, shaking his head gently, and there came to mind a picture of a small boy gagged by hands and bandages and customs and time—a small boy in danger, protected only by imaginary Indians. I have often wondered whether or not Mr. Bartlett noticed he was holding my hand the whole time.

Despite no appreciable change in his belief or behavior, Mr. Bartlett was released from the hospital on the Fourth of July, and our meetings took up where they had begun over a year before.

Every Tuesday morning Mr. Bartlett presented me with problems I could not—and still cannot—solve. Should I take him off all medication as he requests? Watch him come alive? Listen enthralled as great hook-nosed Algonquins parade through my office in gaudy fringed jackets, beating back the sadistic horrors of perverted fiends? Then stand quietly by as "the Razor" drives Mr. Bartlett like a frightened animal through late-night truck stops where a mugging or a bullet may wait for him?

Or should I push the pills, pretend that entering numbers in a library computer two afternoons a week is a good-enough life, and slap a court order of "substituted judgment" on him so that a judge can all but force him to take medication that opens the door to depression?

As the hot weeks pass, and the sun shimmers off the cars in the parking lot outside my window, and the air conditioner buzzes but does not work, I meet with Mr. Bartlett and do a little of each. I help him get back his job. I teach him how to avoid a court order by taking some of his pills some of the time. And I note that in addition to keeping tabs on Bendix, Natalia, Marvel Red-Bone, and Bobby Two-Ton Eagle, there is a second conversation that has quietly and persistently been shadowing the first. In this one, which we do not choose to look at very often, we both understand that Mr. Bartlett's mind does not work as it is supposed to and also that Mr. Bartlett has walked too far with Bobby Two-Ton Eagle and the others to leave them now. To admit that all the people he has ever loved are delusional, and to admit that he still lacks control over his thinking, is to label his entire past insane and his entire future hopeless. Both of us are willing to let the heartbreak take its time in coming.

So we continue, he spinning and weaving his own immaterial past, I listening to a story that is always and in some way about a lonely, endangered kid who was once befriended by an Indian and menaced by dwarfs.

"I heard a new voice over the channel last night," Mr. Bartlett is saying, his rich, lovely voice sliding through the warm air, capturing my imagination. "Marla, I think she said. She told me she'd been dropped on her head as a girl but was discovered lying unconscious by a Kickapoo warrior who had just set forth on a ritual quest. You see, a long, long time ago . . . "

8

IMAGINARY CONVERSATIONS

Philemon and other figures of my fantasies brought home to me the crucial insight that there are things in the psyche which I do not produce, but which produce themselves and have their own life.

C. G. JUNG

IN THE STORIES EXAMINED THUS FAR, THE FOCUS HAS BEEN ON THE social negotiation of meaning. Whether the discussion concerned the working out of explanations for Chuck Willet's or Angie Savalonis's behaviors or the development of a confiding relationship between Charlie Isabella and myself, the emphasis so far has been on stories that two or more people modify through their exchanges. Now I wish to look at stories that are generated privately in our heads and ask first what roles they play and second how they differ from Lloyd Bartlett's Indian sagas.

The average American moves with ease through multiple realities. Every day he speaks with aspects of himself, with imagined replicas of boss, lover, friends, or media figures, and with purely made-up characters as well. Hardly has this ordinary person's head touched the pillow than he leaps into a world of dreams. There he meets and frequently argues with people he knows and with strangers who have come unbidden into his head. When he wakes, he may talk with members of his household before picking up the paper or turning on the television and launching into a running commentary on what he reads or hears. But none of this compares to how his fantasies unfold as he commutes to work. Alone in a car or bus with the steady roar of traffic rumbling around him, he rehearses an eloquent presentation that astounds his colleagues. He chats amicably with himself about being late—"I shouldn't have taken Route 3." "You weren't thinking." "I'll be ten minutes late—you better hope your boss is, too." Then he enchants himself by embroidering an imaginary vacation with warmth, excitement, love, and recognition. As he maneuvers his car into the right lane, small butterflies like airborne violets drift beside a lighter, stronger self who lopes down a grassy meadow toward the sea. He swings onto the sandy road beside the water. He turns off Route 3 in an endless line of dream-filled cars. Although these secret commuters will probably not tell what they have seen, they will continue to spin such fantasies throughout their lives. According to the anthropologist John Caughey, "The evidence is overwhelming that most Americans pass large amounts of time engrossed in imaginary experiences."[1]

Caughey, who has worked in the United States, Pakistan, and the Pacific Islands, is interested in the social relationships that people enjoy in their imaginations. He divides these exchanges into three categories, namely imagined interactions with media figures, dealings with purely imaginary figures both in dreams and awake, and conversations with replicas of real people including aspects of oneself. Except for dreaming and the silent mulling over of problems, none of these activities are generally considered essential in Western societies. In fact, Freud stated flatly that happy people never fantasize, only unsatisfied ones. Caughey does not agree. He argues that we transact important business with the invisible companions in our heads. Take our pseudo relationships with media figures, for example.

1. John Caughey, *Imaginary Social Worlds: A Cultural Approach* (Lincoln, NB: University of Nebraska Press, 1984), p. 26.

The average American "knows" a thousand or more TV personalities, sports figures, politicians, comic book characters, and
movie stars, and together these usually outnumber his "real"
acquaintances four or five to one. In other words, for every person we actually talk to and call by name in the course of an
average year, there are four or five other people like Dan Rather,
the President of the United States, and Jodie Foster whom we
feel we know but have never actually met. Because Americans
spend so much time with their pseudo-acquaintances, their private fantasies are heavily populated by the kinds of people and
behaviors shown on TV. The average sixteen-year-old, for example, has spent more hours in front of a television set than in a
school and in so doing has been exposed to roughly 13,000
killings. Caughey was not surprised to find that "glamorized
violence, predatory sexuality, and selfish materialism" play
enormous roles in the dreams and fantasies of young adults.

Americans of all ages identify with media figures, however,
and in the privacy of their imaginations, they live out the experiences of their favorite fictional characters. Although these imaginary affairs may lead to actual violence in a tiny minority of
cases, for every Mark David Chapman who adulated John
Lennon and then killed him and for every John Hinckley who
fell in love with Jodie Foster then shot President Reagan to
impress her, there are thousands and thousands of apparently
ordinary men and women who actively carry on imagined relationships. These often involve collecting pictures, writing letters,
and discussing their "relationship" with friends. It *always*
involves chatting for hours in "private" conversation.

"We talked to each other endlessly," Lloyd Bartlett told me,
describing his crush on Natalia. "We'd use a special channel and
talk all night."

Having persuaded hundreds of students to jot down their
fantasies for him, Caughey found that a crush on the singer
George Michaels or hero worship of pitcher Roger Clemens did
more than merely provide a substitute idol when a real one
wasn't around, and such a relationship did more than counteract frustration by providing social exchanges that were perfectly
gratifying. The main function of these engrossing relationships,

Caughey maintained, is to enhance the dreamers' self-esteem, and this proceeds by way of a common progression.

An important first step is the selection of the idol.

"The admired figure," Caughey discovered, "is typically felt to have qualities that the person senses in himself but desires to develop further. The admired figure represents an ideal self-image."[2]

"Well, I have to say we *were* a lot alike," admitted Mr. Bartlett after he had listed Bobby Two-Ton Eagle's qualities and compared them to his own at my request. "I'm not nearly as successful or able . . . but at one point I had the potential."

Caughey found that once his informants had "tried on" several stars and settled on one who was like them, they spent a great deal of time picturing the occasion of their first meeting. Over and over again dreamers saw themselves walking into a restaurant, sitting in the front row of a rock concert, attending a Red Sox game, or pitching a no-hitter on the local ball field. Over and over they imagined the star turning and staring, his or her eye caught by some quality that singled out the dreamer from every other person on earth. As "the look" passed between them, the dreamer understood that an important corner in life had been turned.

"It's the moment of acceptance," said one young woman who, dreaming of sailing around the world, repeatedly pictured herself setting foot on the gangplank just as the captain turned and caught her eye.

"It was the true beginning of my life," said Lloyd Bartlett, remembering how his mother handed him over to Bobby Two-Ton Eagle. "He wrapped me in a soft sheepskin and threw me over his head right into the basket."

After replaying the important first meeting dozens or even hundreds of times, the fantasies usually proceed to forming some kind of partnership. Often, the great star falls in love with the day-dreamer or the two take up the star's profession together. Again the scenarios loop back on themselves like coils of heavy rope. Important moments are tirelessly replayed and

2. Caughey, *Imaginary Social Worlds*, p. 54.

feelings of excitement are enjoyed again and again. The dreamers pursue their heroes. They are pursued by them. They save
the star from a burning car. They are saved in turn. They pitch a
no-hitter. They hit the home run at the end of what had been a
no-hitter. And finally, after all this inspired aching and imagining, and after progressing from "I admire them," through "They
accept me," to "I must be terrific," the dreamer attains a wonderful feeling that he or she is truly a unique and special person.
Now, every time a song by George Michael comes over the radio
or Roger Clemens wins a game, dreamers all across the country
feel their self-esteem rise. They are reminded of the special qualities that link them to their heroes.

"I feel better when I hear her voice," said one woman of
Mary Hartman. "She guides my thinking."

"Bobby would always tell me the truth. No tricks. No
games. He was the yardstick for my reality," said Mr. Bartlett.

But isn't this false comfort? If I identify with a media hero or
a purely imaginary figure to the point that songs, events, or
places remind me of our "experiences" together and a happy,
confident feeling is triggered in my mind, isn't this running away
from the real world? Caughey says it is not so simple.

Woolgathering is certainly an escape that may lead to failing
grades, being fired, causing an accident, and other disagreeable
consequences, but, paradoxically, it also reconnects day-dream-
ers to the real life of their society. Caughey found that as he read
over hundreds of fantasies—the city day-dreamer transported to
a silent log cabin in Alaska where she lived off the land, the
ordinary West Pacific Islander reveling in a materialistic Cargo
Cult or Big Man Syndrome, the science student dreaming of the
Nobel Prize—most seemed to reaffirm the very values that the
culture embodied. Charlie Isabella was living out a popular,
albeit ambivalent, American ideal when he reforested a ski slope
and went back to nature with the Indians, and Lloyd Bartlett
was not being subversive of the American way of life when he
recalled writing important books on anthropology and designing pavilions for the World's Fair. His mission to rescue Natalia,
his plan to clean the Grand Canyon, his daring escape from

Razor Rinaldo—all are classic expressions of the standard American fantasy of personal achievement. Caughey could just as easily have been talking about Mr. Bartlett as the girl who wanted to sail around the world when he concluded that when we take time out from the stress of reality to enjoy a fantasy, we are actually playing ourselves a "mental commercial for a materialistic society."[3] Far from leaving America behind or propping ourselves up with false courage, we are giving ourselves a very real pep talk and encouraging ourselves to succeed in exactly those ways that Americans have always admired. Shaking their heads and coming back from their dreams, the would-be sailors vow to work harder, earn more money, and take sailing lessons; the George Michael admirers swear they'll lose weight and buy size 6 jeans. And widows, having consulted their deceased husbands, or "social ghosts" as one psychologist terms them, feel they have the strength now to make difficult decisions. Even in running from the "real world" in fantasy, we strengthen our ties.

Caughey takes this idea—that fantasy enculturates more than it alienates—a step further when he considers the internal ruminating that surrounds actual events. In his studies, he found that this stream of consciousness thinking is crammed with recollections and anticipations of success—mental replays and rehearsals, if you will—but is even more concerned with failure. A critical remark, especially if unexpected, starts ruminations churning.

"Why did she say, 'We've been waiting for someone to put you in your place'?" I found myself wondering insistently after a staff meeting. "Did she really mean 'we'? Or was she the only one who felt I was out of line?"

"What's this 'we' business?" I ask boldly, replaying the incident in my mind but experimenting with an ending I think I'd like better. "No, no, no. That would draw attention to the remark, which luckily no one seemed to hear."

Next I try, "You? Waiting for *someone else* to put me in my place? That's your specialty, isn't it?"

3. Caughey, *Imaginary Social Worlds,* p. 148.

I imagine the awkward silence. "Terrible. Forget it. Silence was probably the best choice at the time."

Caughey maintains that all of us engage in this mental reweaving every day. We play out possible sequences in our minds, and most of the time choose a response that will keep social negotiations moving smoothly. Again, imaginary conversations—our minds' one-act plays, which at first glance seem to lead us away from real situations—strengthen our commitment to the society in which we actually live.

This playing out of possible sequences also serves to fit the unexpected back into the expected pattern of things. Whether I ask myself if a difference of opinion I had with Dr. P. could explain her blunt remark at staff meeting, or whether the kindergartners mentioned in chapter 6 ask themselves if some mistake or lack could explain the topsy-turvy birthday party, our minds tell stories about everything that takes us by surprise. We often get on with the business of living by explaining our way around things that could otherwise, and sometimes should otherwise, stop us in our tracks.

"As usual, the police put me in the one place that Razor and his gang won't go," said Mr. Bartlett, giving me the explanation he had worked out long ago for the always unexpected humiliation of being institutionalized. "A mental hospital."

Caughey maintains that both the rehearsing and explaining of actual events eases the flow of social interactions. We practice our responses to good news and bad, select the responses that help us glide smoothly through, and mark in our minds the impulsive, angry replies that could get us into trouble. We feel our way through alternate scenarios and often reject our first reactions if we see they will cost us too much. Later, when faced with actual rejections or complaints, less takes us by surprise. We have already worked out the kinds of things that are good to say and do, and we have already told ourselves stories that explain why these things happen. In other words, fantasies hold us within the culture both by providing us with a dazzling array of mental commercials for traditional American middle-class values *and* by allowing us hours of private practice that ease the flow of social negotiations. Imaginary companions do more to keep the ordinary individual in the mainstream, Caughey maintains, than to sweep him out to sea.

Before we ask if Mr. Bartlett's imaginary companions do the same for him, we need to examine one more aspect of imagined relationships. This is their ability to uncover, or one might even say to create, useful information. Do dream creatures, disembodied voices, and imaginary companions tell us something we need to know either about ourselves or the wider world? Or do they simply make us feel good and encourage us to work harder for what we want?

Confiding in imaginary characters starts early in life. It has been found that the majority of children between the ages of two and six have imaginary playmates, and firstborn and only children are especially likely to create a "twin," double, or companion with whom they chat openly.[4] (Mr. Bartlett thought the idea of imaginary playmates extremely bizarre. He said he spent his childhood listening to Bobby and didn't have much time for other children, especially imaginary ones.)

Developmental psychologists like the renowned Swiss scientist Jean Piaget have long assumed that the magical playmate is part of a natural progression away from the imaginative and toward the real. Children at the age of three talk to themselves and to imaginary playmates, he noted, but by seven or eight they are leaving this activity behind. Piaget believed that young children create dramatic vignettes, in which they take all the parts, both to practice speaking aloud and to anticipate events that are still novel to them. They openly rehearse all the activities they need to master. After the age of seven, however, they no longer need so much practice, and at that time their dialogues of anticipation—"Now you and I are going to paint a picture"— become the silent conversations of thinking. According to Piaget, as children become more interested in the real world, they leave the imaginary one behind and adopt the logical, abstract thinking needed to understand the real world. If they don't, something is wrong.

Other developmental psychologists have agreed with Piaget

4. Caughey, *Imaginary Social Worlds*, p. 216.

that progress toward adulthood consists in moving from a dramatic, that is, many-voiced kind of thinking that plays with imaginative possibilities to a logical, single-minded style that deals with facts. To think right, they say, is to think logically about the material world.[5] The implication is that spinning fancies produces nothing of importance.

Support for the opposing idea—that it may be natural and informative to maintain a crowd of characters in one's head rather than to think exclusively as a single "I"—is gradually coming to light. For example, recent studies suggest that children who play actively with imaginary pals watch half the average amount of television, have better language skills and are more cooperative.[6] Such children were also found to be less aggressive, better able to concentrate, and less frequently bored.[7] This sounds as if more was going on than the mere practice of speech. Similarly, it was observed in one unusual experiment that, contrary to expectations, schizophrenic patients with hallucinations were more friendly and less defensive than patients without hallucinations.[8] In yet another group of studies, it was found that widows and widowers who maintain an active relationship with a deceased spouse—they talk to them, ask their advice and so forth—enjoy a variety of psychological advantages, such as emotional support and guidance.[9]

A common explanation for the observation that people

5. Caughey and others point out that this progression may say more about Western values than about man's "natural" form of thought, if such a thing exists. As Caughey puts it, if we were intent on raising a generation of playwrights rather than scientists, we would not be so sure that logic is the only form of right thinking. Or as the psychologist Hubert Hermans and his colleagues say more formally, "There is a growing awareness among psychologists that the individualistic and rationalistic character ... of the self reflect an ethnocentric Western view of personhood." Hubert Hermans, Harry Kempen, and Rens van Loon, "The Dialogical Self: Beyond Individualism and Rationalism," *American Psychologist* 47: 23.

6. Caughey, *Imaginary Social Worlds*, p. 216.

7. Mary Watkins, *Invisible Guests* (Boston: Sigo Press, 1990), p. 66.

8. P. M. Lewinsohn, "Characteristics of Patients with Hallucinations," *Journal of Clinical Psychology* 24 (1968): 423.

9. Margaret Stroebe et al., "Broken Hearts or Broken Bonds: Love and Death in Historical Perspective," *American Psychologist* 47 (1992): 1205–12.

sometimes learn from their fantasies is that such people are projecting their thoughts and feelings onto imaginary characters. If they are then led to recognize these feelings as their own, they may gain a measure of personal insight. For example, psychologists routinely use projective tests like the Rorschach (ink blot) test and the Thematic Apperception Test (TAT) to uncover the dynamics of a person's personality long before such an individual is willing or even able to express his or her underlying fears and needs. Take the case of an exceptionally bright thirteen-year-old boy whose mother was overly concerned with his progress at a private school. A TAT picture of a young boy mooning over a violin was given to him, and he was asked to make up a story about the picture:

> Looks like a boy. His mother is making him learn how to play the violin. He has to take very good care of it. —Just sat him down at the kitchen table and told him to practice. Hating it. —Thinking of a way to get out of it without getting in trouble. At first, he fakes that he's sick. Mother gives him Peptobismol. "Go back and play." He doesn't want to say, "I just don't like the violin," because she just spent big bucks to give it to him for his birthday. He ends up hating the violin and getting so frustrated that he kicks the table [that the instrument is sitting on]. The violin falls and the neck breaks. The problem is solved: but he has to face his mother.

Consciously, the boy had little understanding of all that his story revealed. When asked directly about his troubles at school, he said he didn't know why he was getting into trouble. He said his mother had his best interests at heart, and he wished he had a miniaturized model of her that he could carry to school in his backpack to consult. When asked indirectly through fantasy, however, the boy "understood" that his mother was pushing him to do something he disliked. He could also express resentment at the imposition of her goals on his life. Finally, his story clearly explained that his way of dealing with this kind of situation was to disrupt "accidentally" the activity in more and more serious ways until the problem was solved. (This is exactly what he did in private school.)[10]

This process of projecting one's feelings onto an imaginary landscape and then learning from the tales one tells is one kind of learning that fantasy promotes with remarkable success. But projection is not what everyone has in mind when they talk about the benefits of an active relationship with the imagined. When Descartes reported that someone chased him down the streets, urging him not to abandon his search for truth, or when countless novelists insist that the characters they are "discovering" and not "creating" shock them with the unexpectedness of their "lives," these people believe that something more than an echo is coming out of the mouths of their companions. At the very least, then, mental guests are telling the self more than it realizes it knows, and at the most these dream and fantasy figures are bringing new information from who knows where to willing listeners.

It is easier to find examples of the latter belief in cultures other than our own. For instance, in psychologist Kilton Stewart's account of the Senoi, a group of 12,000 persons living on the Malay peninsula, he reports that this isolated tribe has worked out a social system characterized by a surprising lack of mental disorder and physical conflict. There may have been no violent crime among the Senoi for the past 200 years.

The Senoi credit their unusual level of cooperation to the management of dreams. Believing that conflict begins when potentially destructive dream-beings invade a sleeper, they have developed a way of harnessing the power of all dreams, good and bad, for the benefit of the community. The first step in this process is to teach young children to guide the contents of their own dreams. The second is to teach them to interpret these managed dreams themselves.

Stewart reports that the simplest nightmare he found among the Senoi was the dream of falling. When a child anxiously reports such a dream, the elders respond with enthusiasm.

---

10. When Mr. Bartlett was shown the same picture, he told a story of a talented but neglected boy who dreamed of greatness. Although the child tried hard, he was not satisfied with his progress. He dreamed of being discovered by a master musician who would then open the door to success for him.

"That is a wonderful dream," they say, "one of the best dreams a man can have. Where did you fall to and what did you discover?"

At first the children answer in what we would call a normal way. They maintain that the dream was not wonderful at all. In fact, it was so frightening that they woke up crying before falling too far and possibly being killed.

"That was a mistake," Stewart heard the adults reply. "Everything you do in a dream has a purpose. . . . You must relax and enjoy yourself when you fall in a dream. Falling is the quickest way to get in contact with the powers of the spirit world, the powers laid open to you through your dreams. Soon, when you have a falling dream, you will remember what I am saying, and as you do, you will feel that you are traveling to the source of the power which has caused you to fall. . . .

"[Likewise] when you think you are dying in a dream, you are only receiving the powers of the other world, your own spiritual power, which has been turned against you and which now wishes to become one with you if you will accept it. . . ."

To Stewart's astonishment, he found that over a period of time this constant flow of advice and encouragement gradually gave dreamers the ability to control their dreams. Every Senoi was eventually able to turn anxious dreams of falling into flying dreams of discovery. Whether dropping into the spirit world, climbing dangerous cliffs, or making love to someone else's woman, the Senoi move happily ahead in their dreams until they confront the dream figure responsible for the dream and demand from him or her a song or poem or charm that can be contributed to the community upon awakening. In their terms, dreams put them in touch with spirit people who have lives of their own and who are in no way dependent upon the dreamer for their existence. In Western terms, it would be said that the Senoi's permissive attitude toward dreams puts the dreamer in touch with his own subconscious feelings. Regardless of where the insights come from, the problems revealed are handled during daily sessions of interpretation both by prescribing healing dreams and by settling nascent disputes among neighbors.

Stewart concludes his account of the Senoi by admiring the

creative way the tribe has taught itself to think and by wondering if, in "modern civilization . . . people have sloughed off, or failed to develop half their power to think. Perhaps the most important half."[11]

If Stewart is even partly right, and an activity as peculiar as talking back to people in dreams can lead to more harmony and contentment than is commonly found in modern civilizations, then how is it done? Is it the process of talking to ourselves that is important—the dialogue? Or is it the willingness to believe that imaginary companions have minds of their own, which might conservatively be termed the willingness to engage wholeheartedly in dramatic and metaphorical thinking?

"I remember my mother saying, 'Don't bring him back till I tell you. He can't live here,'" Mr. Bartlett said. "Then through the side of the basket I heard what must have been Bobby's voice. 'He may be damaged already,' I think he said. 'A lot depends on his ears.' After that we talked often. His voice would come through the side of the basket and tell me things."

I would like to suggest that the lifelong struggle to harmonize what one *knows* with what one *feels* depends in large part on both internal dialogue *and* metaphorical thinking. As we saw in the chapter that conceptualized understanding as the mutual trading and enhancing of stories, dialogue is a way of expanding and elucidating what is not yet clear or complete in our minds. Metaphorical thinking is also a way of extending the limits of our understanding. And when used together they constitute a powerful, albeit generally unappreciated, way of discovering who we are.

According to Jungians, who have pursued the ideas of sub-personalities and internal dialogues more enthusiastically than other psychologists, imagined dialogue may or may not provide the imaginer with new and useful information. When the self rattles on in a single voice, speaking from a single perspective about what it intends to do this afternoon or how it can balance its chaotic checkbook, it can clarify what it already knows, but is not likely to discover anything new. The situation is altogether

11. Stewart quoted in Caughey, *Imaginary Social Worlds*, pp. 114–17.

different, however, "When self and a voice, or two voices, hold different perspectives. . . . [Then] through inner dialogue, a thought can be expressed by an imaginal other or by the self, questioned or furthered by another. *Dialogue intensifies the way in which language carries us toward what we are going to understand, but as yet have not.*"[12] (My italics.)

"Thought germinates in speech."[13] We have seen how insight springs to mind as one speaks to another, telling the listener that "the same thing once happened to me." Likewise, Mary Watkins, a modern Jungian, maintains that ". . . this is also true of the dialogues of thought." When we converse earnestly with ourselves, we push our understanding ahead.

Metaphor also enhances understanding in a somewhat similar way. The essence of metaphor is that understanding or interpretation from one realm of experience is projected into another domain. More specifically, we use our physical experience of summer, winter, lamb, lion, and so forth to organize and vitalize our understanding of abstractions. "Now is the winter of our discontent" illuminates discontent in a way that a literal discussion of the word is not able to do. Increasingly, metaphor is seen as a process essential to thought rather than merely a figure of speech. In discussing a child who is dealing with an imaginary lion, Watkins argues that, "the character of the lion [is] . . . symbolizing an idea which is not yet known and whose best expression at the moment is the lion. In other words, the symbol does not reiterate what is already known but attempts to give form to what is not yet realized in its particularity."[14] The lion is the child's attempt to understand what he feels but cannot yet fully explain.

In using dialogue and metaphor together, or rather in using dialogue *with* metaphorical beings, we go fishing for what we can dimly sense but cannot see. Imagined dialogues are our attempts to understand what we feel but cannot quite explain. Whether Jungians talk with their rather curiously named sub-

12. Watkins, *Invisible Guests*, p. 54.
13. Merleau-Ponty, quoted in Watkins, *Invisible Guests*, p. 54.
14. Watkins, *Invisible Guests*, p. 64.

personalities, such as "Inner Pig" and "Saint Helpful," or a child shouts to the lion in his closet, or Lloyd Bartlett listens through the side of a basket to the deep and reassuring rumble of Bobby Two-Ton Eagle's voice, all are putting words together in the dark in an effort to understand what they are feeling. To paraphrase Montaigne, what enriches a mind is its being handled and exploited by beautiful language. Metaphors enrich the mind, deepen its meaning, and teach it unaccustomed rhythms. It may indeed be more natural and useful than we generally imagine to maintain an articulate crowd of characters in our heads.

In comparing our use of imagined interactions to Mr. Bartlett's adventures, there are two aspects to consider. One is the uses that the interactions are put to, and the other is the intensity and pervasiveness of the imagining process itself.

Addressing the second of these comparisons first, it is obvious that Mr. Bartlett's internal conversations seem more real to him than most of ours do to us. Whereas he hears voices and sees things that he believes have a material existence that others can detect, we imagine voices and scenes that we almost always understand are immaterial and private. In short, he mistakes what he imagines for physical reality, and today that is quite enough to get him diagnosed as mentally ill. But do we want to say that seeing or hearing things that seem real represents the main difference between Mr. Bartlett and ourselves? If we do, we will be reclassifying a surprisingly large number of ordinary people as grossly disturbed. Surveys made over the past hundred years have found that at least 10 or 12 percent of the general population see and hear things that doctors would call hallucinations.[15] To give just one example, in 1991, 11 percent of a sample of 6,000 Americans said they had seen a ghost with their own eyes. Psychiatrists would be reluctant—at least I hope they would be—to classify 11 percent of Americans as psychotic, not to mention an extra percent or two of poets and visionaries who have out-of-body experiences, hear messages, and have visions.

15. *Unusual Personal Experiences: An Analysis of the Data from Three National Surveys Conducted by The Roper Organization* (Las Vegas: Bigelow Holding Corp., 1992), p. 23.

Thus the apparent commonness of inexplicable experiences poses a problem and leads us to an old, old question: Is every mental experience that is mistaken for physical reality equal?

Before the modern divorce between reason and imagination, when visions and visitations were common occurrences, they were treasured as special messages from the spirit world, but they also posed the problem we have just encountered. Some visions appeared to be much better than others, and it was important to distinguish good, reliable visions from bad, deceptive ones. In the fourth century, St. Augustine declared that the best visions were immaterial and intellectualized. The further they departed from the familiar, specific things we see around us, the better they were. In the thirteenth century, however, St. Thomas Aquinas was categorizing visions according to the part of the supernatural world they came from—namely celestial, natural, or infernal. Obviously celestial visions were best, but it was not always easy to distinguish them from visions that *seemed* to be about heavenly beings but were actually sent by the Devil. By the time of the Inquisition, the criteria had shifted again. If the effect of a vision was good, it was from God. If it led to lewd and rebellious acts, it was from Satan. (As Watkins points out, the modern version of this system goes as follows: "If the person is considered insane, the imagining is thought of as a hallucination and as bad; if the person is considered of sound mind, the imagining is either creative or strange, but not bad."[16])

During the second half of the sixteenth century, bad visions gradually slipped sideways from sin to sickness. It may have been St. Theresa of Avila who first tried to protect her nuns from being burned at the stake by suggesting that certain kinds of imaginings are the effect of infirmities. She argued that some of the sisters had weak imaginations, were melancholy, or were overtired. In these states, they were not responsible for the thoughts that insinuated themselves into their minds, thus they were not committing sins. Unfortunately, this redefinition of bad visions also redefined the visionaries themselves as mentally incompetent.

16. Watkins, *Invisible Guests*, p. 133.

It was a short step to the point where doctors were given the job of treating bad visions, which, in the seventeenth century, began to be called hallucinations. Rather than continue the centuries-old practice of discriminating between inspired, poetic visions and tormenting, destructive ones, doctors simplified their task by declaring that all figures, voices, and messages that were *mistaken for reality* were pathological. Only illusions (brief mistakes) and metaphorical thinking ("It sounded *as if* the Virgin were speaking to me") were left for healthy eccentrics.

By this reasoning, Mr. Bartlett is sick *primarily* because he is out of touch with reality or, to put it another way, he is sick because his imagined adventures are so much more intense than our own. I would like to suggest, however, that although the intensity and pervasiveness of his imagination is a problem and one that potentially endangers him, it is not his main problem— or the one that has to be rectified before therapy can proceed. Returning to the criteria that have been used for thousands of years, it is not the intensity of the vision that primarily distinguishes Mr. Bartlett's delusions from our engrossing imaginings or occasional experiences with visions, but the destructive nature of the imaginings themselves. In modern terms, it is the pathological relationship that Mr. Bartlett maintains both with the process of imagining and with the characters he imagines that is problematical. Not only is he immersed in his ideas with no narrator or reflecting ego that can step back and see himself talking with Bobby Two-Ton Eagle, but he is also locked in destructive and utterly rigid relationships with all his characters. Herein lies the basic problem: Mr. Bartlett does not use his imagined social relationships in the same ways that we do. For us, they help. For him, they hurt.

For us, the silent daily encounters we enjoy with aspects of ourselves, media figures, and replicas of others help us to live in a complex and fast-moving society. When we are of an age to need heroes, we adopt famous persons as imagined companions and share their successes. When our work seems difficult, we play ourselves mental commercials that inspire us to strive harder, or we indulge in a brief escape to a simpler world from which we return refreshed. We rehearse in our minds situations that are unfamiliar, and we replay confusing times to fit the anomalous experience into our repertoire and get on with life. Finally, we play in the fields of our imagination in order to find the words that can explain how we feel or to find the feelings that can infuse our words with meaning. With imagined dialogues we put ourselves together in much the same way that a family or a community holds itself together by talking aloud.

Lloyd Bartlett tries to do these same things with his internal dialogues. With Natalia, Bobby, Armand, Rollo Nomel, and Razor Rinaldo, he embarks upon powerful fantasies that simultaneously provide an escape from and an envious yearning for the American dream. He rehearses confusing situations in his mind.

"I have imagined many things in order to comprehend what happens to me and what I feel," he once said, and indeed his imagination is kept working overtime to come up with explanations that try to reconcile the silent mismatchings and derailments that his brain delivers. Obsessively pacing back and forth through the underbrush of his imagination to find out "what really happened," he tries to integrate what he feels with what he cannot, in fact, know for sure. For Mr. Bartlett, none of these common maneuvers works, partly because his brain betrays him and partly because he maintains such unproductive relationships with his creations.

As Jungians are fond of pointing out, sub-personalities or the imagined inhabitants of our heads come in an astounding variety and are related to the central self in many different ways. Suffice it to say that if we take time to notice who we talk to when we talk to ourselves, we will hear "voices" that praise, criticize, excite, calm, whine, reason, rationalize, bully, and seduce. The relationships are varied, and they change over time. For the mentally ill, however, the range of sub-personalities are typically restricted, and the relationships that these dictatorial, erratic, one-dimensional, and vindictive figures establish with the beleaguered central self are grossly lopsided. Lloyd Bartlett is pushed around mercilessly by terrifying characters, and he is disappointed continually by well-meaning but preoccupied ones. Armand LaCherry as well as Razor Rinaldo move him around like a pawn, and he makes no effort to understand or resist. Used and abused by memory and imagination, voice and vision, it never occurs to him to fight back. This passivity is at the heart of the problem and is the characteristic that most significantly differentiates his fantasy life from our more democratic imaginings.

Two months after the Grand Canyon project had collapsed and Mr. Bartlett had gone in and come out of the hospital, I began to prod him into talking back to his imagined companions. Could he see these relationships as exploitive, express his disappointment, and at least begin to question them?

"You must feel very disappointed in Armand LaCherry," I said. "I can't believe that the powerful head of the Council on Indian Affairs couldn't help you out with Razor and would let you languish in a hospital. He doesn't come through when you need him, does he?"

Wrong, of course. The very idea that someone as powerful as Armand could be criticized was horrifying to Mr. Bartlett. Having caught him as he was leaning forward, my blasphemy stopped him mid-gesture and left him staring blankly in the general direction of my face. Disorganization galloped across his features.

"You don't understand," he finally said, straightening up with a great gasp of relief as he hit upon a way of undoing my sacrilege without offending either me or Armand. "I haven't been allowed to tell you all the things he's done for me."

For at least a month, as Hillsdale shook off its summer lethargy, Mr. Bartlett churned out excuses for Armand, Bobby, and Natalia. Raising his finely curved eyebrows high above his gray eyes as he did when feeling defensive, he pointed out that it made no sense to criticize people who had saved his life forty-four times, paid for his education, opened the doors to fame and privilege, bailed him out of the hospital and so on and so forth. Bobby was too busy to be with him all the time, he explained, Armand too important, Natalia too far away.

Nevertheless, at the end of every hour I would give the refined Mr. Bartlett two or three questions to put to his unreliable supporters. "Why didn't you protect me from the Razor?" "Why do you let me languish unappreciated in Hillsdale?"

Finally, about Thanksgiving, these questions took effect.

"I'm asking far too many questions," he told me one morning when I wondered what Armand's response had been. "I don't want to step out of line and be cut off. They could remove my name from the list, you know."

"But you're acting like a child, Mr. Bartlett," I replied. "At the age of fifty-three don't you have the right to ask for an explanation or express your point of view? What kind of a relationship do you have with these people?"

"I wonder if you could reduce my medication?" he asked, flushing slightly and sitting back in his chair as he spun the conversation 180 degrees.

"I don't know how you tolerate their high-handedness," I continued. "Between doctors who tell you what to swallow and your companions who control everything else that happens in your life . . ."

Mr. Bartlett started to speak, then stopped. He glanced down at the old leather briefcase that sat between his feet. He brushed off his khaki pants. He touched his tie.

"I sometimes wonder," he began softly, "I mean, I may not have given you the whole story . . . may not even know it myself." He paused. "What *really* happened?"

Over the next eight months Mr. Bartlett agreed to write a play in an attempt to set down once and for all what really happened. It was a lovely document, gracefully composed and as stylized as a fairy tale. It was about a lonely boy who grew up in a surreal world where love and protection, like torture and fear, were nothing but ingenious masks that shifted hands even as he watched. The eyes in these masks stared past him. The mouths moved, promising good and bad. The messages penetrated the brain, but nothing was delivered for keeps. Words ran through the boy's ears, but he could not incorporate them into an understanding of his own: "I heard him say he was my father." "They said when I was at Michigan, I had promise."

Over the years he seemed to have overheard the stories of his life from others, and this almost total dependence on hearing, and on other people's words, gave to his articulate adventures an intellectualized quality devoid of touch, smell, and credible detail. His inability to act out the episodes and thus to turn them into personal experience further added to their implausibility. Mr. Bartlett was like a remote-control plane. Asleep or awake, he swerved and veered, flew and nose-dived according to invisible signals that ran through his head.

And this was not the only problem with the relationship that Mr. Bartlett maintained with the powerful people in his head and with the less imaginative, but also fairly powerful, people in the mental health system. He had no idea at all what any of these people thought and felt. They were opaque. Not that Mr. Bartlett was insensitive, but as to why Bobby Two-Ton Eagle wanted to help him, why I enjoyed talking with him, and why Rollo Nomel or the hospital psychiatrist wanted to sedate him, he had not the foggiest notion. Years before, he had apparently given up as impossible the ordinary business of figuring out what people around him were thinking. This helpless immersion in his own ideas isolated him in what he called a "sleep cocoon," and because he so seldom put himself in other people's shoes (even Bobby's or Natalia's) and could not get to know them as real people, their negotiations with him were unintelligible. Neither Bobby Two-Ton Eagle nor I were real to Mr. Bartlett in the sense that we had needs, desires, fears, hopes, and our own outlook on life. Like the protagonist in a modern absurdist novel, my patient could not see through others' eyes or understand or trust. He never asked anyone a question.

As Mr. Bartlett worked on his play, which, among other helpful things, forced him into a position of unambiguous authorship, he finally asked a question. It was a very small question, barely a sentence, but one morning when we were reading the parts aloud together, he paused and asked, "I wonder why the Commissioner didn't send me to graduate school."

"Hmm," I answered absentmindedly, eager for him to continue reading about the mynah bird that carried messages to Lloyd in his sleep when he was lost, as he now was, in some orchid-encrusted portion of the rain forest.

"I was disappointed," he mused.

Waiting for Mr. Bartlett to resume reading, my eyes continued down the page to where Bobby Two-Ton Eagle was perched on a high branch, wearing a homemade parachute of leaves and smoking a pipe whose smoke rendered Lloyd unable to see or remember "except for the songs he allowed the bird to sing into my head."

"You know this writing business is taxing," Mr. Bartlett went on. "Getting it all down where I can actually *see* it raises a lot of questions. It's hard to determine what may be delusional." He laughed briefly. "Do you think I should call this thing 'Inside the Head of a Lunatic'?"

"No," I blurted out, finally realizing that I was listening to a person who had stepped out of himself and was questioning his imagined life in the way that ordinary people question theirs. "No, that's disrespectful. It's too easy. I mean, that's the problem."

"What are you talking about?" Mr. Bartlett asked kindly, in a puzzled tone of voice.

"Mr. Bartlett," I replied primly, "the goal is not to show that everything you've ever done or thought is either totally delusional or completely factual, but to integrate your experience of both realms. In your play you must show us what it feels like to live on both sides of the fence at the same time—how hard that is."

"I'd be kicked off the network, if I revealed their secrets," he said, understanding correctly that I was suggesting that Mr. Bartlett the playwright be given power over all the rest of the characters. "I'd lose my . . . my life."

"Yes, you would," I replied. "You would lose the Mr. Bartlett who tries to do great things but is thwarted by Rollo Nomel and let down by Bobby and Armand. But at least some of the time you might join another group and have a different life. You'd be a storyteller."

"From listener to teller?"

"No, from told-about to teller. From character to author. Don't you think it's about time?"

Mr. Bartlett thought a long while before getting what he surmised was the joke.

"Dr. Baur," he said, laughing in his most charming way, his silvery gray hair falling slightly out of place, "you have no respect for reality. You can't just write out a life for yourself. I mean authors write stories, not lives."

≈   ≈   ≈

At the time of this writing, Mr. Bartlett is still teetering on the edge of a difficult and unpromising decision. At times he retreats into his delusions and steadies himself with the illusion of love, but other times he considers writing his own story and living his own life. For the past thirty years delusions of great accomplishments and great dangers have rooted him on the edge of our society. He is intensely envious of exactly the kinds of achievement and success we most admire, and he is rigidly reluctant to attempt anything on his own for fear that his brain will scramble the facts and make a fool of him. Nevertheless, Mr. Bartlett is making a curious kind of progress with his captors. When he assumes the role of author, as we all must do, he cautiously moves his characters around, now giving credit, now gently reprimanding. He begins to talk back to the voices in his head, and strange as this may sound to us who fantasize so discreetly on the way to work, this kind of talking moves Mr. Bartlett closer to the common way of thinking.

"You know, Bobby was a victim of the system as much as I was," he said not too long ago to my intense astonishment. "His hands were tied by every rule and regulation in the book to the point that he couldn't do his job. He was so happy to finish his patrols."

"Finish?" I asked, my mind jumping to where I'd last seen the overweight Indian sitting in a tree in the rain forest, his hair sprouting like wet ostrich feathers from the top of his head. "Retired? Bobby?"

Mr. Bartlett leaned back comfortably in the old corner chair and laughed in his fullest, richest voice. "He'll be back," he reassured me. "But only part-time. He's getting old."

Stranger within me, stranger at my side, we walk together like the body and its shadow, we sit down in the square among vagrants and visitors from farms or foreign countries, we listen to the man with the pompadour and fluttering blue lips, follow with our eyes the girl with the turkey head.[17]

17. Artur Lundkvist, *Journeys in Dream and Imagination: The Hallucinatory Memoir of a Poet in a Coma* (New York: Four Walls Eight Windows, 1991), p. 126.

9

THE MAN WHO SWALLOWED
RHODE ISLAND

*Falsehood flies, and the truth comes limping after
it, so that when men come to be undeceived it is
too late; the jest is over, and the tale has had its
effect.*

JONATHAN SWIFT

THERE IS A FORLORN STRIP ALONG THE WESTERN EDGE OF RHODE
Island that extends, as you would expect, not from someplace to
someplace else, but from a cluster of nameless, abandoned sheds
in the north to parking lots in the south that are crisscrossed by
well-established lines of weeds. It is the narrow portion of a narrow state where everything has run out of gas. No current runs
through electric lines here, no water along the sides of roads.
Summer and winter, mailboxes rest atop S-shaped chains on
either side of unrepaired highways, and in the yards of small
ranch houses, flowers or their dried remains stand wearily in
everted tractor tires that have been made to look like squat,
black tulips. Even the colors of this indecisively rolling landscape have seeped away. Houses built during a time when rocks
along walks were painted white have faded from baby blue and
pink to a chalky and unpromising pastel. Pines have grayed,

grass browned, and concrete roads bleached into cracked squares of an unremarkable tan. Overall, it is a dry and porous region, and it is here that my memories of D. Edward Bennett have apparently gone to rest.

I first met Ned Bennett, as he was familiarly called, when I held a part-time job in a clinic that specialized in outreach programs for the rural poor. I was an older than average graduate student with no experience. Four years my junior, he was one of four senior therapists. I seem to remember—or at least I can easily picture—walking into the storefront clinic on Maple Street many Junes ago and seeing for the first time a slightly rotund, sweet-looking man emerge from the corner office.

"Oh, Ned, will you have time this afternoon to review the Santobal case?"

"Hi, Ned."

"We're on for lunch, Ned."

"*Ned*, you shouldn't have done them all by yourself. C'mon, man."

Mr. Bennett nodded and smiled, or rather the round, sandy-haired man actually looked at one person, smiled at another, cocked his head, touched a shoulder—in short he paid attention all the way across the beige-carpeted space from his office door to the secretaries' desks in the far corner of the building. There he stopped, sitting casually on the corner of a desk, swinging a leg. My memory stops there, but I bet he leaned forward with that quiet, puzzled smile of his and took in the mood of his clinic. And I bet I thought to myself, what a champion listener.

"June 5," I wrote in my notebook. "First day at the Maple Street Clinic. Met the director, an attractive but rather distant woman, and was shown around by Betty P. She is giving me Tom, a case she describes as 'one of my failures.'

"Sarah gave me three cases, two schizophrenics and a bi-polar, manic depressive who doesn't speak English (??). I'll get more next week including a thirty-year-old man who wants his seventeen-year-old girlfriend to move in with him and his mother and live off the latter's social security. . . .

"June 7. Met with Mr. Bennett who will supervise my work. We meet every week for an hour in the office with the purple plant. He said, 'Everyone is employed' (meaning the clients), and that one of my jobs is to figure out which ones will change careers, from a depressed person or an alcoholic, for example, to a dishwasher or a contented person. Useful concept. This is going to be good."

And so I began, and we began. During my time at the clinic, I picked up a great many useful concepts from Ned Bennett, and I absorbed, more than observed, the character of the man himself as I met with him every Wednesday from eleven to noon in the corner office with the sprawling purple plant.

Typically, I sat across from Mr. Bennett at a large table covered with papers, books, and curios. I don't remember looking at him, and perhaps I didn't much. In any event, I have a much better sense of how he made me feel rather than how he looked or possibly felt himself. At the beginning of each hour, I remember that he would close the wooden door behind him and call the secretary to instruct her not to disturb us till noon. Rather symbolically, it seems to me now, he would clear a path through books and papers so that we were linked by a cleared stretch of table about two feet wide. Only then would he sit back with his typical half-smile and ask me whom I wished to present that day. Pleased to be on stage, I would spin for him as psychologically-minded a tale as I was able to construct from such resonant facts as "forty years old," "divorced," and "unemployed, male." I would sing, for example, of a Mr. Molson who was interested in getting off the dole, but who only wanted to be a doctor, lawyer, or architect.

"I'm sure he isn't smart enough," I would confide, shaking my head, "or rich enough. I'm sure he won't make it."

"And that is the point," Mr. Bennett would say quietly. "There is no disgrace in failing to become a doctor—it's such a difficult profession, you know—and meanwhile Mr. Molson is spared the humiliation of getting, and very well losing, a job in the local hardware store that he doesn't believe he can handle."

Every scrap of knowledge I had gained about success and failure—or about whatever Mr. Bennett was talking about at the moment—had a way of flying into my head as he spoke. Almost faster than I could think, I held up the insights we discussed to each of my clients, to myself, my family, my friends, and of course my enemies. If I'd read an article on high self-esteem in men used as a defense, or one on fear of success in women, I thought about it then. If I was peeved at a rather dreadful man I dated after my divorce, I asked myself if our shortcomings could be explained by fear of failure or fear of whatever Mr. Bennett and I had discussed with such intensity.

Mr. Bennett suffered my eagerness with dignity. He thanked me warmly when I brought him clippings from the *Journal of Nervous and Mental Disorders*. He seemed pleased when I told him that I had added the question, "Where do you see yourself in three or four years?" to each of my initial interviews. Hopes too high, too low, or absent, provided an index of my client's apprehension. I was learning.

Mr. Bennett went out of his way to help me learn. He augmented supervision by seeing clients with me, by including me in training sessions and staff meetings, by saving articles for me, and by lending me books from his library. The collected sayings of Eric Semrad was a favorite of his—he had actually studied with this famous therapist—and the book became a favorite of mine.

"Sorrow is the vitamin of growth," I have underlined in my copy. "People grow only around sadness. It's strange who arranged it that way, but that's the way it seems to be."

True for the big insights, I thought at the time, again trying the idea out on my clients and myself, but not true for learning how to be a therapist on Maple Street. Mr. Bennett made that a surprisingly positive experience. For instance, although I have totally forgotten telling him about the thirty-year-old Jeffrey and his skinny girlfriend Nina, my notebook says that I explained to my supervisor that I couldn't keep the couple in focus. Sometimes I seemed to see them clearly—Jeffrey limping in on a cane wearing his Harley-Davidson shirt, Nina crossing and recrossing legs shaved so close they glistened—then, suddenly, the picture went out of focus, and I was alone in a room with strangers. I assumed that experienced therapists could stay focused for fifty minutes at a time.

"Mr. Bennett is surprised that I see myself as making mistakes," I wrote on that particular Wednesday. "He says that when I think I'm losing touch, it is actually Jeffrey showing me how he drifts out of reach whenever he is uncomfortable. In other words, I'm *supposed* to feel this unfocusing. Mr. B. seems to be saying that as long as I'm awake and respectful, every interaction is potentially therapeutic. He says new therapists typically make up in energy what they lack in experience."

At the same time that Mr. Bennett learned how I thought, I learned how he lived. Initially, I got most of my information from his colleagues, for although he was forthcoming in supervision and sometimes touched on cases he had handled, the man possessed an enviable modesty that made him suddenly go shy when his own accomplishments came up. He once told me he'd taken on a case that Eric Semrad had dismissed as untreatable.

"But that's neither here nor there," he had said and changed the topic.

So mainly I learned from others that Mr. Bennett lived in a suburb of Providence by himself (and liked it that way), was a particularly astute diagnostician, and didn't know how to drive a car. Betty told me in the ladies' room that he had juvenile diabetes, which accounted for the bruises and red marks on his hands and all the sick days he took. It probably accounted for his precocious maturity as well. I also learned that he collected carved meerschaum pipes, especially those with birds on them, and that he had lucky charms from thirty-four different countries. That he had a sizable collection of unusual tie pins, I could see for myself.

Mr. Bennett was admired and beloved by the entire office. I don't know quite how his colleagues communicated their feelings so quickly, but to walk into the Maple Street Clinic was to believe he was a champion. Perhaps they whispered their admiration—"Isn't he a wonderful clinician?" and "He got another personal letter from the commissioner"—or perhaps they expressed their affection by wanting time alone with him. There was always a tug-of-war for Mr. Bennett at lunchtime, which as far as I can recall was never settled by going out as a group. He had standing lunch dates with certain people that went back seven or eight years. And then again, maybe Mr. Bennett told me himself that he was terrific. Looking back, I remember several times when Betty was annoyed with him.

"What's with Betty?" I asked.

I bet he sat on the corner of his desk then, smiled, and said, "I'm glad you noticed."

"So?"

There would be a pause—an earnest struggle behind the eyes—then, "I'm not free to explain, but . . . Betty's a pretty competitive person right now."

"*I'm not,*" I'd say to myself, faster than sound, and as I noted mentally that competing with another therapist is a very silly thing to do, any thought that Mr. Bennett himself might have mishandled the situation left my mind.

But nothing brought out the affection that the Maple Street clinicians felt for Mr. Bennett like a medical crisis, and these were on the increase. I remember the first time tests were run on his kidneys. I walked into his hospital room and thought it was a cocktail party. Pots of fragrant herbs rather than flowers jammed the window ledge of his private room, a dozen visitors spoke cheerfully above Peruvian music that had been smuggled in on a portable tape deck, and tasteful get-well cards lay like a giant solitaire game on his sheets. There were new curios to add to his collection, too, new amulets. No doubt about it. Mr. Bennett brought out the best and most creative in everyone, and I was not terribly surprised to learn from him later that the charming dark-haired nurse I'd seen hovering outside his salon had all but proposed to him.

Now this is probably the point where I should admit that I am a hypochondriac. I could give you one of several explanations for this malady that I have painstakingly worked out over the years, but suffice it to say that at certain times in my life I become convinced that the most horrible thing in the world is to be diagnosed with a fatal illness that disables its victims in some horribly painful way, then leaves them to die slowly in a dark empty room. (I shudder to think what analysts will make of this, but there it is.) Once every several years, I become convinced that this fate awaits me within the week, and I am afraid.

Ned Bennett, on the other hand, was not afraid of his diabetes or of pain or of being alone. He hoped he had ten good years left, he told me as he pinched back the purple plant that had been overwatered in his absence, and although he didn't look forward to being blind, his doctors said they would hold his eyes together for as long as they could with laser treatments. Dialysis, with its accompanying depressions, he continued matter-of-factly, would come sooner. He knew two people who had committed suicide rather than undergo the wracking moodiness and the inability to think that dialysis can produce.

"How do you stand it?" I finally asked, when after a year at the clinic I, too, had a standing lunch date with Ned Bennett at Ken's Lunch.

He adopted a faraway look with which I was becoming increasingly familiar. "*Primum vivere; deinde philosophari,*" he said to the distant figures who walked past the small windows of the state's only diner-with-a-dormer. "First live, then think about it."

"Meaning in this case?" I replied.

"Meaning that I don't wish to live in my thoughts as in a besieged city, as somebody said. I plan to keep *doing* as long as I can." He paused again, and I noticed that he was slightly freckled and that the tie pin he wore was a Celtic cross. In fact, he'd worn crosses all week. "I don't believe anyone dies one moment before they are supposed to."

"I couldn't stand it," I said.

"You won't have to," he assured me mysteriously, finally looking at me. "You're not the type."

Ned and I became friends then as well as colleagues. He gave me books instead of lending them to me, and I gave him undisguised admiration and support. I gasped when he showed me his blood profiles (he kindly refrained from showing me subsequent ones), and I spluttered when a stupid, insensitive resident let him overhear the news that his eyes were starting to go. Ned was urged to work only four days a week, but he would not give in. He used all his sick days and then some, and on the days he was out, the clinic seemed to wait and listen. We functioned, of course. The same slow parade of sideburned Walters and Everetts trudged in across the beige carpet shadowed by their silent Lucys and Irenes and trudged out holding their appointment cards in front of them. But the clinic lost momentum on days that Ned was out sick.

"I wonder what Ned means to the different people here," I wrote idly in my notebook. "It's hard to figure out." And indeed it was. What I noticed at the time was that I was becoming one of Ned's special friends, and that he picked such people from different parts of his life. He spoke often of Jonathan, for example, a curator of a folk art museum who helped him learn about the charms he loved to collect, but I never met him. Ned also spoke of a former colleague, Dotty Beerstadt, and of a member of the Audubon Society, Madeleine Somebody-or-other, but I never met them either. A traveling companion, a commissioner, a cousin—both the Northeast where he lived now and the Northwest where he'd been raised were alive with people who loved Ned Bennett and who stayed in touch with him. I would say he received three or four cards a week during the time I was at Maple Street, and these he piled so high around the purple plant that some of its viny branches grew over and around the good wishes. Ned always spoke favorably of these kind people, and I think this characteristic gave to his acquaintances the feeling that he would speak favorably of them, too. I have tried to copy Ned in this.

What I notice now, however, is that although Ned built his friends up, he did not bring them together. In fact, his network of supporters was divided into sections like food on an old-fashioned child's plate. There was little chance that the psychologists would spill into the museum people, for example, or that the commissioner and his staff would trickle over into the neighbors. This compartmentalization gave Ned a subtle kind of privacy, I imagined, and was accomplished by means that sailed right over my head at the time.

"Dotty was fascinated to hear of your work with schizophrenics," he once said, smiling at me with obvious pride. "I described your approach as best I could—wish you'd been with us—and told her about the changes you've wrought in Tom." He paused to smile some more, his round, rosy face lighting up from within. "She was impressed."

I probably smiled back across the Formica table at Ken's, and I'm sure I felt the invigorating warmth of being studied and understood by Ned. I probably said, "I'd like to meet her."

Ned chuckled as if remembering part of their conversation. "Dorothy is a character." He paused again and became serious. "She said an interesting thing, you know."

"Hmm?"

"She said that one of the saddest comments on the state of mental hospitals today is that they are afraid of innovative people like you. She said she admires your work, but that she and her kind would never hire you."

Jerk, I thought to myself. See if I go out of my way to meet her.

"Interesting," I said aloud, and tried to wiggle back into the warm complimentary place I'd been in a moment before.

In retrospect, I can see that there was another way in which Ned separated his friends into audiences of one. This involved his fondness for assigning numbers to emotions in order to clarify terms that generally remain vague. It is a useful technique, especially with children, and I have adopted it myself.

"On a scale of one to ten," he would say, "how much do you like this guy?" Or "What's the percentage of perceived empathy? How well do you feel this person understands you? Does he get fifty percent of your ideas? Eighty?"

After a time, the numbers became a kind of code between us as well as a rating scale in a game that might have been called How Well Do We Understand Each Other?

When Ned told me about a client, for example, or his latest trip to the emergency room, he would often imply that I could understand what he was going through better than a Jonathan or a Madeleine. I had a higher number.

"They are so good to me," he would typically say. "I marvel at Jonathan's knowledge of nutrition. We ran a health food store together years ago. But, oh dear, when it comes to figuring out depression . . . fifty, maybe."

In these ways Ned cultivated his friends in individual plots. Each had a special gift that he admired and enhanced. Each gave to and received from him in different ways.

Over the next three or four years Ned got sicker, although not at a steady rate, and we drew closer. I had a not-so-miserable relationship at that time, and Ned became my confidant and advisor. At the same time, his illness was dredging up old childhood hurts, and, as one of his supporters, I listened to many tales of his past and growing up.

One lazy summer afternoon we had left work after lunch to walk through town—or rather to walk along Suskatchett Road, which had run through a town until the rail service pulled out and the town disappeared. Turning off Maple Street with its ranch houses and tire-tub gardens, we strolled onto Suskatchett where slightly larger houses had been converted into laundromats, pharmacies, and other small businesses, then sometimes reconverted again into private homes. Ned never wore cologne that I could detect, and I remember noticing that even in the heavy heat of this July afternoon, he kept all his essence contained within his well-cut but slightly old-fashioned and oversized seersucker jacket. He was always like that—loose but contained.

I don't know why I should remember this, but we eventually made our way to a rutted road that climbed out of town through woods and overgrown fields. We were ambling along, he talking idly about his family, when we reached a chain-link fence that ran for some distance along one side of the road. There he stopped, turned to me, and heaved a sigh.

"I might as well stop kidding myself—and you," he said quietly, his blue eyes glancing off mine and looking into the woods beyond the fence.

Looking at this puzzled man who stood, slightly damp with exertion, slightly hidden within his jacket, I suddenly felt great compassion. I waited, and waiting I watched the old battle behind the eyes. It was the place, I imagined, where the pain of dying of diabetes is strung into the wire and woven into the fences that hold a mind together at times of unbearable stress.

"You'd never believe . . . " he began, turning and starting to walk back toward town, "how awful my family was—and still is—to each other."

Over the next hour, as we walked slowly past split-rail

fences, picket fences, and scraggly hedges, Ned told me a story of loss and disappointment. The youngest of six children growing up in the Pacific Northwest, he had lost his mother at the age of four and his father seven years later. The family had then been split up among aunts and uncles only to be reassembled when the oldest sister married and took her brothers and sisters in. The new arrangement was far from ideal, however, and Ned found himself tormented by his sister's insecure and jealous husband. Ned implied he had been beaten, and later added that he had also been locked in the cellar as a punishment. Later still, he admitted to being sexually abused.

On and on the story went, fascinating in its baroque tortures and more fascinating still in its pervasive mystery of its dark, water-soaked forests and its deep family secrets.

"The usual," Ned would say, modestly veiling the climax of an alcoholic brawl with a shrug and leaving me to fill in horrific details. Or, "The same old story," he would conclude when speaking of the punishments he received, "only with spiders. I remember sitting on the cellar stairs with spiders and wondering if they could hear me breathe."

There were threats of military school, too, I remember, and formidably silent dinnertimes. There was slave labor when the young Ned was indentured to various uncles after his parents' deaths. In one household, he told me, he had to cut and stack firewood every day after school whether or not it was sleeting outside, and whether or not he felt sick from the as yet undiagnosed diabetes. No pile of logs by the back door, no food on his plate at dinnertime. As in all Ned's stories, it was the child's silent acceptance of these barbaric practices that was more distressing than the cruelties themselves.

"How can you speak so matter-of-factly about sitting at the dinner table with no food and watching your cousins eat?" I would ask.

"That's the way it was in those days," he would answer, smiling quizzically at my distress, which was always greater than his own. "I'm afraid I've made it sound worse than it was . . . or perhaps I was numb in those days."

"But, Ned," I would say, "but, Ned," and the rest of my

words would dive silently back into my head where they would struggle to arrange themselves into a story that would explain how so unsupported a little kid could survive such malicious neglect. "Maybe he had been numb," I concluded, "but now?"

Whether Ned's stories were specific or general, cool or luke-warm, I took them all in and gave them life. The bitterness of an existence without health and without family grew up around us during that summer walk and those that followed like the monstrous berry patches of his youth. As each blackberry cane with its purple thorns further ensnared us, I felt more sympathy for Ned and more pure joy in being whole and unabused and alive. I *loved* not having diabetes.

There were other good things about being with Ned. I was about to say that I got to watch him in action, doing therapy, but actually, it only felt that way. Supervision had become a two-way street, and I heard more and more about the handful of special and very difficult clients he kept for himself. One was a gangster from Federal Hill in Providence, I recall, who promised Ned he would put a hit on anyone who bothered him. Another was a Hungarian poet who drove two and a half hours each way just to visit Ned. And several were Cape Verdeans because Ned spoke Portuguese and no one else in the clinic did. Local clients loved him, too, and every year the Knights of Columbus gave him their "Credit to the Community" award. The year after I left, he was given a prize by the commissioner for the eloquent way in which he explained the clinic's mission. The office was full of "Bennett stories" like these.

It was never entirely clear to me how much these honors reflected Ned's fine ways of caring for the disenfranchised and how much they reflected his personal bravery. No one at the clinic would have considered that pity played a part in his celebrity, but the fact remained that after I left the office and Ned became sicker, the prizes and honorable mentions increased. Toward the end, he was particularly pleased to be elected to an advisory board whose members were charged with rethinking the care of the mentally ill and were being paid for doing it. But I am getting ahead of myself.

While still at the clinic I learned, like everyone else, that

Ned's favorite words were "empower" and "champion," and that his charismatic brand of client-centered therapy, which has so influenced my own, rode on these complementary concepts. The goal in every case at the Maple Street Clinic was to empower the client—to give him or her more of a say in how life was to be lived—and to champion each person as if our own future rode on his or her successful rehabilitation. It made for a very respectful place, with the clients' interests kept at the center of each transaction.

And so, during my two years on Maple Street, I gratefully imbibed a double message: first, that the poor and the disabled count, whether they are the mentally ill off the street or the clinician with diabetes who has no family. Help is at hand. The Lord tempers the wind to the shorn lamb. And second, that helpers count. Whether they believe in themselves or not, they will rise to the occasion and meet the need. And it was true, too. With no one was I a better friend than with Ned Bennett.

After a couple of years at the clinic, I left to obtain the different kinds of clinical experience that are required of a psychologist. Naturally, I kept in touch with Ned. Our weekly lunch date became biweekly, then monthly, but in between those times we wrote notes or chatted on the phone. Then I would drive up to Maple Street on a Wednesday and sit down again in a booth at Ken's. It was wonderful to regale the supervisor with supervisor stories.

"I wish you could meet this guy," I would say, hitching forward on the red vinyl bench. "You would find him intriguing. And Dr. Stone . . . Ned, she is indescribable. Last Thursday, she drove down from her university and gave us a lecture on the *dangers* of therapy for women."

On I would go, heaping new ideas on the table, tumbling my gripes in among my pleasures, and generally having a wonderful time. Often—increasingly often—Ned was in pain, and at these times he seemed to value my stories twice as much.

"Tell me another Dr. Stone story," he would say, leaving his tuna untouched. "I get such a lift from your energy."

His letters told much the same grateful story, and rereading them now, I can discern two different patterns. The more common was "Hi, Susan. In spite of two trips to the emergency room, I have made considerable progress in the cataloging of my New Guinea 'treasures.' Ha, ha." (He had personally collected most of his lucky charms and believed several to be quite rare.) Or, "Hi, Susan. I visited Boston yesterday with my old friend, Dotty Beerstadt, and what a time we had catching up on our accomplishments and, yes, our deterioration.—Found I couldn't get up from the table at the restaurant. Embarrassing."

In contrast to these all-is-well-in-spite-of-terrible-trouble letters, which left me speechless with compassion and admiration, there were sadder letters in which Ned seemed to drop to his knees. These were long wrestling matches that chronicled his dealings with exactly those fears that seemed most daunting to me. What if he could no longer work at Maple Street? What if his health insurance ran out? What if the despondency that sometimes floored him wouldn't lift? What if he became totally dependent on people who didn't like him very much? I shuddered even to think of these questions, and I marveled that he continued to have such trust in life.

Ned's happy letters were the perfect opposites of the sad ones. It was amazing how his job continued, his insurance paid thousands, and his friends fell over each other to support him. At the beginning of one letter he told me that four people had already dropped by in the morning with food and four others had called.

"Make that seven and ten!" he wrote in a postscript late in the day. "No wonder I have no time to write."

But whether the letters were up or down, and whether they described lonely times or busy times, I see now that there was always a sentence or two in them for me. "I learn so much from you," he wrote in one. "You're a generous person." "You are better than you imagine." "You're a champion." "You are my champion."

By this time I had known Ned Bennett for exactly five years, and I was indeed one of his champions. I was still one of his students, in the sense that I continued to expect to learn from him. Others felt the same. Even Betty agreed that Ned's misfortunes had pushed him far ahead of us on the road through life, and she, too, felt flattered to be let in on such hard-won knowledge of the human heart. We agreed that he was "a born teacher," by which we meant that he had an amazing way of discovering each person's secret dream and helping him or her to "get on with it," as he liked to say. Of course, Ned's help was intimately involved with empowering and encouraging. To be instructed was to be praised, and I never met a person who didn't love the combination. No one since my parents had so influenced my thoughts or so resolutely supported my endeavors.

In August of that year Ned's health deteriorated dramatically. He began passing out—at work, at home, in Ken's Lunch—his kidneys failed, blood sugars ran riot, and his eyes weakened. There was talk of transplants and amputations, of leaves of absence and moving. Ned grew confused, too. Over the phone, he would tell me about his most recent hospitalization or seizure or transfusion and then forget that he'd told me. In person, it was just as bad. When we met at Ken's Lunch, he would frequently leave for fifteen minutes, return, and act as if he hadn't left. Most of the time he was in pain now, and although I thought he was a wily old expert with pain, there was a new component—something in the stomach, perhaps— that finally squeezed the truth out of him. Only that's not right either.

This new attitude or perspective emerged on the day I thought he was going to die. I had driven over (with my delightful new partner, who had, himself, become quite a friend of Ned's) to visit Ned at his home outside Providence. I was appalled to see how uncomfortable he was. Unshaven, and wearing a long bathrobe of some pale, silky stuff, he let us into his apartment that overlooked a neat little line of backyard gardens. When I had visited him before, Ned and I and whoever else dropped in used to sit in white canvas chairs on a narrow stone terrace and look into Mr. Contini's pole beans. Ned would brew the strongest, most wonderful coffee I ever drank and serve it in glasses that sat in shiny brass holders, which he had brought back from Istanbul. In winter, the same ritual was carried out in his small living room. Paintings, beads, headdresses, plaits of dried flowers covered all four walls of the room, but the furniture was spare. Two dark blue love seats sat opposite each other with a low table between on which lay only a photograph of his smiling young parents in tennis clothes. A beautifully patterned grass mat covered the floor, and a big throne of an easy chair sat near the window. Into this, Ned now lowered himself with care. Without saying a word, he propped his arms on his knees and continued the struggle we had interrupted. Almost nothing moved—not his head nor his hands, not the fringe on the sash of his bathrobe—yet I had the impression of great turmoil. Sweat broke out all over his face. I handed him a linen napkin.

"Ned, let us take you to the emergency room," I finally said.

There was a long silence.

"Been there," he said between clenched teeth, as if he were afraid of moving anything. "Heard the doctors outside the curtain." He stopped for a time, still struggling, almost crying now, I thought. "Said, 'Might as well let him go.'"

"Ned!" I exploded, then immediately reined myself in. "Ned," I started again calmly, "I'm calling an ambulance."

So accustomed was I to following Ned's directions, however, that I did not call an ambulance, but I did not agree with his decision either.

"This time you're wrong," I found myself saying silently as I sat for what seemed like a hundred hours on first one love seat and then the other. "This is wrong."

My friend and I stayed with Ned all day. We rarely spoke. There was nothing to do. From time to time I would think back to the dozens of talks Ned and I had quietly enjoyed in this same room. He always sat in the big chair, slumped casually in its well-worn arms, his feet propped on the end of the coffee table. He would often smoke one of his meerschaum pipes, tiny ivory-colored birds spiraling up its slender bowl, and I would watch him from the love seat by the window. At first these occasions had felt like a treat—the professor meeting with his favorite student—but later they felt like the meetings of friends. We had learned each other's habits, and together we went rowing in unison across such topics as memory, therapy, and dreams. Central to our conversations, I remembered, was the concept of community, and although I had not recognized it at first, we were negotiating a "deal" of sorts whereby Ned promised to boost my self-confidence while I promised to keep him "doing" for as long as his illness would allow.

And it worked, this deal. Based on his evaluation of my skills, I had taken on the most difficult cases in the clinic. Based on his evaluation of my interests, I changed departments in graduate school. He even circulated chapters of a book I began writing after I left Maple Street and sent me pages of encouraging feedback. With Ned on my side, I prospered. On my part, I agreed to accompany him to Philadelphia where the kidney transplant would probably be performed. I expanded a Godspeed Fund that had been set up to help him with medical bills. And I urged him to use our home in the woods whenever my partner and I left for a week or a weekend. In short, we were well on our way toward becoming indispensable to each other, and the talks in his living room were the way we made good on the bargain. Ned would sit back in his chair, eyes closed, thin legs dangling over one arm of the chair, listening as only Ned could listen. He praised. I organized. He got sicker. I expressed devotion.

But now Ned was bent double in the easy chair listening to nothing but his own excruciating pain. He ate nothing—threw up when he tried to sip a little brandy, clutched his stomach, and occasionally repeated, almost deliriously, what he had overheard at the hospital.

"Let him go. Let him go," he would croon to himself and then, turning some corner in his mind, cry out, "not yet. Oh, please."

"He's going to die," I said to myself. "Not today perhaps, but within the week or the month. My best friend is going to die."

But whenever I talked to myself like this and returned to the obvious conclusion that Ned should be hospitalized, a strange thing would happen. Ned would relax his grip on his stomach and straighten slightly in the big chair. He would notice that we were still in the room and, as if taken by surprise, he would start to talk about New Guinea or his kidneys, Istanbul or injections.

"Nothing is lost," he once said defensively. "We have all the pieces."

"Ned, save that for later," I said, not knowing what he referred to and further puzzled at his tone of urgency.

"But you need to know I have them," he continued, avoiding my gaze. "I can list them for you. The carved head . . . the spotted lizard . . . the paintings. . . ." And on he would struggle, almost visibly displacing the physical anguish so as to make room for a different conflict. It was a heart-wrenching and thoroughly alarming performance. Ned would take a deep breath, straighten, and almost physically lift the sharp, unworthy stomach cramps off his lap and allow a broader argument to squeeze in. Then down he would crumple against these alternate torments with their strange connections to amulets, aborigines, pain medication, and poets. Perhaps the painful procedure changed Ned's focus and pushed the cramps aside. The change was not, however, a relief for me.

I remember a strange discussion about injections. It seems that the indiscreet doctor in the emergency room who thought Ned should be allowed to die had given him a shot of painkiller when Ned refused to be hospitalized, and this shot now figured prominently in Ned's thinking. When we first arrived, he claimed that it didn't have any effect on the pain. Several hours later, he claimed he hadn't gotten an injection at all. Finally, taking another of his deep breaths, he insisted that my friend and I search along his spine to see whether or not there was a needle mark.

"Spine?" I asked.

"Don't ask," mumbled Ned. "You don't want to know."

Ned stood by the window and loosened his bathrobe. It slipped easily off his shoulders revealing a broad, slightly pink back covered with blond fuzz. We found no needle mark or scar. We found no evidence of anything.

"I can list them," Ned repeated. "They're all there."

I remember watching him walk gingerly into the bathroom at the end of the hall, his bathrobe still draped around his waist and with God knows what thoughts running through his head. He was no longer sending signals that made sense to me, and I

was emphatically not in the 80 to 90 percent range of understanding.

I was relieved when Ned's friend Alan showed up. He looked
like a kind young man, although as usual, I didn't know Ned's
other friends unless they came from the clinic.

Alan took up the vigil on the love seat. My friend and I
returned home. We left Providence and drove west and then
south along routes 44 and 102. I'm sure we talked about Ned,
but all I remember now is rolling up and down the long hills as
the sun went down and depositing the memories of the day
along the roadside. A white-painted chain holding a mailbox
became Ned Bennett's spine. An old gas station filled to the ceiling with broken wagons and wardrobes, carts and carriages,
bassinets and bicycles all rolling on airless tires up the inside of
the dirty window became an incestuous conglomeration of Bennett memories. Open auction sheds became the clinic and, in
some strange and unintended way, a fine old Presbyterian
church with an ugly addition in Necco-wafer green became Ned
himself. Up and down over the hills we drove, past dark houses
reluctant to separate themselves from the shadows of surrounding trees, thinking of Ned. As we proceeded, I sometimes felt the
old warmth returning and told myself that I would try still
harder to help this beleaguered man, but sometimes I hit a
pocket of confusion and felt peculiarly cool. And so I continued, swimming home alone as if through the unevenly heated
waters of a spring-fed lake.

Alan called at midnight, concern in his voice. Ned still hadn't
eaten anything and was largely incoherent. Did I think he
should be hospitalized against his will? Yes, I did, but no, he
wasn't. Ned didn't give a reason for his refusal. He simply
would not go. At one A.M. I told Alan I would drive up at six to
relieve him. As one of Ned's three or four closest friends, I was
ready to force him into a hospital.

Early the next morning I retraced my steps—north on 102,
east on 44. In the gray light of dawn, the houses still sat motionless and unlit as I drove along the empty highway. My tires hit
the cracks with a rhythmic bumpa-bump, bumpa-bump.

As I pulled up in front of the small apartment building, Ned appeared at the door looking pale and beaten.

"I'm going to work," he said, as a cab drove up to the curb.

"No you're not," I replied calmly. "You're going to the hospital."

"Can't," he said, looking past me, and, to my utter amazement, staggered around me and fell into the cab.

"Ned," I called after him, "I have not driven two hours to see you do something stupid like go to work when you can't even walk. What in hell is going on?"

"Maple Street," he said, looking neither at me nor the driver. "Maple Street."

Standing on the walk in front of his apartment, I watched the cab gather speed as it rolled down the hill. Ned's door wasn't completely shut, and as the cab disappeared around the corner at the foot of the hill I could see the door open slightly and shut again.

"What?" I asked myself. "What?"

The following day Ned and I began to unravel. Still actively searching for an explanation for his bizarre behavior, I was describing the poor man's pain to a friend who knew Ned slightly, when I mentioned the shot in the spine.

"Not possible," she said simply. "Not where you put painkillers."

"Not possible," confirmed a physician friend who I consulted later in the day. "He made that one up. Also, your friend wouldn't be sipping brandy if his kidneys were failing. Something's wrong there, too."

"Actually, you must have the wrong person," said Ned's own doctor when I phoned. "Ned hasn't been to the hospital in ten months."

"Hasn't been to the hospital in ten months?" I repeated stupidly. "But the tests for the dialysis. The coming kidney transplant. I mean, what about all those trips to the emergency room?"

"We use a computer to keep track of all our services," the doctor replied, now becoming cautious and confused himself, "and Mr. Bennett hasn't used any of them. Perhaps you have the wrong Ned Bennett."

I hung up in a daze. No trips to the hospital in . . . ? *No trips?* But the bills he complained of. The "let him go" doctor with his terrible prediction. The medications from the emergency room. The calls he made from the hospital . . .

I called Betty, who had left the Maple Street Clinic a year before to start a private practice.

"Did Ned Bennett speak Portuguese?" I asked her.

"Not to my knowledge," she replied. "In fact, no, because he couldn't talk to the lady in Pina's Bakery."

"Did he break his back the year before I came to the clinic?" I continued.

"Of course not. What's going on?"

"I don't know," I said. "I have no idea what's going on."

My next call that evening was to Ned. I told him of my conversation with his doctor but not of my call to Betty, and I wonder now what I thought such a confrontation would accomplish. Ned didn't wonder anything. He knew.

Taking the offensive, he angrily requested that I not call his physician again. The poor doctor had called Ned at the clinic, he told me, complaining that a hysterical woman had phoned babbling incomprehensively about kidneys and spinal injections.

"I understand that you're squeamish," Ned said, trying to sound forceful. "But no more calls on my behalf, got it?"

"Don't do this, Ned," I remember saying, begging him to stop as I stood at the kitchen phone and stared at the linoleum. "Don't do this. I know what I said to your doctor."

Ned continued to attack, and I was reminded of a phrase he used many times in supervision when I asked why some people seem eager to burn their bridges. "Only the builders know what the bridge is worth. Some bridges need to be burned."

Ned torched his end of the bridge with "the hysterical woman" accusation, which I knew wasn't true, and he fanned the flames with statements like "I'm tired of helping everyone else feel strong and healthy," which I knew was true.

I lit my end of the bridge with "What about the kidney

transplant? Your doctor said your kidneys are fine now. What about speaking Portuguese? You can't even talk with the lady in Pina's Bakery. And what about your hospital bills this year? You don't have any." It was amazing how discrepancies I hadn't consciously noticed started coming to mind.

Still staring at the linoleum on which I had superimposed a picture of Ned's listening face, I also challenged the very lies I had enjoyed the most. "What about learning so much from me, trusting me, relying on me—me the champion, remember? Is that made up, too?"

There was a pause, and Ned's voice became deeper and quieter. I think he said, "No, there's some truth to that, but it is also true that your weakness has been a burden."

I was stung. Slapped. Ned Bennett had *never* in the course of our five-year friendship said anything derogatory about me, not one thing, and now he admitted that all the time he'd been saying "champion," he had also been thinking wimp.

"Oh, I am so sorry," I said sarcastically, and added, with absolutely no understanding of how close to the truth I came, "but if you don't like burdensome people, why encourage them, Ned? Why collect them like . . . charms?"

Somehow the awful conversation ended and we hung up. I stood in the kitchen awash in confusion.

Had I heard right? Had our friendship of five years just ended? Had Ned been lying about himself . . . and me? Why? Why lie about illness? *Ned* lie?

Except for my thoughts of Ned I remember very little of the following days or weeks. At first I was preoccupied with reevaluating the medical stories, then all the stories I had heard from him.

"He told me about four trips to the emergency room," I would say to myself, putting four of my fingers on my desk as if beginning a complicated equation. "Now his doctor said that *no* visits had been made in ten months, but Ned described the 'let him go' trip just before he became very sick, the one when he called me from the waiting room asking to be distracted by a Dr. Stone story, a trip for a shot of Demerol right after his vacation, and, yes, at least one other visit made straight from work. Four."

Convinced that the part of the Bennett stories having to do with acute pain should be broken off the main body of information that pertained to the "real" Bennett, I could almost picture Ned-in-pain go floating off into a different category, perhaps to become part of a different tale.

"But I saw him throw up," I remembered, and as Ned in his silvery bathrobe reversed his direction and came back into view, doubled over in pain in the easy chair, groaning and throwing up brandy, then the truth of Ned-in-pain flowed back into the original story. Illness, accomplishments, childhood trauma, romance—back and forth rocked the wispy bits of information in my mind, never holding together for more than an afternoon, never making sense. It was like putting the north ends of a hundred magnets together. It was like "Ching-Chong Chinaman sitting on a fence/Trying to make a dollar out of fifteen cents."

During these weeks I called Betty several times and nailed down a few more inconsistencies. Ned had, indeed, told different medical stories to different people and outlined different financial sagas. He had not run a health food store with Jonathan but in fact had bought a piece of property, which he lost through foreclosure. Nor did the story of his education square with the facts we had. However, neither Betty nor I could discover much about his family, travels, or famous friends. Maybe he had been forced to chop wood for his dinner. Maybe he had graduated from college at nineteen. Maybe he had traveled to Istanbul and New Guinea. And maybe he had taken a course with Eric Semrad. We did discover that Ned was now taking an extended leave of absence from the clinic, but the reason given was, naturally, "health."

From frustration and confusion, I dropped abruptly into thorough-going doubt, and for a time I distrusted every single thing about Ned I could remember. He had a perfectly nice family, I thought to myself. He never went out of the country. And those awards? I never actually saw them. I found, however, that like confusion, cynicism did not produce a satisfactory account. I could not "take as certain the opposite of what the liar said," for, as Montaigne knew, "the reverse of truth has a hundred thousand shapes and a limitless field." Or as Swift predicted,

"You . . . will find yourself equally deceived whether you believe or not: the only remedy is to suppose that you have heard some inarticulate sounds, without any meaning at all."

From a place of honor, my memories of Ned Bennett tumbled not into disrepute or compromise but into silence. Most of what he had told me about therapy, about myself, about him, about illness, and especially about believing in other people sat dumbly in my head, cordoned off from the rest of my experience by shame and disappointment. I had no way of understanding what my years at the Maple Street Clinic supervised by a kind and utterly untrustworthy man might mean, so I ignored the experience as much as I could. Within a year, I rarely wondered why Ned had told lies or why I had believed them. Only occasionally when a man or a woman in my office would lean forward, shaking with the humiliation of betrayal, and say angrily, "*Why* did I believe so many lies?" would I think back to routes 44 and 102 and the memories of Ned that lay along those highways like so many dead raccoons.

ON LYING AND BELIEVING

The truth is something too harsh and devastating for the majority of men to bear. In their secret hearts they know themselves, and they can suffer the thought of themselves only by idealizing the facts. The more trivial, loathsome, and degraded the reality, the more powerful and relentless must be the idealization.

H. L. MENCKEN

Most liars can fool most people most of the time. Our research, and the research of most others, has found that few people do better than chance in judging whether someone is lying or truthful. We also found that most people think they are making accurate judgments even though they are not. . . .

We lead our lives believing that there is a core of emotional truth, that most people can't or won't mislead us about how they feel.

PAUL EKMAN

SEVERAL YEARS AFTER NED BENNETT AND I BROKE OFF OUR FRIEND-ship, I found myself piecing together an explanation of our relationship. I did this both to reassimilate those five curious years into the rest of my experience and to discover how my beliefs about lying had evolved. For one thing, I found it increasingly impossible not to believe *something* about Ned, and for another, in order to deal with the confusion of betrayal that my clients brought to me, I needed to understand why a nice man like Ned would lie and why I and his other, ordinarily sensible friends would believe him. As I set out to investigate what psychologists call the "literature of deceit," a lot of memories came back.

I remember one winter afternoon sitting in a library and squinting against sunlight that bounced off the snow outside and slid in across the dozen or so books on deception that lay open before me. In one, the author contended that lies are conspiracies and that people who tell lies are striking bargains with the people around them. He further contended that such pacts are patterned after bargains first struck in early childhood. I tried to formulate Ned's "deal" as I read on—something like "As long as I seem to perform outstanding work in spite of terrible pain, you will admire me and care for me." A complementary bargain, struck by friends intent on maintaining fictions of their own, might have been, "As long as you keep going against such terrible odds, then surely I can overcome my troubles, too." Such bargains, I learned, exist on both a conscious level and, more darkly and perversely, on an unconscious level as well. They are maintained by both parties for the benefits they seem to provide and the fears they allay. Political lies that delayed World War II were cited as examples, as were lies told by an alcoholic and accepted by a spouse to keep their marriage intact. Then, for no apparent reason, there came to my mind a picture of Ned receiving mail. I saw him again as he opened greeting cards in his office and, smiling, tucked them around the purple plant, and I recalled him arranging an impressive display of birthday cards on his dining room table.

"The postman told me he'd never seen anything like it," he had said, "had to make two trips in from the street."

Suddenly I remembered the Christmas cards I'd seen on my last visit to Ned's apartment, and the concept of lying as a conspiracy became clear. Just before Ned left the Maple Street Clinic for his extended rest, my partner and I received an impersonal note asking us to pick up some paintings we had loaned him. A precise time was arranged when Ned himself would not be there. We would be let into the old, familiar apartment by a housekeeper.

On a wintry morning, we drove into Providence and parked in front of Ned's apartment. A silent woman in her sixties let us in. As usual, the apartment was spotlessly clean and neat, and in the middle of the living room was a stack of our belongings tied in a bundle. As I approached them, I noticed that the hangings behind the love seats were gone and in their place were two matching cascades of Christmas cards. Some fifty cards had been attached to six or eight ribbons that hung from the ceiling all the way to the floor. I walked over to the nearest cataract of cards.

"For our champion. Merry Christmas!"

"Hope this helps, Ned. Courage."

"For a terrific guy at Christmastime. Sorry I couldn't send more."

"I pray for you nightly. You are always in my thoughts."

"You're a champion. Keep up the fine work."

"Happy Holidays, Champ. Our thoughts are with you."

On and on and on it went, this outpouring of good wishes, this great long string of half-conscious contracts.

"Don't worry about me," read another. "You make our cares seem trivial. Take care and God bless."

"Friends forever! Hope the enclosed helps."

"Merry Christmas, dearest friend."

"If you can do it, I can do it. Keep fighting."

"To the Champion."

About half of the names I recognized. Madeleine the bird-watcher who had never married. Jonathan the folk art curator who was wrestling with homosexuality. Estelle who was depressed. Anthony who hated being short. Bill who was in debt. Nancy who was trapped in a miserable marriage. Lou who was on his third wife. Here they were, the addictive conspiracies; here, fluttering down from the ceiling, the bargains of choice.

It seems to me now that Ned Bennett cut bargains with his friends on at least three levels. In exchange for sympathy, he embellished a difficult life to make his troubles seem more terrible and his accomplishments more wonderful than they really

were. For what is usually called friendship, but for Ned was
more like oxygen, he schmoozed with his listeners as only an
experienced therapist can. And for an intense and encapsulating
loyalty, he convinced each person he befriended that he or she
was the one superior and essential friend he needed.

It is easiest for me to see how Ned's bargains worked with
the people I knew or knew about at the Maple Street Clinic.
There he befriended a great variety of individuals who had talents, which perhaps he admired, but who also had fears. Ned
was the expert on fears. According to his own descriptions, he
was seriously ill, in debt, living alone, childless, and unsupported by family. He was the victim of accident and abuse, and
there was hardly a misfortune he had not suffered. My feeling
now is that if he had met someone afraid of snakes or heights,
he would have fabricated—modestly, hesitantly—a simply wonderful tale about being terrified by a skein of poisonous snakes
that slithered after him up a tall tree in New Guinea—and then
left! Ned insisted that he survived each of his tragedies by a
great effort of will, and this gave to the guru of pain not only
the power to console and advise but also in many minds the
magical power to protect. Standing next to Ned was like standing by a tree that has already been hit by lightning, like diving
into a brand-new bomb crater during an attack. On a somewhat
less magical level, Ned's friends believed that he could show
them by example the way to conquer their apprehensions, and
they further believed that as they themselves helped Ned with
devotion, companionship, money, or whatever else they had to
give, so he would help them with wise words reported directly
from the front. They would not be alone, for Ned had gone
before them.

If Ned and his companions could have stopped with this
exchange—if his need had been only to cut a better figure and
ours only to have a charismatic leader—we would remember
ourselves as gullible students and him as a skillful and ultimately
outrageous dramatist. In my mind, at least, he would have
joined the lonely ten-year-olds who boast of meeting famous
baseball players and joined the scrambling adults for whom, as
Samuel Johnson wrote, "Nature is hourly working wonders

invisible to every other eye, only to supply them with subjects of conversation."[1]

But Ned's needs and ours were greater, and the contracts we made were more inclusive. In addition to seeming more important and more experienced than he really was, he also wanted to be sustained by adoration, and this inspired him to distort his listeners' lives as well as his own. These were far more hurtful lies, for unlike the broken-back and injected-in-the-spine stories, the steady infiltration of exaggerated compliments strained something far more intimate than credulity. Like the viny purple plant growing among the greeting cards, Ned's carefully selected tributes exploited each crack and channel of self-doubt and self-deception. Skilled therapist that he was, he sensed immediately what each person wanted to believe, and he provided observations, dreams, and hunches to show that it was true. The resulting accounts were as fascinating as they were satisfying. His earnest and carefully worded compliments seemed to explain so much more than the truth, which, if it existed at all at that moment, was too complicated and disorganized to be useful to his listeners. In exchange for supporting his friends' fictions, Ned was given not just allegiance and the power that it implies, but vitality. His losses in childhood—however extensive they might have been—had numbed and wounded him, and it seems to me that only by telling increasingly terrible tales could he generate in others the emotional reactions that should have been his own. We, his followers, took his stories to heart. We gave them life with our sorrow and indignation. We lent Ned our tears for a day or a night.

In retrospect I see a third conspiracy, which I find hardest to understand. Although the cascades of Christmas cards seem to argue the contrary, I don't think Ned's primary goal was the collection of a devoted band of auxiliaries. I believe he wanted a *best* friend, and because he couldn't feel that closeness even

1. Of course Ned was not in the league led by George Psalmanazar who, in the 1700s, presented himself in London as a Japanese converted to Christianity. There he supplied ready listeners with a fictitious history and geography of Formosa to which he added an alphabet and a language. Phyllis Greenacre, "The Impostor," *Psychoanalytic Quarterly* 27 (1958): 359–82.

when it was offered, he kept trying with everyone in hopes of connecting. He worked very hard at this and overlooked a lot to gain a best friend. He told us stories. He gave us compliments. And he encircled each with a distrust of all the others. His thoughtful disparagement of so many of his acquaintances—I can think of no exceptions save a friend of his who had died— not only kept us apart and therefore unlikely to compare stories, but also gave to each the erroneous conviction that he or she was essential to Ned's well-being. We each believed we were his number one best friend.

I think that when any of Ned's followers needed him less and began drifting away or when Ned's own troubles and insecurities increased and he needed us more, he would intensify his tales of deprivation, intensify his compliments and accomplishments, and intensify his efforts to keep his friends apart. This last may have been the most destructive of all his prevarications, for it encouraged in us not merely credulousness and wishful thinking but a false sense of intimate superiority as well.

I remember a fragment of conversation that Ned and I exchanged when he was doubled over in pain at Ken's Lunch. He had been repeating himself alarmingly and had made one of his mysterious fifteen-minute trips to the men's room, trips I now believe were taken to treat his discomfort with alcohol or pain pills.

When he returned, sliding into the booth in his slightly awkward way, resting his head in his hands briefly, he told me that he had dreamed about his mother and was distressed that he could recall nothing more. He gazed outside then as he often did and finally said, to no one in particular, "Everyone has a career, you know, and everyone has a place, I think. . . ." His voice trailed off, and he remained staring out the window. Perhaps a couple walked across the glaring parking lot just then, perhaps a mother passed by with a child.

". . . a place in the family," he continued. "I want to come first in somebody's life."

I don't think Ned ever came first in anyone's life—or not for very long—and the longer I work as a psychologist, the less I am sure that there is a remedy for so early and so grievous a lack. I think to myself now that Ned's exaggerations did not exaggerate how miserable he felt, and his compliments did not overstate his need for my energy, as he would have put it. I think there were things in his life, like a reliance on alcohol, for example, that he did not feel he could tell his friends without losing their respect. Thus he transposed each pain that could not be spoken of into one that could. In a similar manner, because he could not criticize his friends for fear of losing their allegiance, he transposed the natural frustrations inherent in any friendship into quiet asides aimed at the shortcomings of absent colleagues. In these and other ways, he guided us past the discomforts of truth in hopes of being loved. And as for us, we followed for similar if less desperate reasons, and we kept on following until we didn't need the illusion of loving ourselves or Ned so perfectly. We never learned how to detect his lies any better. We simply stopped needing the deals he offered.

When I try to imagine how Ned originally became caught up in conspiracies—that is, when I go in search of the underlying and largely unconscious aspects of the bargains—I am entirely on speculative grounds. The best I can do is match what I think I know of my former friend with instances of childhood deception that I have read about or encountered.

Most definitions of lying include the ability to distinguish truth from falsehood so that deliberate deception is kept separate from delusions or misinformation. In addition, the notion of a goal, either conscious or unconscious, is essential. A liar knowingly and purposefully deceives. Roughly defined, lies stretch along a continuum, from white lies at one end through altruistic lies, hypocrisy, swindling, cheating, and the like all the way to *pseudologica fantastica* or pathological lying at the other. At this extreme are found individuals like Ned, who lie regularly and without compunction about matters that on the surface, at least, have little immediate practical value to them. Accounts of a woman who unswervingly insisted that her clothes cost two or three times what she paid for them and of a man who asserted that he sniffed, smoked, and injected enough material to kill three or four average men have about them a compulsive and fantastic quality. So, I believe, did Ned's insis-

172   CONFIDING

tence that his eyes, kidneys, spine, and circulatory system all put
him in critical danger or that his family had beaten, starved,
exploited, and abused him. The longer I knew him, the more
dramatic these complaints became.

There is disagreement among those who study pathological
lying as to how responsible these individuals are for what comes
out of their mouths. Sometimes these people resemble patients
with Korsakoff's psychosis who, having damaged their brains
with years of excessive drinking, are powerless to stem the tide
of misinformation that comes boiling out of their imaginations
to fill gaps in their besotted memories. At other times pathological liars behave like con men—the old psychopaths, the current
"antisocial personalities"—who clearly understand that they are
lying but do it anyway. In short, pathological liars seem to
waver between inspired self-deception and outright deceitful-
ness, between believing and pretending. At least initially, they
seem to be aware of their deceit, but the urge to believe their
own exaggerations is so great that when they are confronted
with the truth, they often become mentally confused to a
remarkable degree. This confusing combination of lying and
self-deception is nicely captured by Scott Snyder, who has
described the mixture as it existed in one of his patients, a
twenty-six-year-old woman who complained of insomnia, emptiness, and boredom, and who, when he met her, was depressed.
As usual, the woman was asked to describe her childhood.
Where had she grown up? Who were her parents?

A detailed developmental history . . . indicated that she was
from an extremely wealthy family in northern Africa and
that her father had been away from home much of the time
during her developmental years because of his duties as a
high-ranking military officer. During her father's absences,
her uncle would often sexually and physically abuse her, she
said. Her mother was unable to protect her because she was
ill with cancer. The patient said that she had provided primary nursing care for her mother for 3 years, until her
mother died when the patient was 14 years old. She then left
home, she said, and drifted from town to town supporting

herself through prostitution, theft, and drug smuggling. She left the country at age 19 when she married her husband.

Interviews with the patient's husband and close friends indicated that she frequently . . . fabricated events surrounding her early years. Her father was actually a low-ranking clerk assigned to the defense department. Her mother had had arthritis and had been only partially disabled before her death. The husband stated that the patient would frequently glamorize and romanticize her early years, but that she would seem to convince herself that what she was saying was true. In this country, she would tell friends that her clothing cost two or three times its actual purchase price. Whenever her husband would question her about these statements, the patient would remain convinced of their authenticity until she was shown sales slips of the purchase price. She would then either enter a dissociative state [as if hypnotized or disconnected from her body] punctuated with rage, or become depressed and withdrawn.[2]

There are as many explanations for how this woman and others like her can know and not know something at the same time as there are major schools of psychology. For now, suffice it to say that although the mechanisms used to explain this blend of lying and self-deception range from Freud's concept of repression through behaviorists' bad habits and cognitive psychologists' biased judgments to Sartre's idea of bad faith, most agree that prevaricators combine believing and pretending when they set about convincing themselves and others that what is, isn't.

One way to accomplish this sleight of hand is to pay more attention to the emotional truth of an experience than to the facts. Ned may have fully believed he was dying on the day we last visited him in Providence and so concocted the story of overhearing the doctor in the emergency room to more dramatically get across his feelings. The story may have *felt* true to him.

2. Scott Snyder, "Pseudologica Fantastica in the Borderline Patient," *American Journal of Psychiatry* 143 (1986): 1287.

It may have had what psychologists call "affective truth." In a similar manner, although on a different scale I hope, former President Reagan convinced himself that he had never said, in reference to California's attempts to preserve their redwoods, "A tree is a tree. How many more do you have to look at?" The comment had been captured on tape, but as Lyn Nofziger wrote in his memoir, "We didn't tell him or anyone else, so he was free to do one of the things he had always done best—convince himself that the truth is what he wants it to be."[3]

Another way of blurring the distinction between *is* and *isn't* is to repeat the lie so many times that it becomes true in the sense that you can't remember any other version of the story. Psychologists agree that this can happen, but disagree whether or not it represents the loss of original data—as if the fabrication had permanently pushed the facts out of mind—or is better described as the addition of a second account that co-exists with but generally preempts the first. Whichever it is, experiments have shown that when these wishful-thinking kinds of lies deal with moods rather than experience, and an individual energetically "whistles a happy tune" rather than boasts of owning a condo in Acapulco, they often work. In fact, resolutely pretending to feel the way one wants to feel but doesn't is the basis of a technique known as fixed-role therapy.

There are other, less common, methods of blurring the distinction between truth and falsehood, and together they stymie our attempts to ascertain exactly when the pathological liar is deceiving only us and when he is deceiving himself as well. And this creation of uncertainty is an important aspect of lying. As M. R. Haight points out in *A Study of Self-Deception*, liars leave us guessing and hesitating, unable to act, for all are playing for time—time to escape, time to understand, time to change, time to recover whatever it is they have lost.[4]

Although lying is considered so destructive to every society

3. Lyn Nofziger, *Nofziger* (Washington, D.C.: Regnery Gateway, 1992). As quoted in *New York Times Book Review*, 18 October 1992, p. 9.

4. M. R. Haight, *A Study of Self-Deception* (Atlantic Highlands, NJ: Humanities Press, 1980), pp. 109–19.

that even "the devils do not tell lies to one another,"[5] psychologists consider lying one of the most significant occurrences in the development of the individual. Before age four or five, children don't distinguish clearly between truth and falsehood, and without knowing what is true, a person can unintentionally misinform, but cannot lie. Further, preschoolers have a fuzzy idea of how lie detection works. They commonly believe that their mothers and fathers are mind readers or even mind controllers who know and influence what their progeny are thinking. But at about age four a child learns he can say something that isn't true and be believed. The existential psychologist Donald Keene maintains that the child enjoys a tremendous increase in power at this point and gains a new and profoundly important sense of independence.[6] He or she is no longer a transparent extension of Mother or Father but a separate, secret self—an autonomous being with a separate identity. At this point, whether the child experiments with what Anna Freud called delinquent lying—whose goal is securing material advantage and escaping punishment—or with fantasy lying—whose goal is spinning fantasies to ameliorate intolerable realities—an important step has been taken on the road to individuality.[7] Another psychologist puts it this way: "The striving for the right to have secrets from which the parents are excluded is one of the most powerful factors in . . . establishing and carrying out one's own will."[8]

Thus when Ned told me about running the health food store with Jonathan or described the horror of being in the emergency room listening to doctors discuss his imminent demise, he could boost his self-esteem both by pretending to have experienced

5. Samuel Johnson in his essay "The Lie of Vanity," quotes Sir Thomas Browne as saying, "The devils do not tell lies to one another: for truth is necessary to all societies: nor can the society of hell subsist without it." Quoted in Philip Kerr, ed., *The Penguin Book of Lies* (New York: Viking, 1990), p. 163.

6. Donald Keene, *Toward a Clinical Existential Psychology* (1968), p. 44.

7. Anna Freud, *Normality and Pathology in Childhood: Assessments of Development* (New York: International Universities Press, 1965), pp. 114–16.

8. V. Tausk, "On the Origin of the 'Influencing Machine' in Schizophrenia," *Psychoanalytic Quarterly* 2 (1933): 519–56.

what he had only imagined and also by putting (another) one over on me. The satisfaction we experience when we pull the wool over someone's eyes, either innocently as part of a poker game or practical joke or maliciously as in an out-and-out lie, is called "duping delight," and it apparently draws its power from the excitement we felt in preschool years when we took a giant step toward independence by learning how to lie.

Regardless of how a young child first comes to experiment with lies, his or her parents and the culture in which they all live will influence the child's future use of the skill. If parents punish lies with excessive severity, it has been found that children will continue to lie but learn not to admit it. If, on the other hand, the parents themselves lie to the child, either by breaking promises—"We'll go to the store tomorrow"—or by outright deception—"We're just going for a ride in the car," meaning we're taking you to the doctor for shots—the child learns that it is neither important nor safe to say what you really mean. They learn to lie in any situation that makes them uncomfortable. Also, if the environment in which the child is raised is chaotic or traumatic, children sometimes use fantasy lies to deny the danger they feel and transport themselves to a happier place. This is seen a great deal in sexually abused children, who create alternate lives for themselves, at least while the abuse is going on. It is hypothesized that if the trauma is severe and long lasting, these other lives will actually be adopted in lieu of reality, at which point the child is said to suffer from a multiple personality disorder. Although it is impossible to reconstruct Ned's childhood, the death of his parents and subsequent reshuffling of the family have been verified, which seems quite enough sadness to make fantasy lies attractive.

In addition to the distinct styles of lying found in families, different class and cultural groups treat prevarication differently. The upper class is said to admire honesty (Thomas Szasz points out that this is a luxury only the powerful can afford[9]), whereas

9. Thomas Szasz, *The Myth of Mental Illness* (New York: Dell Publishing, 1961), p. 248.

the working class admires smartness, meaning the cleverness to con others and the shrewdness not to be duped. Among cultures, the Irish Catholics, for example, love the flamboyant excesses of a tall tale; English Protestants are more comfortable with reliable facts. In a friend's family—half-Irish, half-English—the children were exposed to both extremes so regularly that her brother, John Carroll, wrote a poem about being caught between his mother's painstakingly accurate accounts and his father's spellbinding but inevitably misleading tales. "No one believes what Dad has to relate," he begins, "he's known to embellish, to prevaricate. . . ."

> Yet Mother looks TRUTH straight in the eye,
> She'd rather eat worms than utter a lie.
> She's ever meticulous, always correct,
> Plain facts are for Father a pain in the neck.
> So tell me who's right, and tell me who's wrong.
> Mom keeps the records, and Dad sings the song.

Regardless of whether a child grows up exposed to singing or accounting, the motives that prompt his lies are likely to evolve as he or she matures. As already mentioned, lying to maintain a sense of independence starts early, and lying to gain power and control is quick to follow—misinforming being one way to tip the balance of power in one's favor. (Of course, once a liar is discovered, even the accurate information he possesses is suspect, and the individual suffers a loss of power.) Schoolchildren also learn that lies can hurt or devalue a person. Lies of flattery develop later. Finally, the great majority of lies are prompted by the need to regulate self-esteem—lies of vanity, Samuel Johnson called them.

"It is apparent that the inventors of all these fictions intend some exaltation of themselves . . . : their narratives always imply some consequence in favour of their courage, their sagacity, or their activity, their familiarity with the learned, or their reception among the great; they are always bribed by the present pleasure of seeing themselves superior to those that surround them. . . ." In short, "He, to whom truth affords no gratifications, is generally inclined to seek them in falsehoods."[10]

Such lies, used when a person wishes to close the gap between what he wants to be and what he feels he really is, attempt to hide the impotent degraded self.[11]

A number of psychologists have wondered what lying does to the liar. In addition to the obvious irony that lying subverts the very goals that the lies were designed to obtain, existential and humanistic psychologists believe that lying focuses a person's attention so squarely on others that prevaricators lose a clear sense of themselves. They are said to develop a "false self" that is based on what they believe is expected of them—be it a tower-of-strength, a delinquent or a perfect child—and, like an impostor or an actor, they don't dare take their eyes off the audience. As a result, development of the real self stops and only the roles mature. To reinvigorate this stunted growth, the impostor needs to start leveling with someone, be it a best friend, therapist, or lover, but as Donald Keene points out, the longer a person puts off experiencing the guilt or shame that prompted him to twist the truth in the first place, the harder it is to unlock the true but secret self and experience the shame.[12] Not surprisingly, liars rarely seek treatment. In my experience, husbands and wives bring a prevaricating spouse in on the eve of divorce proceedings. Schools and courts coerce delinquent liars to attend therapy, and occasionally one will come in under his own steam, briefly and without funds, to boast of putting one over on spouse, lover, kids, employer, or IRS.

Pulling the observations together from this quick tour of pathological lying that are relevant to Ned, I speculate that the unconscious dynamics that started his pattern of lying was an early and genuinely desperate need to be a "good boy."

10. Johnson, "The Lie of Vanity," in *Penguin Book of Lies*, pp. 166 and 164.

11. Quoted in C. V. Ford, B. H. King, and M. H. Hollender, "Lies and Liars: Psychiatric Aspects of Prevarication," *American Journal of Psychiatry* 145 (1988): 559.

12. Keene, *Toward a Clinical Existential Psychology*, p. 47.

Believing that his bad behavior was responsible both for his parents' death and the breakup of the family—a common mistake made by children—he may have escaped from this overwhelming guilt by trying to become the perfect child. When he fell short, I surmise he lied to bring himself up to par and to ingratiate himself with anyone who would care for him in those chaotic times. Eventually he may have developed an uncontrollable compulsion to appear quintessentially good. The adults around him, when they paid him any attention at all, probably encouraged this false but easily manageable behavior for reasons of their own. Especially when the boy's father died, it must have been easy to accept Ned's bargain of, "As long as I seem to perform outstanding work in spite of terrible pain, you will admire and care for me," even if it was obvious that the little boy's outstanding works were desperate fantasies.

If he established this unrealistic and grossly idealized self-image in response to his early losses and insecurities, the young Ned would daily be faced with the choice either to maintain the deception through apparent good works or to come clean and face what felt like both guilt and pain. He apparently chose to live a lie, and eventually he deceived himself into believing large parts of his fantasies because they felt true, because he had told them so often, and because it seemed too late to unravel forty years of might-have-beens. Curiously, when I think of Ned now, I find my attention shifting away from the process of deceiving toward that of believing, as if an inability to believe rather than a readiness to lie lay at the root of his problems. I find myself wondering whether he failed to believe our words of affection because he lied so much himself, or whether he lied so much because he could not believe his friends when they told him that he was, without exaggeration and ingratiation, a gentle and talented person.

So now let us turn to believing, which is beginning to feel like the more important of the two processes to understand. In a fascinating article, "How Mental Systems Believe," psychologist

Daniel Gilbert asks an innocent question. Is it true, he wonders, that understanding is one thing and believing is another?[13]

"Everyone knows the difference . . . between supposing a proposition and acquiescing in its truth," wrote the famous nineteenth-century psychologist William James.

Nonetheless, replies Gilbert, "what everyone knows may be . . . wrong."

Since ancient times, most philosophers have maintained that believing involves two processes: the first is the comprehension of an idea and the second its assessment—is it true or false. René Descartes, the first modern thinker to formalize this division, maintained that the mind passively receives ideas—the way wax receives impressions—then actively considers them by studying, comparing, and analyzing until an assessment is made as to their veracity. He was very clear on this point. We comprehend first, without judgment, and then we "give or withhold our assent at will."[14] The idea is still with us, perhaps the more so because computers process information in exactly this way. Load it in first, process it second.

Some thirty years after Descartes published his *Principles of Philosophy* in 1644, Baruch Spinoza dismissed the idea that believing is a two-step procedure and argued that comprehending and accepting occur simultaneously. In other words, the very act of comprehending involves accepting. Spinoza agreed that one could subsequently evaluate a proposition and decide it was false, but one could not skip over the initial believing phase, no matter how ridiculous the idea. Translated into computer language, Spinoza claimed that believing is the mind's default or normal mode of operation whereas doubting and disbelieving is a function that has been added on.

Both philosophers' systems account for people holding huge numbers of beliefs and for holding doubts and disbeliefs as well. In fact, if a pair of Cartesian and Spinozan computers were designed, each with unlimited processing capability, the belief

13. Daniel Gilbert, "How Mental Systems Believe," *American Psychologist* 46 (1991): 107–19.

14. René Descartes quoted in Gilbert, "How Mental Systems Believe," p. 108.

system built up in each would be similar. But neither natural nor manmade mental systems have unlimited processing resources. Neither has every bit of needed information, and for people, especially, there are often other operations going on in the mind at the same time. We figure out what we believe while we are hurrying for a train, dodging puddles on a sidewalk, and talking with a fellow commuter. As a result, the ideal, complete processing of information gets compromised a great deal of the time. The progression from receiving an idea to assessing it or from accepting an idea to reconsidering it a moment later gets cut short. The result of this common overload is that the two philosophical systems produce somewhat half-baked beliefs, but not the same half-baked beliefs. A Cartesian machine would have gaps in its understanding. A Spinozan machine would be gullible.

To understand why this is so, Gilbert explains how mental systems operate when they are overloaded. The models we have of minds and computers all involve subsystems that work together serially to produce everything from adding two numbers or lifting a finger to writing a biography or dancing the tango. In simplest terms, information is passed along from subsystem to subsystem. In each, the information is modified in some way, then sent along to the next subsystem. Although all information-processing systems involve this flow of data, some simple ones are what Gilbert calls a "single exit system." That is, "the answer" or product of the thinking can only emerge after all the steps in the progression have been completed. In general, however, sophisticated systems allow answers to emerge at a number of different points in the process. Gilbert gives the example of a pancake-making machine whose job it is to convert messy, irregular pancakes into perfect, circular ones. The first subsystem in this machine cuts a square out of the irregular pancake's center. This square pancake can either travel to a blue box or go on through the machine's second subsystem, which cuts a circle from the square and drops it into a red box. This is an example of a "multiple-exit system," and it is capable of producing several products.

An interesting feature of this kind of system, Gilbert says, is that because resources like time and energy are required to send the information (or, in this case the pancake) from one subsystem to the next, any depletion in resources will cause the system to prematurely deliver the answer or product. When the multiple-exit pancake trimmer doesn't have unlimited resources, it will produce square pancakes (the product of the first subsystem) but not round ones because the latter depend on the former but not vice versa. This tendency for an information-processing machine to produce answers from its early subsystems when under duress is accentuated when later tasks are more difficult than early ones. Thus we can see that under stress a Cartesian mind might only have time to receive an idea but not to make any judgment about its truth or usefulness, whereas a Spinozan mind might only have time to register belief but not to reevaluate.

"Now," says Gilbert, "it is possible to begin asking the question . . . : Are human beings Cartesian or Spinozan systems?"[15]

Observations from several areas of psychology bear on this question, and I will mention just a few briefly. Studies of developing children suggest that credibility precedes doubt and seems to be easier. It is a common observation that young children are suggestible and believe almost everything they are told. Skepticism comes later. This does not fit well with the Cartesian model of thinking, which would predict that the positive and negative evaluations of neutral ideas would proceed simultaneously and with equal ease.

In psycholinguistic studies, investigators work on the assumption that complexity in thought tends to be reflected in complex language and that simple thinking is reflected in relatively simple linguistic forms. In a very rough way this is like saying that a person's "normal" or default method of operating will be tagged with simple, straightforward words like believable, happy, true, tall, correct, whereas the override or less usual operations that require extra effort will be tagged with the more complex "marked words" such as unbelievable, unhappy, untrue, short, and incorrect. Marked words, which signal complex thinking,

15. Gilbert, "How Mental Systems Believe," p. 110.

must meet two criteria. First, they generally have more morphemes (which are meaningful linguistic units such as child*hood*, boat*s*, *dis*belief) and second, they cannot be used neutrally. "How untrue is that statement?" or "How unhappy and how short is she?" are not neutral questions. They imply that the speaker already knows the general nature of the answer. On the other hand, "How true is that statement?" or "How happy and how tall is she?" are neutral, if a bit peculiar. There is a great deal more to this argument, but students of English generally agree that to the extent that words for mental operations suggest something about the operations themselves, they tell us that the rejection of ideas is more complicated than their acceptance. Related experiments have shown that it takes less time to affirm a true statement than to deny a false one, again as if we were programmed to expect the truth and have to go to extra trouble to reassess an idea when we suspect it is false.

Other lines of research converge on the idea that doubt develops later and is a more taxing operation. It has long been known, for example, that when prisoners are being brainwashed, their ability to doubt or hold off bogus confessions is severely compromised by stress and lack of sleep. In other words, doubting and arguing against a proposition takes so much energy that the process can be subverted by draining an individual's resources. When exhausted to the point of not being able to think or remember, prisoners relate that they find themselves believing whatever their captors say.

In the laboratory, a mild version of this overloaded state is simulated by asking subjects to evaluate dubious statements while at the same time listening to irrelevant information or performing a second task. The distracted subjects' ability to reject untrue statements is markedly reduced compared to subjects who are able to give their full attention to the statements. If subjects had Cartesian minds, they would register the propositions but, if distracted, not have time to decide if they were true or false. With Spinozan minds, the overloaded subjects would believe many of the doubtful propositions and not have the time to reassess them. As in the developmental and linguistic studies, distraction experiments suggest that comprehension and acceptance occur together. In less scientific terms, studies suggest that under ordinary circumstances, people are biased toward believing what they hear. This is especially true when "what they hear" are personal statements coming out of someone's mouth. Even when statements are paid for, as in advertising, or are part of a debate, which often forces participants to argue for a position they don't personally espouse, research has shown that the overwhelming tendency is to believe that speakers tell us what they truly feel.

"After decades of research activity, both the lie-detection and attribution literatures have independently concluded that people are particularly prone to accept the autobiographical propositions implicit (or explicit) in others' words and deeds."[16]

If we are persuaded by Gilbert and his colleagues that "people are credulous creatures who find it very easy to believe and very difficult to doubt,"[17] then why is this so? No one would build a computer with such a bias. What are we doing with credulous brains and what does that tell us about lying?

Although we cannot peer inside a mind and identify the specific neurons involved in doubting, believing, lying, or any other process, we do know that for a creature constantly surrounded by things that move, it is essential that seeing is believing (ditto for hearing, tasting, smelling, and touching in their fundamental forms). In other words, we know that for an organism to survive, it must believe its senses, even if they trick it occasionally, and we are no different. Our brains are wired to believe our sense organs and not to question them. Gilbert speculates that the same is true for social exchanges. As our brains evolved from a relatively simple organ that dealt directly with sights and sounds to the complex ones we possess today that deal with all manner of verbally communicated second-hand experience, he surmises that Nature, as is her way, used the old sensory circuits to handle the new communications and simply evolved extra subsystems to deal with doubt. In theory, this jury-rigged system

16. Gilbert, "How Mental Systems Believe," p. 112.
17. Gilbert, "How Mental Systems Believe," p. 117.

would have a much easier time evolving than would a completely redesigned brain. Of course, like other modifications, say
upright posture with its attendant low back pain, the improvements would not be without cost. In the case of social communication, the expansion of mankind's experience from "hear it,"
to "hear *about* it," may have given us the tremendous advantage
of hearing about what others experience at the price of being
too ready to believe what we hear. Apparently, this is not a bad
bargain in evolutionary terms. Judging from the extent that the
faculty of language has developed among human beings, being
gullible does not noticeably compromise survival. In fact, a
small body of research, much of it done by Bella DePaulo, suggests that believers actually get along better in this world than
doubters.

Even before DePaulo decided to focus her academic career
on the study of lying, she was running experiments on deception
in order to discover how good her subjects were at reading verbal and nonverbal cues.[18] She showed children and young
adults, from sixth grade through college, videotapes of people
describing their friends and enemies. Some tapes were honest
descriptions. Others were designed to mislead. Somewhat to her
surprise, she found that two quite different skills emerged: one
was the ability to detect deception, and the other was a particular sensitivity toward feelings. Subjects with the first skill identified the liars who were praising their enemies and deriding their
friends but were not very good at identifying the specific emotions that the truthful speakers were feeling. Subjects with the
second skill were poor lie detectors, but excelled at tuning into
feelings that were openly conveyed. DePaulo's experiments suggested that males, and especially younger males, are the best lie
detectors, whereas older females are most attuned to the feelings
a speaker wishes to convey. DePaulo called this second skill
"politeness," meaning that "females appear to be polite and

18. Bella DePaulo, "Success at Detecting Deception: Liability or Skill?"
Annals of the New York Academy of Science 364 (1981): 245–55. Also Carol
Toris and DePaulo, "Effects of Actual Deception and Suspiciousness of
Deception on Interpersonal Perceptions," *Journal of Personality and Social
Psychology* 47 (1985): 1063–73.

accommodating in their judgments, as they refrain from eaves-
dropping on those cues that other people do not want them to
perceive."[19]

DePaulo's investigations also show that as we get older and
more fully socialized we lose some of our ability to detect lies
but we gain politeness. Such a progression suggests that society
somehow rewards empathy so that as people mature, most are
encouraged to move away from blunt, truthful exchanges and
cultivate polite and rather credulous ones instead. Intrigued by
this movement toward credibility, DePaulo correlated her subjects' abilities to detect lies or remain politely unaware with
other qualities such as social understanding and popularity. She
found that students who were rated by themselves and by their
peers as being popular and having good relationships were the
subjects who were polite but who could not detect deception.
Conversely, the subjects who were good at detecting lies were
rated (again by themselves and by their peers) as less popular
and less pleased with their interpersonal relationships. Apparently being constantly on the lookout for deception creates
uncertainty both in oneself—"Am I reading the signals right?"—
and in others—"What are they really saying?"—that leads to
uncomfortable relations. Gilbert would add that in overriding
our usual tendency to believe, we expend considerably more
time and energy as well. In most purely social (as opposed to
business) exchanges, it is quicker, easier, more comfortable, and,
in the end, safe enough to lean toward believing.

Not long ago an attractive couple came into my office, the
woman berating herself for not discovering earlier that her husband had had an affair. She told me that the moment she found
irrefutable evidence, she was able to see dozens of other clues
she had not noticed before.

"Why did I believe him for so long?" she asked angrily
through her tears. "I am so ashamed of myself for being
duped."

"I feel terrible myself," her husband said earnestly, missing

19. DePaulo, "Success at Detecting Deception," p. 253.

the point of his wife's concern. "I've apologized a hundred times, but it doesn't do any good. When is my wife going to trust me again?"

I looked at them both for a long moment, each securely trapped in a separate dilemma, and I found myself wondering where routes 44 and 102 run through a person's brain. I pictured goldenrod and wild asters blooming in dusty drifts along those highways, and I imagined abandoned auction sheds alternating with windowless bars and grills that had not been opened in forty years. I also pictured networks of neurons laid out across the landscape, their patterns dictated by useful old habits like believing and staying close to others that extended back in time tens of thousands of years—old pathways deeply imprinted in our minds.

"It's an old problem," I found myself saying slowly, "and not uncommon. When you literally can't believe your eyes, when you experience an earthquake or the first big lie, the whole brain, the whole world is thrown out of kilter."

I stopped as confusion descended over both their faces, but I knew what they needed to hear, and I knew how many months or even years it would take them to hear it. In whatever terms I couched it, they needed to learn what Ned's sad loss of faith had finally taught me about lying and believing—that needy conspiracies invite lies and that self-confidence does not; that trusting yourself enough lets you keep on believing and interacting. One way or another I would tell them that not believing is a far greater problem than lies.

BABY FISH-EYE DEMELLO

As I swept the kitchen floor last Saturday morning, my eyes fell on a pack of matches and I thought how strange it is that such a small, ordinary object can burn down an entire house.

"Didn't I just dream about that?" I asked myself, and, pausing in my sweeping, I reconstructed a barely remembered passage in which a smiling, bespectacled arsonist dressed in old-fashioned flying gear complete with full-size, fold-up wings and decorated with red, white, and blue banners went fluttering around the Hillsdale Clinic trying to set us on fire.

"And that dream turned into the one—" I stopped, immobilized in the middle of the kitchen by a sickening sensation. "Good God, that was no dream. . . . That was the real Baby Fish-Eye DeMello and his twin mothers. And I was one of the fires."

Four days before Lorna and Lola DeMello tried to kidnap my reason and I ended up stealing Baby Fish-Eye's dream, I came down with a violent summer virus. One hour I was happily swimming across a pond and the next I was shaking uncontrollably with chills. I showered, I put on sweatshirts, I nearly chipped a tooth drinking tea, but nothing warmed me up. The next morning I had a fever of 101, and for forty-eight hours I went banging back and forth between chills and a temperature of 103. My head ached horribly. No thoughts of a happy nature baked in my oven. But there were plenty of miserable ones. As I lay on my bed sweating, I found myself remembering earaches I had suffered more than forty years before in my grandmother's spare room—clean, light, and populated by dangerous spiders—and I thought of having the measles in a small, dark room in New York City. The memory of a mustard plaster emerged, tangled in a remembrance of pulling taffy in New Rochelle, and behind these dribbled spoonfuls of cod liver oil and little packets of powder, which I now suspect were sulfa drugs. On and on the procession wound. Fever triggered memories of fever, chills of chills, and aches of aches as I lay face down across the foot of my bed wishing for an Ice Age.

To my amazement, the fever ended. Drove itself up late one afternoon, gave me a shake, and then disappeared. The headache did not. It hung around trying out various positions—above the eyes, behind the eyes, at the base of the skull, over the top, and so forth.

It is well known that any emotion of great strength brings with it the illusion of permanence, and the pain of a headache, like the pleasure of love, is no exception. So when I cautiously ventured out of the bedroom and down the stairs, the two days I'd spent in bed felt like ten. Worse, those two scorchers had blown a hole in my calendar making the events of the preceding week—a swim with Betty, a meeting with the DeMello family—seem to have no relevance to nor connection with my new life as a person with headaches. I'd been too far away for too long a time simply to pick up where I'd left off. So when the phone rang that evening and the secretary at Hillsdale Clinic said, "The DeMellos need you to call the emergency squad at the police station because they won't do anything for Frankie until you tell them what's going on," I did not know exactly which me was going to make the calls.

Readjusting the blue ice pack that I had secured around my head with an elastic bandage, I called the Hillsdale Police Department. I tried being formal.

"This is Dr. Baur from the Hillsdale Clinic calling concerning Frankie DeMello. How may I help you?"

"Help us?" roared a Lieutenant Trotter, amid little beeps

that let me know that my attempts to be serious were being recorded. "Lady, you're the one who needs help with this guy. Tell us he's got a medical problem—medical, you know, like a coma, a broken leg—and we'll take him away for you, but we can't just scrape the kid off the living room couch and dump him in the bin for nothing. You get my meaning?"

"Certainly do, Lieutenant, but give me a little background. You received a—"

"The kid's mother or aunt—couldn't get that straight—some lady with a loud voice has been shouting at us to take him away because he smokes on the couch and is going to burn the house down. That's not a medical problem, I told her. So she says, 'Yeah? Well it soon will be.' Not good enough. So I says, 'Does he want to leave?' No, he don't, so we're not going to pull this kid off the couch and dump him in a hospital. He's twenty years old, see?"

"I agree. He's not your problem. Nice talking to you, Lieutenant."

Hanging up, I called the secretary at the clinic.

"I suppose you want me to call the DeMellos."

"Oh, please. A lady with a loud voice has been calling every fifteen minutes, no exaggeration."

"Lola? Loud?"

"No, it's Lorna, isn't it?"

"No, Lola's the mom."

"Are you sure?"

"Well, give me the number."

"Numbers. They live in a couple of different places."

Pausing to take aspirin, I settled down to talk with Baby Fish-Eye and his mother about what I guessed was the nth chapter in the struggle they had been waging for most of Baby's twenty years. In briefest terms, Lola and her family were living out a common scenario in which the mother identifies one of her children as The Problem then makes a career out of getting the child fixed. Doctor after doctor is asked to prescribe medications to calm him down, and hotlines are kept busy five or six times a year with requests that the child be taken away for a while. To the surprise of no one except the mother, the problem thrives on this treatment. Everyone in the family, and soon in the community as well, learns to play their part, and in short order The Problem functions as an effective regulator for the entire family. At the first hint of any change or disruption that might break the fragile family apart, Baby would go into action. He would drink, steal, disappear, ignite, or in some way attract everyone's attention and pull the family back together again. Reunited, they would work together to fix Baby until such natural dangers as growing up, sadness, employment, and the like had safely passed. Baby Fish-Eye was a lifesaver for the entire DeMello clan.

With my head feeling a little better, I called the first number the secretary had given me. The phone rang and rang, but there was no answer. I called a second number with the same results. The third number put me in touch with Baby Fish-Eye himself.

"What's going on, Frankie? You shaking people up?" I asked.

"Not me," he drawled in his super-cool, laid-back voice. "I'm just layin' here watchin' TV. Been doin' a little studyin' through the day . . . some chemistry."

"Frankie, it's July. You haven't been in school since you were sixteen, four years ago. What are you talking about, studying chemistry?"

"Yeah, Dr. Baur, yeah, I'm just studying a little every day. Goin' t' look for a job tomorrow."

I was never able to tell if Baby Fish-Eye was on weed or if his outrageous denial of the world around him was a one-hundred-percent-natural, no-additives-needed defense. I could picture him lying on the couch, his head wrapped in a red bandana and the rest of him draped in black. He was a dark, heavily muscled young man given to slumping in chairs and bending his fingers back one by one. Descended from the black Portuguese who came to this country as whalers or gardeners, Frankie's features had an interesting foreign flavor to them. His mouth was full, and he had lovely slanted brown eyes. He was also given to pulling his shirt up and rubbing his darkly tanned stomach, as guys that age seem to do.

"Frankie," I continued, "I gather Lorna is pretty upset and wants you to get some help."

"She always say that, Dr. Baur. I don't need no help."

"OK, Frankie. Stay in touch."

Hardly was the phone in the cradle when the secretary at the clinic called back.

"Please call the DeMellos," she begged.

"I'll try again," I promised, and called what I guessed was Lorna's number. Again no answer. After calling the operator and the telephone repair service, I redialed the Clinic.

"Tell Mrs. DeMello to turn the ringer on her phone back on if she wants to talk with me," I told the secretary.

I figured I had fifteen minutes of peace now, and as I leaned back in my chair, I had the sudden urge to go back to bed. I could practically feel the pillow, the cool darkness, the drift toward sleep and dreams. I flopped on the couch for a ten-minute nap then walked myself into the kitchen and made a cup of tea. Fearing success, I tried the number again.

The phone rang only once.

"YES! YES! HELLO!" a woman's voice blasted through the receiver. "DR. BAUR?"

"This is Dr. Baur," I said quietly, setting my tea down as if it were in danger of being knocked from my hand.

"GOT HER!" shouted the voice to someone at the other end of the world. "I DON'T KNOW," it continued, "THE LITTLE SKINNY ONE OR THE SHORT DOCTOR FROM EGYPT."

I could not hear the replies above the background noise. A television was going in the same room, and farther away I could hear a man yelling at one or possibly two children.

"DR. BROWER, DID YOU CALL THE POLICE AND TELL THEM TO TAKE BABY TO THE HOSPITAL?" she shouted.

"Who am I talking with, please?"

"LORNA! LORNA, BABY'S AUNT. DID YOU CALL?"

"Lorna, I'd like to speak with your sister. I'd be speaking out of turn if I discussed the problem with you."

"YOU WOULD NOT!" she roared back, and in the background I could hear the sound of running feet. "LET'S GET THIS CALL ORGANIZED. NUMBER ONE—DID YOU CALL THE POLICE. YES? OR NO?"

"Lorna, yes, I called the police and they would be willing to help you if Frankie had a medical problem, but he doesn't."

"DON'T HAVE A PROBLEM?" she shrieked. "YOU SEEN 'IM. HE'S GONNA SET THE HOUSE ON FIRE AN' HIS MOTHER AN' THE LITTLE CHILDREN ARE TORN TO PIECES WITH WORRY. THAT'S A PROBLEM, DR. BROWER, AN' YOU NEED TO FIX IT."

"Why do you think he'll set the house on fire, Lorna?" I asked before she swept us both away on a wave of complaints.

"'CAUSE HE'S ALL A TIME FOOLIN' WITH MATCHES AN' THIRTEEN-YEAR-OLD GIRLS! THAT'S WHY. BABY LAYS ON THE COUCH WITH METAL MUSIC AND PLAYS WITH FIRE EVERY CHANCE HE GET."

There was a resounding crash in the background and the sound of shattering glass.

"Lorna, are you safe?"

"OF COURSE I AM. I DON'T LIVE WITH HIM."

"Who?"

"BABY! ARE YOU MIXED UP AGAIN?"

"Lorna, it sounds as if there's a fight going on in your house."

"DOCTOR, THAT'S WHAT I'M CALLING ABOUT. MY HUSBAND IS GETTING VERY STRESSFUL 'CAUSE NO ONE IS HELPING US WITH BABY. HE'S GOIN' TO EXPLODE, IF YOU DON'T PUT BABY AWAY."

"Lorna, I must speak with Lola."

The conversation became increasingly confused. I talked with Lola, who was crying.

"Lola, are you there?" I found myself repeating. "Could you get Frankie to the emergency room tonight for an evaluation?"

"Hi." A soft little voice came back over the line. "My name is Sheena."

"Sheena! Where's Lola?"

Where indeed. Sweet, muddled Lola, who, when overcome, was apparently handing the receiver to one of the children as they ran past. The violence and sadness of a dozen generations had rolled down on her and had inspired in her unimaginative soul two simple pictures of peace. She could see herself on a white cruise ship in an empty square of blue sea or she could envision Baby asleep on the couch "at the regular times of night."

"Either one would be a real fine vacation for me," she had said the last time I saw her, glancing past me as she always did and swinging her head back and forth in gentle figure eights.

"WHO'S TAKING BABY TO THE HOSPITAL, DOCTOR? TELL ME THAT."

It was Lorna again, and by now she was so worked up that she could only capture and process one word per sentence. Thus when I tried to explain confidentiality to her, she thought I had no confidence in her, and when I said it was a question of legality, she thought someone was trying to put her nephew in jail.

"Lorna, could you stop shouting?" I asked at one point as my headache returned, starting at the base of my skull and leaping to a commanding position over my eyes.

"NO, I CANNOT!" she roared, louder than before. "MY SISTER, SHE JUST WHISPER, BUT I COME CLEAR AN' THAT'S HOW I GET THINGS DONE."

I wondered then if they were identical twins, but I could not imagine such an overpowering voice coming out of a woman who looked like the round, sweet-eyed Lola. What the voice finally made clear, however, was that Baby Fish-Eye had indeed been acting up. He had started a small blaze in his wastebasket, which Lorna described as "a smoker's fire." He had pinched the lady who reads the electric meter so hard she threatened to cut off their service. And all on the same day, he had painted his face red, white, and blue with his mother's cosmetics, and ridden his brother's tiny bicycle down the middle of the road. It reminded me of the time he had rolled across the clinic's parking lot upside down on a skateboard wearing only a bathing suit and beads.

"Lola, Frankie is always doing these things," I said when I nabbed her once more. "But you seem more upset than usual."

"I have a new job starting tomorrow and I haven't slept for three nights worrying what will happen when I leave," she replied.

"Big change," I agreed.

"Yeah. All the kids wants the extra money, but they don't wants me to leave."

"It's a common problem, Lola," I answered. "Has Baby figured out a way of keeping you home?" I hoped she would see his threats and shenanigans in a new light.

"No, he only figure out how to upset me again and again."

"Listen, Lola, this is what we're going to do. I'm going to order an emergency evaluation of the situation right now. You sit tight and a worker from the team will call you within half an hour. Can you do that?"

"NO!" roared Lorna, who had grabbed the phone. "IF THAT EMERGENCY GUY DON'T GET HERE IN FIFTEEN MINUTES, IT'LL BE TOO LATE. I'VE BEEN CALLING EVERYONE IN HILLSDALE FOR TWO HOURS AND ALL I GET IS FRUSTRATION. YOU HEAR ME? FIFTEEN MINUTES!"

Did I hear her? My head was pounding and I wanted to lay it down in a bowl of crushed ice. It was all I could do to say good-bye civilly before hanging up. I ordered an evaluation, which the worker estimated would not even begin for an hour or two.

"Put the clinic phones on the answering machine," I advised the secretary. "Lorna is not going to be happy fifteen minutes from now, but I am going to bed." And I did.

Two nights later, after learning that Baby Fish-Eye had told the emergency team that he was teaching himself how to build houses by reading flyers from the hardware store, and that they had given him sleeping pills that Lola and Lorna thought were too strong, I dreamed that a dark, smiling arsonist was flying over and around the Hillsdale Clinic trying to set the place on fire. Over the windows, behind the windows, at the base of the foundation, on top of the roof, the cheerful fellow fluttered and flew with his matches. Inside the clinic, I remember turning to Ralph who ran up and down the corridors and to Nancy who emptied ashtrays and shouting, "Get ice water!" But for some reason we were all more interested in the acrobatics than the fireworks. Running from window to window, we watched this airborne character who was now whizzing over the building on a saucer. High above us, red, white, and blue banners slapped smartly against a sunny sky, and as we watched, he changed first into a black Frisbee and then into a huge yellow and green balloon.

The dream wandered off into some other story as far as I can remember, and I didn't even recall the flying arsonist part or connect fever to fire until reminded the next day by the pack of matches lying on the kitchen floor.

What seemed strangest at that moment and what intrigues me still, is how the crazy Lorna and Lola phone calls were cataloged in my mind as a dream, and even now the shouted conversations seem more closely related to the flying arsonist than to earlier meetings in the clinic. Perhaps it was the fever or the headache, but that late-evening episode with the shouting Lorna, the weeping Lola, whispering Sheena, a glass-bashing man, and the cool, fire-setting Baby Fish-Eye remains in my mind as a dream—as a story I have heard, but not one I have participated in or influenced in any way. It is a curious feeling, pleasant—or more precisely "easy" in its lack of authorship. It is the feeling you get after watching a modestly chaotic late-night movie that washes over you without making much sense. But now I have a problem. When I think ahead to next Monday at two P.M. when the short doctor from Egypt (who is actually an Israeli) and the little skinny doctor will together meet with the DeMello family, I know I will have to weave the events of the past week into the ongoing story of this family's life. I will need more energy than I have right now, first to shake free of the spell and then to synthesize the markedly dissimilar episodes into a vaguely coherent account.

I remember reading a research paper on how we distinguish our dreams both from reality and from other people's dreams, and I remember that after several weeks, when the subjects in this experiment were given transcripts of their own dreams and of the dreams of their partner or spouse, it was impossible for them to recall accurately which belonged to which. As they read over parts of various dreams, there was no sense of authorship to mark certain passages as their own as there would be if they had been reading transcripts of their own conversations or papers they had written. The investigators surmised that because dreams seem given rather than produced, the dreamer lacks the usual cues that tag chunks of thinking as belonging to him or her. Such tags are the mental residues of effort—subconscious memories of "I tried to figure out if . . . " "I imagined" "I thought"—that are stored with the memory of the experience itself. Without the effort, and the tags that such mental activity produces, experience becomes a series of disjointed, depersonalized episodes—a confusing movie made up of other people's dreams. Effortless, perhaps, but not meaningful.

. A week after I returned to the clinic, the DeMello family came in to complain for the millionth time that Baby was disrupting the family by acting strange. He liked the sleeping pills and wanted more, but Lola was as uneasy as ever because now she never knew when Baby would wake up and get into trouble. She wanted a pill that would make Baby normal and "make his mother proud."

"I just don't get it," she said, swinging her head lightly and sending her silver earrings tinkling and clinking over her round shoulders. "My life in this family seem like one long dream that play itself over an' over again. No matter what I do, it just go where it wanna go. That's what's wrong with this family, but I don't think nobody on the outside can understand."

"Must be a lonely, frustrating feeling," I said out loud while privately thinking, We agree! For the first time. We're talking about the same thing.

Lola nodded, tears starting to her eyes as they did every session.

"I don't like dreams much," she began, "except for the cruise—"

"I love dreams," broke in Baby Fish-Eye, who had apparently been dozing with his feet on a file cabinet. He opened his slanted, speckly eyes and studied the ceiling without moving a muscle. "Last night I dreamed I was flying up and down—anywhere I wanted to go. No pressure on me."

"And where did you fly to?" asked the short doctor from "Egypt."

"Disney World," said Baby without hesitation. "All my dreams take me right outta this world—take the family, too. Ready or not."

12

MAPPING THE FAMILY STORY

> *The little world of childhood with its familiar surroundings is a model of the greater world. The more intensively the family has stamped its character upon the child, the more it will tend to feel and see its earlier miniature world again in the bigger world of adult life.*
>
> C. G. JUNG

ONE YEAR AFTER FRANKIE "BABY FISH-EYE" DEMELLO FLEW OFF in his imagination to Disneyland and ended up to everyone's dismay in Newtondale State Hospital, the short doctor from Israel—Alan Flashman—told me the following story about families. It began some sixteen years ago when Dr. Flashman was a resident at the Albert Einstein College of Medicine. There, his duties as a young psychiatrist included creating a team of specialists to care for patients in the Burn Intensive Care Unit at the Bronx Municipal Hospital Center. His role on this team expanded from the ordinary one of helping patients and families adjust to their painful misfortunes to the subtler role of psychological detective. Why, he asked himself, were so many of the spouses of burn victims furious as well as appalled? Why did these angry family members talk as if the accidents were inevitable or even planned? Was he actually dealing with what he calls "covert suicides"—the subconscious wish to die that leads individuals to take risks and to be careless until finally "an accident" just happens?

"What got me into this business of mapping family stories," he said, "was a man—a janitor—who came to the unit with a hundred percent of his body burned. He died, and I interviewed his wife. She was a wonderful storyteller, as the Irish often are, and it became clear to me that she was telling a story of a very long power struggle."

In this family, Dr. Flashman learned, women were traditionally obedient. They lived within the home, and they followed their husbands' advice. It had been like this for generations until the janitor's wife and daughter got other ideas. One chapter in this long debate involved the daughter's wish to go to college and the wife's decision to use family collateral to support this experiment. The father said no. He felt that his role as head of household and as a man was being challenged. Months of arguing ensued. Finally, his wife marched down to the neighborhood bank and secured a loan. While she was there, the janitor, who had handled cleaning materials all his life, cleaned the wooden steps of their home with flammable cleaners and a propane torch. He caught fire himself and nearly burned down the house.

"'Oh my God,' I said to myself when I heard this, 'the man got so angry, he just went up in smoke.' What I saw then, was that the 'accident' could not possibly be understood without knowing how several generations in this family had dealt with one another. The fire had a special meaning for this family that would not hold for other fires or other families."

As Dr. Flashman continued talking with the janitor's wife, he further realized that they were engaged in a kind of reciprocal storytelling (the kind we saw in chapter 2 that Roy Schafer was experimenting with and calling narratives). Again and again, the wife would retell the events leading up to the accident, but each time the account was expanded or in some way clarified by the insights that Dr. Flashman's listening fostered. Conversely, with every retelling, Dr. Flashman's own story of what is important to know about an accident was expanded and clarified by the wife's tale of how the members of her family worked or failed to work together. Some stories, he concluded, can only be understood if their distant beginnings are uncovered.

Naturally, Dr. Flashman carried these insights to new cases. Regardless of the type of burn, he now collected information on every member of the extended family—uncles, cousins, grandparents, stepparents. He tried to see how the whole unit or family system operated to keep itself going. To parallel this, he developed what he called a systems approach to the emotional management of the burn team itself. This group, too, functioned as a family system, meaning that the activities and feelings of each member of the team caused reactions in all the other members. Also, the jobs the team undertook and the progress it made—both physical and emotional—were all shared.[1]

"Keeping track of all these people and events got pretty messy on paper," Dr. Flashman remembered. "The conventional genogram, developed in the late 1960s by such family therapists as Murray Bowen and Monica McGoldrick, wasn't capable of handling the passage of time. The old genogram is a snapshot—here's a square for Dad, a circle for Mom, symbols for the kids, and a bunch of lines for divorces and deaths—but there is no way to look back and see patterns of behavior that may be repeating themselves."

So Dr. Flashman devised a way of following the progress of a family, called Family Developmental Tracking, which is why when he met Frankie and his several mothers and brothers he began drawing circles and squares and lots of dates. His objective was to map the characteristic behavior of this particular family system, starting as far back as possible. For example, what did Lola, her brothers, and one sister do when it was time for them to leave the nest? Did each get a job and move into an apartment? Did they go to jail? Did the girls get pregnant and move into someone else's house? And would these patterns then repeat themselves in Frankie's generation?

Looking at Lola's family of origin in the expanded genogram

1. Michael Kerr and Murray Bowen, *Family Evaluation: An Approach Based on Bowen Theory* (New York: W. W. Norton & Co., 1988).

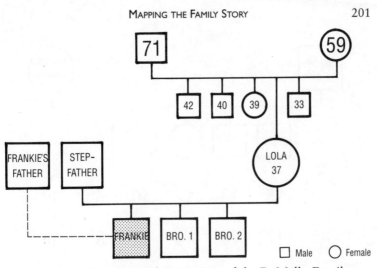

FIGURE 1. Conventional Genogram of the DeMello Family

(Figure 2), it is evident that it was strangely difficult for each of the five children to leave home. Several of the boys went in and out of jail before marrying and moving out. It was almost as if they had broken the law of the home, been sent away, and were allowed back only to break their parents' rules again and be sent away once more. In a similar fashion, Lola's sister, Lorna, ran away and returned repeatedly before marrying and moving out. Lola adopted a different pattern. She became pregnant at fifteen and was allowed to stay in the home with little Frankie until she married some five years later. Somehow she managed *not* to break the rules of the home and *not* act out her rebellion. During her tumultuous marriage, however, she returned to her parents' home many times. The youngest brother—"the good one," as Lola calls him—moved out a couple of times to live with girlfriends, but he soon returned for good. At present, he lives with his parents—and, we learned later, his uncle had lived with *his* parents a generation before.

"Just like the novels," Dr. Flashman said when I told him. "You know, the writers of family sagas have known for years that it takes three or four generations to bring out the family drama."

In simplest terms, then, the genogram that Dr. Flashman devised suggests that Lola grew up in a family that had parts or roles in the family drama for "bad," rebellious kids and another

FIGURE 2. Family Developmental Tracking: Lola's Family of Origin

script for dependent ones who seemed to want, or at least accept, protection. Both ways of behaving strongly suggest that the family was run according to a set of rules so rigid and inflexible that an adolescent with the natural need to modify family rules so that he or she might become more than a family clone was given no room for negotiation. Either the teenager knuckled under and was kept at home as a perpetual child afraid to grow up, or he or she broke the rules, started growing up, and was kicked out with the message that "rebellion and growing up are bad."

"Conventional genograms can't reveal these ways of acting in a family," Dr. Flashman explained. "In addition, they can't answer the question, 'What do these actions mean now?' Why did Frankie get put on Ritalin for hyperactivity at age five? Why not at six or eight? Why did Lola have a breakdown at age twenty-four? We can begin to answer these questions when we see what else is going on both in Lola's family of origin and in the new family she's starting with her husband."

For example, we can see in the genogram of Lola's new family (Figure 3) that when Frankie is four years old, he gets a stepfather. Lola tells us that her husband had a violent temper when he drank, and would strike out at those around him. This behavior began shortly after Lola was married, and it does not seem surprising that within the year, Frankie became unmanageable and was put on Ritalin.

In a similar fashion, Lola's breakdown at age twenty-four is more understandable when we see that just as Frankie was taken off Ritalin and Lola's second child was ready to get out of diapers, the young mother gave birth to a premature baby. Now she had an eight-year-old who was becoming increasingly restless off his medication, a two-year-old, and a preemie. In addition, the house where she and her children were living while her husband was in and out of jail burned down, and her life went up in smoke again. She was forced to return to her parents, but this was no longer a solution. Her position as the dependent, obedient one had been taken over in her absence by her youngest brother. Lola with her three young children were not welcome. Feeling angry and rejected, she fought violently with

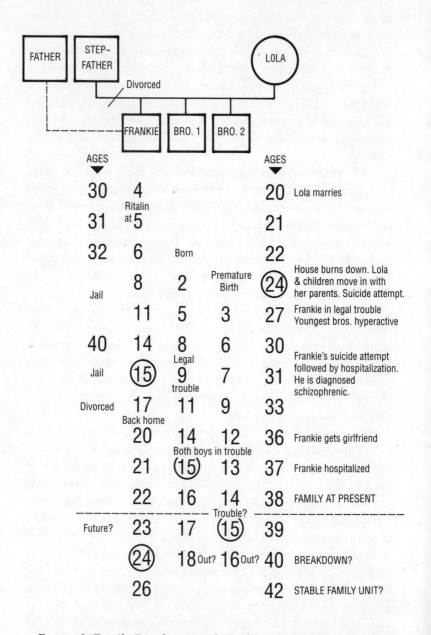

FIGURE 3. Family Developmental Tracking: Lola's New Family

her father, twice kicking a door down, and once drinking alcohol and taking all her father's heart pills in an angry suicide gesture. Although Dr. Flashman had begun mapping families like the DeMellos in order to organize multigenerational data and to answer the question, "What does this action mean now?" he realized that the maps could be used as a guide to the future as well as the past. In other words, if he saw that Lola or a brother was kept at home as a fragile or obedient child, he could look at Lola's children to see if any of them were on the same kind of journey. Sure enough, there was Frankie making a serious suicide attempt at fifteen (the age Lola had become pregnant) and suffering a breakdown at seventeen, at which time he was diagnosed as schizophrenic. Both gestures labeled him "fragile," and suggested that he might be the one the family chose to stay home.

"Where do you think Frankie will be ten years from now?" I asked Lola recently.

"With me," she answered without hesitation. "I knew Frankie was my boy from the time of his first breakdown, and he say he'll be mine till he get a hundred years old. When the others are gone, I'll be with Baby. Peoples used to take us for brother and sister, you know."

Had I used Family Developmental Tracking when Frankie was eighteen and the DeMello family first came to me, I wouldn't have been so surprised by what now seem to be a more understandable series of events. I would have expected Lola to want to keep Frankie at home. I would have expected the second brother to get in trouble at age fifteen—he did. I would have expected trouble with the law. And I certainly would have paid attention when Frankie got his first serious girlfriend at age twenty—exactly the age his mother married and moved and began to be abused. But I did not map the family back then, and I was unprepared for what seemed like its sudden disintegration.

When Frankie turned twenty-one, he and Tanitia decided to marry. He looked as good as I'd ever seen him that fall, and the prospect of being out on his own for the first time, yet protected by the well-organized Tanitia, seemed to interest him a great deal.

"We'll work at a job that pays good money, an' I can play my metal music whenever I want," he said. "Tansy better learn how to cook fast."

Frankie started to work out at a gym and dress smartly. This so alarmed the family that both brothers made trouble at school and came in for counseling as if to take Frankie's place.

Several months before the marriage, I began meeting with Lola, who openly encouraged Frankie and his girl to marry but confided to me and her sister that Frankie was too fragile to move out of her home. I also met with Frankie and his girl. Tansy sensed Lola's ambivalence and was hedging her bets by trying to get pregnant several times a day. Frankie was delighted. As the date approached, however, he grew quiet, and when the couple rented an apartment and actually moved in together, he became physically ill. For several weeks he threw up frequently and was treated for the flu. A month before the wedding, Frankie began canceling his appointments at the clinic. It became apparent that he was either not taking his medication for schizophrenia or was throwing it up. A new supply was obtained, and a loading dose (or catch-up dose) administered. For a day or two he seemed to rally, but with hindsight I can see we were opposing the momentum of at least three generations with a couple of pills. Our efforts were useless. One morning Frankie received a phone call from his mother, ostensibly about his benefit check. That afternoon he rang all the fire alarms in Hillsdale, ignited his wastebasket (more smoke), and turned himself in. Within two days he was at Newtondale. Mute, immobile, and incontinent, he was a true baby. He remained hospitalized there for nearly nine months.

Now he is coming home, "Where he belongs," Lola says, "an' he's given up on girls. The other boys miss him. They're starting to settle down now because they know he's coming back." The pattern continues uninterrupted.

Referring again to Figure 3, it is clear that a number of hurdles confront the family in the coming years. Will the third brother break loose at fifteen? Will Frankie break down again at age twenty-four, as his mother did? Will his brothers leave home then?

"It would not be too farfetched to predict some very dangerous or pathological transactions, say from the time Frankie is
twenty-four to the time he's twenty-eight," Dr. Flashman specu-
lated.[2] "These years will give the family its last natural opportunity to free themselves from the unchosen necessities of their
common path—from their old pattern of living where any gesture or statement that is spontaneous and truly expressive of
how someone is feeling sets off so many reactions in the other
members of the family that it gets smothered. As a result, the
people in Frankie's family feel trapped. They have the sense that
they are doomed to go on living exactly as they have been living.
They have no feeling of authorship for their actions. They feel
controlled by the way things are and have to be. That's the way
myths represent life—as inevitable. Will the family stay in the
myth? Or will it struggle to regain a measure of freedom, and
enter the realm of history?"

One thing is clear, if the myth is continued, either Frankie
will stay at home as a child, as both his uncle and great uncle
have done before him, or, if he is placed in a halfway house
against Lola's wishes, one of his brothers will be sacrificed to
the role of fragile child in need of protection. Of course, no one
in the family consciously understands why it is so dangerous to
grow up or why one child must remain at home. The original
problem, for which keeping a child at home was the solution,
has been forgotten generations ago.

"Now you can begin to appreciate why one of the problems
in treating families is that a family's time scale is very different
from the time scale used by therapists," Dr. Flashman said.
"Professionals see clients like the DeMellos getting better or
breaking down within a span of several years—maybe a
decade—but actually families live and grow, suffer and heal
within the slow passage of *generations*.

"Consider Murray Bowen's provocative pronouncement that
it takes three generations to create a schizophrenic. That's like
saying it takes three generations for a family to become trapped

2. Alan Flashman, "A Systems Approach to the Emotional Management
of the Burn Team," in J. Nicosia, ed., *Manual of Burn Care* (New York:
Raven Press, 1983).

in a myth of its own making or three generations to break free of its problems."

But how does this actually happen? Why is it that when patterns of living are rigidly handed down from generation to generation, they become increasingly confusing. Studying many families, including his own, Murray Bowen was able to appreciate that his mother and father interacted with their children *not* primarily on the basis of the characteristics or needs of their sons and daughters, but more on the basis of the earlier relationships they had experienced with their own parents. Of course, as children Bowen and his siblings had no idea that they were being recruited into a drama that was already under way. They did not realize that when their mother sang a lullaby, she was singing as much to her own mother (and to herself, as if she were again the listener) as she was singing to her children. Bowen believed that this unacknowledged carrying forward of past relationships affected the way parents punished, praised, comforted, instructed, and generally treated their children. To the extent that these past relationships were problematic and remained unresolved, the unconscious carrying forward created confusion. (To the extent that the relationships were productive, they forged family cohesion.)

"Think of Frankie as playing a part in a play that has been running for three generations," suggested Dr. Flashman. "In the original drama the players actually read the script; that is, they experienced the loss or the problem firsthand, be it loss of a parent, a house burning down, or an unexpected pregnancy. They see the original props—say the house that is now in ashes or a piano that must never be played. As the years pass, members of the original cast die or move away. They are replaced by Lola and her siblings and later still by Frankie and his brothers. These replacements are never told what the old problems were or how to think about them. They certainly aren't told what to say. But they are praised if they say the 'right lines'—the lines that made sense twenty years ago—and punished if they say something too different, even if it makes sense in the present situation.

"It's important to understand that when a player says the

right lines—like Frankie saying, 'Ma, I feel sick,' which he believes is his own idea—he experiences a special 'click.' That click is the sense of belonging, of things coming together the way they're supposed to. However, if Frankie says the 'wrong lines,' and starts talking about moving out, then he will experience an unpleasant drop as he hits a gap. The gap is a sense of speaking a foreign tongue, and of saying something that no one will recognize. Something starts to fall apart.

"This maneuvering becomes increasingly confusing with the passage of time because after a generation or two the entire cast is made up of people who have never seen the original script or experienced the original problem. They still walk carefully around 'something' that isn't even on the stage anymore. [The piano.] They may even speak the right lines to 'someone' who it was very important to placate or comfort in the past, but who is now both gone and nameless. You see the confusion? I mean here's a rough description of psychosis for you—a person whose actions don't fit the present reality in an understandable way. In a milder form the same muddle is familiar to all of us. Yet from the player's point of view, he is simply trying his best to play a needed part. Out of loyalty for his family, he is unconsciously agreeing to remain no one—a blank and self-erasing slate that accepts the inscriptions or lines of prior generations."

Given this ongoing drama, Bowen wondered how it could be changed—how the actors could be "differentiated" or broken free from their traditional roles. He found it to be extremely difficult. If therapist-as-director tries to redirect some of the scenes, the family tends to assimilate the role of director into the drama as well. If therapist-as-audience gives feedback, the same thing happens. The therapist mysteriously finds himself onstage caught up in the same old play. Bowen concluded that the best way to change a family was to coach one member until that person was able to refuse to honor the traditional exchange of lines. "I'm part of this family," that person says, "but I'm not continuing the old play." This daring sabotage does not create a new drama, but it brings the old one to a halt. It forces members of the family to face each other and begin to speak lines that fit the present reality.

"There are cultures such as Latino and Yiddish," Dr. Flashman continued, "where every baby girl is called Mommy and
every boy, Daddy. 'Sing to me, Mommy,' a mother will tell her
daughter. 'Take care, Daddy,' she will say to her son. I think
they are giving the child a hint that he is going to play the role
of parent as well as child.

"This may help to explain what Bowen meant by saying that
it takes three generations to create a schizophrenic. We can see
that with each generation of DeMellos there is more confusion
and an increasingly narrow range of solutions or options. Perhaps all that is left for Frankie's children is to remain unborn."

Looking at the other side of the coin—the gradual differentiation and loosening up of family roles—Bowen believed that
there are particular points in a family's life cycle when its members have a natural opportunity to grow and expand. The most
obvious of these windows is adolescence, which is when most
children start making their own decisions.

In every family with children, parents have a pretty clear
although often unstated idea of what roles the children should
play. Some parents expect tomboys or little scholars. Others
expect strong ones or weak ones, bad ones or good ones. There
are family mascots and pranksters. There are little Mommies
and little Daddies. From the age of about four years old to
twelve, children accept the roles given to them, and learn how to
play them. During adolescence, however, they begin to strike out
on their own and change these roles. No longer content to be a
chip off the old block, the fourteen-year-old adds and experiments. Cigarettes, makeup, beer, preppie clothes, untied shoes,
messy rooms—all kinds of props are used to put on new pro-
ductions. Not only does each adolescent change the person he or
she wishes to be, but the teenager changes the rules for making
the rules that the family lives by. It is not enough for parents to
allow their children to alter the way they speak and dress; they
must also allow their sons and daughters to assume a more
equal role as partners in determining their emerging lives.

I once heard a psychologist say that adolescence is a fight
over who knows what is best for the child. "One of the important things to remember in this fight," he said to parents, "is—

lose!" In other words, adolescents need to emerge at eighteen or twenty believing that they are different—or as Bowen would say, "differentiated"—from their parents' expectations, *and* that they themselves know how to regulate their lives.

It is at this point, when children reach adolescence and start rocking the family boat, that *either* they will be allowed to make new roles and set new rules, which will open up the family system for everyone, *or* great energy will be expended to keep them in their more obedient, preteen position. To some degree this shuts down the family's options—again for everyone. There is no way for a family *not* to change one way or the other. The entire system either becomes more flexible or more rigid.[3]

Naturally, not all aspects of family life become better or worse when a family changes, and it is common to hear people say that their families are "lucky in love" or "losers when it comes to work—not one of us has had a job we really liked." These are common ways of saying that a family has or has not had problems in certain areas of living. If asked, the speaker will usually go on to admit with surprise that this piece of "luck" or that inability is indeed generations old. Although they may wish to "fix" their own problems and hand down to their children an entirely different pattern or attitude, such transitions cannot be rushed.

Returning to Bowen's formulation of family growth, and using it in conjunction with Flashman's Family Developmental Tracking, we can now look at the DeMellos and see the family's pattern of increasing rigidity. We can speculate even further into the future. When Lola was fifteen, she spent a day in the city

---

3. In chapter 14, "The Record Keepers," we will see that institutions such as university departments and teaching hospitals are also systems. Here, too, students and junior clinicians come into the system to learn a role that is clearly formulated by their seniors. For a year or two, beginners are fairly obedient, but then they enter a kind of adolescence. They wish to expand and modify their roles as psychiatrist, psychologist, or social worker, and they wish to have a hand in making the rules that govern their behavior and training. Like a family with a dozen fifteen-year-olds, the hospital system is challenged. It will either open up and allow greater flexibility for all, or, as we will see, it will find ways to discourage rebellion and innovation. Often these ways of *not* changing are called "being professional," just as in the family *not* changing is often called "being good."

and came home pregnant. Her father, who beat all the kids when they disobeyed him, beat Lola and then made a deal. You can remain at home with your baby, he told her, as long as you never again break another rule in our household. In other words, I'll feed and protect you, if you agree not to grow up. (This apparently solved a problem for Lola's parents.) Having few resources, Lola accepted the bargain. For all intents and purposes she remained a child of twelve both in her father's home and then in her husband's home, where she was again beaten. Fifteen years later she struck the same bargain with Frankie, again to solve an old family problem that she couldn't even name. Although his stormy adolescence gave the entire family—Lola and her three sons—a second chance to disentangle themselves from each other and experiment with independence, it seemed too dangerous. Frankie shut down. Bowen might speculate that each of Frankie's two half-brothers will again try to pry open the family system as each goes through adolescence. If all three fail, the troubles will be passed on. Like his uncle and great-uncle before him, Frankie will stay with his mother until she dies. Each of his brothers may pass this "solution" on and have a son who is expected to remain a troublesome child—a distraction, a reason for the family to stay together.

"In a family like this a clinician must understand that the treatment will take several generations," said Dr. Flashman. "Let's say that hope for this family means letting out the secrets about abuse, whatever they may be. You might work for fifteen years with Lola simply to stop Frankie from abusing his unborn children. That's where your focus might be. If it worked, the direction of the family would change—away from enmeshed rigidity and toward differentiation."

This is what Dr. Flashman means by "doing therapy in the family's time" rather than forcing the problem into the clinic's much shorter periods of treatment.

"Therapy is always somewhat artificial," Dr. Flashman continued, as he began returning the DeMellos' six-page genogram to Frankie's chart, "just as case histories are artificial stories. But by mapping the family story in family time, therapy can sometimes fall into step with real life. Mapping lets us recognize and respect who the clients are now, this minute, who they are capable of being in the next year or so, and who they can become together in the future.

"And this is good for the therapist as well," he said with a smile. "She has time to be curious, time to choose and reflect more freely among a variety of strategies for facilitating change—including *no* change just yet—and time to learn. She needs to figure out what therapist she can become with the family as they go off on this slow journey together."

At the end of the summer, Frankie "Baby Fish-Eye" DeMello finally got out of Newtondale Hospital, and Dr. Flashman went back to the Hebrew University in Jerusalem where he teaches Family Developmental Tracking as part of a course in systems theory. Before he went, he told me a story that, he said, most poignantly illustrated that changes in the lives of families proceed according to their own slow timetables.

"I was once asked to speak to an entire kibbutz about families," he began. "It was arranged that they would gather in the dining room, from the oldest to the youngest, and that I would stand at the end of the room and, as therapists do, try to put into words something that they felt but perhaps could not quite say. I hesitated a very long time, wondering if I should tell them what I saw happening in their communities, or whether I would be causing them pain and retarding their healing. But I went ahead, and this is what I told them.

"I said, 'Many of the kibbutzim in this region of the Negev were founded in the last years of the 1940s by young people who had recently survived the Nazi Holocaust in Europe. They came to Israel as refugee-pioneers with the most extraordinary mixture of personal tragedy, burning identification with their people, intense idealism, and an adolescent passage—a phase of growing up—that was brutally cut short. All of these people had suffered overwhelming losses. Most were all alone in the world. On this desolate emotional landscape they built the kibbutz, and this community took the place of their families—not of ordinary families with many generations, but a horizontal family with everyone in a single generation. As much as humanly possible these people in their late teens and early twenties turned their backs on what they had lost, and began again. Of course, they could not forget their parents and siblings, but all the rest—the aunts, uncles, and grandparents—were allowed to recede into some inner recess of their hearts that remained locked and silent.

"'Soon the kibbutz began creating children, and naturally these children formed another horizontal generation. For practical as well as ideological reasons, they were raised together with their age mates and seen as children of the kibbutz. No one seemed to notice then that in real time—in family time—an entire generation was growing up with parents but with no grandparents—no mothers and fathers of their own mothers and fathers. Now imagine twenty, twenty-five years of group life without a single grandparent around. How could children possibly come to see their parents as "children of" and begin to understand the family drama of which they were a part? They couldn't. In the kibbutz adults were "mommies and daddies of," but beyond that, they were only rather abstractly "members of" the kibbutz, as if they had been born to it.

"'And then,' I told these people sitting in the dining hall, 'just add the years as they move slowly along—and you will come to the early 1970s. The first children of the kibbutz themselves become parents. For this society at this time, the birth of the first grandchild in each family is a double birth, for with the birth of the child, the first grandparents are born. For a generation, the words "Grandpa" and "Grandma" have not crossed the lips of anyone. But with this first utterance of "Grandpa," voices that have long been silently locked in the heart begin to speak, and memory returns. The voice that returns is that of children long ago in Eastern Europe whose cries and squeals abounded with "Grandpa" and "Auntie." It is the voice, rich and vibrant, of large families who shared real family time with each other. It is the voice of family life as once lived by these now graying once-young pioneers, and it brings back to them their real families where parents were always both "my mommy" and "daughter of." All the grandparents, uncles, and aunts who had been lost in the Holocaust and who had been locked away in the hearts of lonely teenagers began to move then, and without warning the old pioneers—weeping—regained the memories of their families. Images that had receded generations ago arose anew. The enormity of the loss, its boundaries, expand. And with that deep and unexpected shudder of pain every generation on the kibbutz was changed. "My mommy" plain and simple is shaken, and everyone feels the secret and the richness of the family drama in which my mommy has a mommy just like me.'

"That is the story I told them as I stood before that group in the dining hall, facing three generations in fact, and two more in emotional reality. And as I said the words—'and then the first grandparent was born,' I felt that shudder move again through the hall as it still does through me.

"And do you know what has happened since the early 1970s?" the doctor from Israel concluded. "By the time the first grandchildren on the kibbutz became teenagers, community living had returned to its natural state. Children are no longer raised in groups. They have all moved home. There are many factors involved in this shift, but I cannot help but think that one factor—one meaning—was the shudder that shook the hearts when the first generation of grandchildren and grandparents faced each other. This moment could not have been hurried into existence any earlier. It is good to remember that therapy needs to fit itself to life and not the other way around."

13

"I WOULD TELL MY WHOLE DAY ON PAPER"

I regurgitate all the words in my subconscious,
Unconscious, conscious, and after-conscious mind,
Brain, heart, soul, mind's eye, afterlife, vibrations,
Eyes, kiss, and more.
Tell me how one writes.
I do it through pencils.
I spill out words beyond control.

PEGGY STEIN

He is not dead because he can sustain names.

CARLOS FUENTES

FILED IN THE BACK OF HEAVY MEDICAL CHARTS, WEDGED BEHIND steel mirrors, crumpled between mattress and bedsprings and crammed into messy envelopes lies the silent correspondence of the back ward. Whether addressed to the world in general or to a particular person, and whether offered directly or hidden for posterity, these scraps of paper carry messages that in one way or another are meant to set the record straight. These writings, some would claim, are the originals, the primary sources on which all other accounts must depend.

The writings I have encountered in hospitals and clinics vary considerably—not only from the official records that purport to describe the writers' lives but among themselves. They range from simple lists of names or words, through diaries of various kinds, to letters and poems meant for the outside world. Some are magical in nature and are meant to ward off harm. Many are relentlessly autobiographical with strings of sentences that document every breakfast and shower and nap and seem to bind a fragile self together. Some are letters. And a few are great bellowing cries of outrage whose words go scrambling across splattered sheets of newsprint, sneak out the hospital gates, and shockingly collide with unsuspecting readers. But back to the lists.

In a course I once took on the ancient Sumerian epic of Gilgamesh, a legend which is believed to have evolved in the third millennium B.C., my professor contended that lists are the oldest known form of writing—of marking existence with words. Even before Gilgamesh was cut into clay tablets around 1700 B.C., there had long existed a "King list," purportedly written to record the names of all the kings who had ruled since the Flood. (Gilgamesh was fifth.)

In Mountain Valley Hospital, we had two practitioners of the ancient and satisfying art of making lists. One was Yolanda, a young woman who kept a "Dictionary of Autographs and Forgeries," which was, in part, a list of words that she divided in an effort to decode what people meant. "This, t-his," her dictionary began, "Elucidate, (h)e-luci-date," it continued, "Will-i-am." There were also lists of divided and undivided words that reminded me of poems by e. e. cummings, and wonderful accounts of slippery words and duplicitous pages that

> had I known it was yours
> O peals, liota deantist
> I would people the next president to die as
> possessing the gift to which I, cercerian in retrospect,
> speak for granted as a fried potato might say, "easy come,
> sincerely yours."

Yolanda would also type and retype the letters of her name in various combinations, and when asked why she did this, she explained that she was "recording" herself. At the age of twenty-three she was put on the then experimental drug Clozaril with good results. So much of her confusion cleared that she was able to live in a residence and hold a part-time job. She told me that she rarely writes anymore.

Our second list writer was a hermit whose sister discovered that he wrote out nothing less than lists of kings.

Willie Otis was a wizened old Yankee in his late sixties who, when hospitalized, kept himself apart from other patients and, when living on the outside, kept himself apart from everyone except a sister who cleaned his apartment twice a year. Spring and fall Mary Otis would drive over from Franklin with buckets of soaps and brushes and a large box of three-ply garbage bags. Into the last she dumped the accumulated refuse from her brother's apartment and no one, not even Mary, could estimate how many hundreds or even thousands of lists she may have inadvertently thrown away before they came to her attention. In fact, since Mr. Otis himself persistently declined to comment on the lists of kings that he wrote in code and hid around the house, perhaps for his sister to find, perhaps to ward off a premature death, or perhaps to inform the next tenants, much remains a mystery.

What is known, however, is that Mr. Otis used mirror-writing to list the names of kings, and occasionally queens, on small pieces of paper, which he then hid within balls of string, between the pages of old magazines, inside his mattress cover, and under books that stood on the top shelf of a tall, dusty bookcase. It was this last collection that tipped off his sister. She was whisking the books off the shelf by fives and sixes (the better to dust, I assume) when she noticed that each armful of books launched a flutter of small, carefully folded notes. Only when she had finished dusting the entire bookcase, did she decide to open and read the little packets.

"ⁿomoloƧ," she began and got no further. Realizing that her brother was writing backwards and thinking that this reversal might have a bearing on his illness, she dropped the lists off at the clinic. Her brother, of course, stayed home.

The discovery and delivery of notes eventually became part

of Mary Otis's cleaning job, and by the time I arrived at the Hillsdale Clinic dozens had been delivered and nineteen saved. These eventually found their way into my mailbox then onto my desk.

"Louis XIV," I read with difficulty. "King Arthur, Queen Elizabeth, King Ferdinand, Oedipus Rex, Napoleon, King Alphonso, Leopold I, and Ann Boleyn."

Each name was written backwards in a sharply slanting hand, and each list, with many repetitive entries, was inscribed on a piece of paper the size and shape of a small envelope. Some included only eight dignitaries and others had as many as nineteen. Each had Mr. Otis's name tucked in among the kings. There was also a number, like "seventeen," or a phrase such as "golden scepter" written out on more than half the lists. On four of the nineteen, Mr. Otis had appended to the names of kings numbers that I suspected were their ages. This last practice gave me the only hint as to why he may have written the lists. The numbers indeed turned out to be the age at which each king died, and Mr. Otis included his own age after his name as well. On the back of one old envelope he was 64. On two scraps of lined paper he was 65, and on a recent index card, 67. It seemed to me, gazing at these little paper markers arranged row upon row on my desk, that the annotated lists were like a field of tombstones, each proclaiming that Willie Otis had got this far. And perhaps there was more to it. For all I know, Mr. Otis gained a sense of accomplishment in pulling past King Albert I of Belgium, coming abreast of Leopold I of Hungary, and heading with silent resolution toward Louis Quatorze. He, too, was "recording" himself, in a modest Yankee manner. I was reminded of a date board I had seen in an antique shop. On one side was painstakingly carved "Nov. 21, 1800," and on the other, "snowy, cold & windy."

Quite different from these lists were the inventories of evidence that paranoid patients kept, which were meant to prove the existence not just of themselves but of the conspiracies that ran their lives. Like commonplace books, such inventories contained notes on what the individual had seen, newspaper clippings, pamphlets, telephone numbers, and letters. In some fashion, each entry sustained the belief that dangerous forces were at work in the outside world. One collection that I was urged to study belonged to a man named Harold Peters and contained hundreds of newspaper clippings, each of which included the heavily underlined name of *Peter* or *Peters*. When this man could no longer stand being deluged by all these thinly veiled references to himself, he would write the editors and urge them to stop harassing him. Although the paper never responded—further proof that a conspiracy existed—Mr. Peters said that it felt good to put his grievances in writing.

"It forces them to pay attention," he told me. "Even if they don't answer me, I know they've read the letter. They can't completely ignore me now."

Another compiler who both collected evidence and sought to engage in a dialogue, focused on the hidden meanings expressed by the poses of models in jewelry advertisements. These the patient shamelessly ripped out of library copies of *Vogue* and *Bazaar* and stored in a shopping bag inhabited by a rag doll. An advertisement with a sharply twisted head or an assertively raised chin was all the proof he needed to convince himself of women's cannibalistic contempt for men. Later, this muttering, disheveled man discovered a veritable treasury of disdain lying on the cosmetic counters of a department store. Thereafter he added nothing but glamorous skin care and cologne pamphlets to his collection. The conclusions that he drew from his now-perfumed delusions he communicated to presidents of the United States. He urged one after another to guard against the influence of women and illustrated his arguments with vicious cartoons of women with pointed teeth and barbed-wire necklaces, which he claimed were merely copies of the jewelry ads. Although this curious old man did not say that his career as a collector of evidence gave him any measure of satisfaction, it was evident that his life revolved around his compilations.

Before turning to narrative—that ceaseless substitution of meaning for bare facts—there is one more mysterious form of writing that is occasionally encountered among the mentally ill and that is even more prevalent among epileptics. A small minority of these unfortunate individuals suffer from what is known as hypergraphia, or the tendency toward extensive and oftentimes compulsive writing. Hypergraphic patients write letters, diaries, prayers, poems, and lists like the rest of us, but there is a desperate repetitiousness or a compulsively detailed quality about their accounts, as if they were flinging out or tightly confining an invasive terror. In one of the original articles on hypergraphia in temporal lobe epilepsy, Stephen Waxman and Norman Geschwind gave the example of a young man who documented his seizures in diary entries that he wrote daily for five years.[1]

> March 19, 1969-Thank "*GOD*" none.
> March 20, 1969-Thank "*GOD*" none.
> March 21, 1969-Thank "*GOD*" none.
> March 22, 1969-Thank "*GOD*" none.
> March 23, 1969-Thank "*GOD*" none.
> March 24, 1969-   6:05 A. M.
> March 25, 1969-   7:00 A. M.
> March 26, 1969-Thank "*GOD*" none.
> March 27, 1969-Thank "*GOD*" none.

Over the years he gradually elaborated on this style so that the long regimented columns read "I thank '*GOD*' no seizures," and finally, "I do thank dear '*GOD*' above, no seizures."

The same authors gave examples of excruciatingly detailed diaries and rambling aphorisms. One young patient found that once he started writing, it was hard for him to stop. He reported writing the sentences "Why Can't A Man Live Before He Dies?" and "God Bless the Child That Has Its Own" many hundreds of times. When he couldn't find blank paper, he wrote on newspapers or on the pages of books. Like many hypergraphics, he hid most of his writings throughout his home.

A final example of this obsessive ruminating in longhand, or rather of the related phenomena of automatic writing (on paper) and "spirit writing" (in the air), concerns a secretary who was

1. S. Waxman and N. Geschwind, "Hypergraphia in Temporal Lobe Epilepsy," *Neurology* 24 (1974): 629–36.

beset by unexpected orgasms as she typed. On one occasion her doctor reported that as Miss B. sat working, she experienced intense sexual arousal.[2] It was all she could do not to writhe and rock as the unwanted pleasure washed over her in waves. Finally she reached a silent, embarrassed orgasm. Twenty minutes later, still feeling stimulated, she automatically began spirit writing, which she described as writing out messages for the spirits who possessed her. Later still she began writing automatically. During these spells she typically produced some twenty-five pages of mystical material which she showed to no one.

The Argentine writer Julio Cortazar was not, to my knowledge, waylaid by unexpected sexual storms, but he has described in detail the sensation of being attacked without warning by a sudden feeling of estrangement. At these times he felt invaded by "obsessive creatures" or permeated by great tension, which he could throw off only by writing.

"To avoid something much worse," he said, he wrote these inexplicable feelings out of himself and into the world of universal existence.[3] He neutralized the nightmare. Cortazar argued that stories thus produced come from an ominous, undefinable territory, and are the product of a trance-like condition that according to convention would not be seen as normal. The goal for the author—as for the reader—is to pass through and emerge safely from a too-intense and compelling reality into a more tolerable and familiar world.

This brings me to the story of T.M., who was unwittingly trapped in a brutal reality and who, somewhat like Cortazar, tried to write himself beyond the reach of invasive memories. A reclusive man, T.M. was institutionalized on and off from the time he was a teenager. In his twenties, voices in his head told him to attack people, and when he did, he was confined to a prison for the criminally insane. He emerged nine years later, a drooling, jabbering idiot who had apparently taken complete

2. Anthony B. Joseph, "A Hypergraphic Syndrome of Automatic Writing, Affective Disorder, and Temporal Lobe Epilepsy in Two Patients," *J. Clinical Psychiatry* 47 (1986): 255–57.

3. Julio Cortazar, "The Writer in a Trance: Anguish, Anxiety and Miracles," *New York Times Book Review*, 26 January 1986, p. 26.

leave of his senses. He paced. He sat. He laughed grotesquely. He babbled on about pain rays, needles, meat picks, helmets, grids, sex changes, robots, and electric chairs. He said he was a girl, a tomato, and the egg of a dinosaur hatched in a bad dream. And he wrote.

"ARE YOU A DANGER TO OTHER PEOPLE?" the prison psychologist printed in block letters on a big pad some three weeks before T.M.'s release.

"It's because of the fact that I went through a super huge magic drug," he wrote back in a grade-school hand.

"WOULD YOU HURT ANYONE NOW?" the psychologist persisted.

"No they'd hurt me with that kind of a threat."

"WE ARE GOING TO MEET WITH STAFF FROM THE HOSPITAL TODAY."

Prisons routinely release their burned-out schizophrenics who, by the age of forty, have generally put on weight and lost the energy required for a consistently violent life. These men trickle through the mental health system—from hospital to halfway house, if possible, or at least from locked ward to open ward. At thirty-eight, the gray-haired, round-shouldered T.M. was about to start this journey. On a winter afternoon, he was given a paper bag full of clothes and driven to Mountain Valley Hospital.

When T.M. began meeting with me, he was still aiming streams of gibberish at anyone who came near him. He would sit folded up in a chair, his small eyes set deep in his face and his pointed nose drawing his face forward in a bewildered expression that reminded me of a mole. The moment I approached, however, he would start for his bedroom and fire a slurry of sentences in my direction as he left.

"Grew up in hell," he would say in a rapid, singsong voice, his rubbery face contorting into a deep frown that hid his eyes. "Pain rays. Ray jobs. They got rid of everyone—everything going dead. Crashing down. They had 'em gassed and John was hollering—that's right—hollering at me and the lightening bolt goes BANG and I'm in for big trouble. Big trouble. Just kill me and I'll go kaboom, bye-bye.

"Robot," he would mutter, as he wandered off shuffling his feet in agitation. "Robot. Robot."

"HOLD IT!" he shouted at me one afternoon as I approached. "When I'm incompasated, why make a problem with the pill bottles. THE HELL DRUGS. I'm in for the black crab nebula death which nobody can tell how serious that is, so ENOUGH!"

"Enough what, T.M.?" I wrote on a sheet of paper, which I cautiously handed to him across the six or eight feet of space that I was not supposed to invade.

He fished a pen from the pocket of his faded flannel shirt.

"Enough up to 100,000 cinavillian people," he wrote back hurriedly. "Been all over the cosmos from Queen to Ditch Digger or worse. I have springs inside me made of plastic. It's like fear and it's not like fear."

"Let's go to the cafeteria," I wrote back. He nodded, and without further ado, off we shuffled down the long corridor, T.M. still muttering "Robot" under his breath.

All interviews with T.M. were conducted in writing, for it was well known that he could not stand the anxiety of conversing. His early writings were no clearer than his monologues, but the act of writing apparently calmed him down and enabled him to remain in the same room or even at the same table as his interviewer. Similarly, when he was upset by some happening on the ward, he would ask for paper and start writing. If he was criticized, he would write, and if trash cans reminded him of pain rays, he would write. A few of these pages found their way into his chart, but none explained why describing a thousand years of torture in terms that no one could understand made T.M. feel better.

For two years T.M. and I wrote to each other for an hour every week. We had started in my office, but the quiet there was too stressful so we moved to the cafeteria. On one particular day we straggled into the bright, high-ceilinged room together, he wearing his favorite dark blue sweatshirt with a screeching eagle flying off the front, and I carrying an armload of pads and papers. We went straight to the table nearest the dishwasher, swung out the chairs (which are attached to the tables so that

neither can be thrown), and sat down. The noise level was just
right. The kitchen radio played while a social worker and an
indignant patient argued loudly. A doctor rattled quarters into a
snack machine, and the hospital's raspy-voice cook and a gray-
haired "salad girl" wrangled amicably over the dishwasher.

I pulled out a fresh pad of paper and a couple of pens. "How
was your week?" I wrote.

Bang, went the rolling door of the big machine. T.M. took
the pad and nodded briefly. Steam billowed from the kitchen.

Bending earnestly over his work, he answered, "Nero
ordered this one, and I am in for super-endless torture."

"What pills, Lovey?" sang out the salad girl. "The nitro?"

"No, my mother will take care of me," the patient across the
cafeteria said crossly.

Thump, *thump*, went the snack machine delivering its little
packages.

As T.M. wrote on and on about calamities, his first sentences
floating just above the pad's sky blue lines and those that followed wavering downward across the page, his jaw fell open
and he began to drool. When he got to the puddles, he wrote
around them. He leaned hard on the pen. He started a new
page.

"Who's Nero?" I asked out loud.

T.M. glanced around the room apprehensively then returned
to his writing with urgency.

"I don't take—"

The dishwasher clattered into its second cycle.

"But you'll need the operation?" the salad girl warbled
above the noise.

"Never!" shouted the patient. "Never, never, never."

As the doctor crumpled cellopháne into the trash container
at my elbow, T.M. wrote on nervously.

"May I see?" I finally asked.

T.M. held up a finger and completed a long paragraph. With
a sigh he pushed the pad across the table and collapsed on his
folded arms.

"Nero has ordered this one," I read on page one, and went
on to read about the kinds of torture that the emperor had in

mind. As always, T.M.'s words fell off the lines, got smaller at the bottom of each page, and started on the other side with a burst of capital letters.

"Are you worried about Mr. Montero who has just arrived from Newtondale?" I wrote.

T.M. nearly leapt back onto the pad.

"Yes, you could say that 10 to the 9th times. He is a super-doom machine with me, and I am in for the transatlantic electricity charge. Like *super-endless death*!!!

Each time a new patient arrived from the prison, T.M. became upset and never more so than with the tall, blank-faced Mr. Montero. He acted as if he had been terrorized by this man, but, as with the others, no one knew for sure.

People around us got up to leave.

"Time To Go," T.M. wrote in large letters. "Robot. Robot."

Just as we threw our soda cans in the recycle box and headed for the door, four new patients, including Montero, burst into the cafeteria talking loudly. With a scream of terror T.M. dove under the nearest table and began beating his head on the underside. The men swirled around him, laughing and shouting. Two aides jumped into the scene.

"T.M.!" yelled one. "Come out from under there!"

Banging his head one last time, T.M. staggered up from the floor and lunged for the aide. He yanked the clipboard from the man's hand, dropped to the floor, and began to write. Faster and faster the words went, slanting across the page like hard rain, then slower and slower until they pattered steadily onto the already-written-on paper. T.M. sat on the floor in the cafeteria. He did not look up. He wrote with a fierce and encapsulating concentration.

And suddenly I remembered being on a train in Italy in springtime, sitting in a compartment and being inundated by a sea of preadolescent girls. A thousand mouths, two thousand sticky, grabbing hands, lipstick, brushes, hair flying into the air, laughing, torrential bursts of incomprehensible language all engulfed me without warning. Arms, bread, cookies, scarfs, gum, giggles, candy—I was about to go under from the smell of oranges and the stickiness of little mouths. Like T.M., I grabbed a pencil, and began to write. And I can still recall the sensation of encompassing the turmoil with my pencil. Catching up with the commotion, my words took up the dance the girls had started and I was able to choose such fast, such tricky words that the turmoil was nearly left behind. With words I led the mouths and hair flying down paths of my own choosing—with words that served as fences, as names, as ordinary explanations. The bobbing flood of young girl parts subsided around me and their babbling flowed into the steady clack and rumble of the train.

I looked down at T.M. still writing on the clipboard.

"Stay away from Italy," I said gently.

His pointy, mole-like face turned upward in surprise.

I could not read what T.M. had scribbled back and forth across the clipboard, but I think it served him well. Perhaps he led his would-be torturers into outer space and regained some small measure of control by at least anticipating their torture. Perhaps he merely drowned out their voices with noise and confusion of his own. In any case, the act of writing had contained his anxiety.

Some six months later, T.M. cautiously experimented with using writing in another way, namely to communicate.

"How it all started:" he wrote. "I was caught by the clock tower."

"How it all started:" he wrote again. "I was Montgomery's fingers. Come here, Honey, they'd say, then beat the shit out of me."

In this roundabout way, I slowly learned about T.M.'s years in prison. I gathered what I could from the records—his early attempt to smother a guard (a "screw") on the intake unit, his reassignment to Block D when his unwillingness to speak intelligibly led him to be placed among mentally retarded murderers, his gradual withdrawal from all contact, and his inexplicable decision to write.

"What I remember: ALL ORDINARY THINGS BECOME INSTRUMENTS OF TORTURE," he once printed—then savagely broke the pen.

As T.M.'s memories began to surface, I visited Newtondale myself. I arrived on a raw March afternoon and stood in the empty yard that slopes down to the "houses" with their cell blocks then drops another couple of feet to end against an enormous brick clock tower with a lookout station on top. High above me I could see the motionless shape of a guard behind the tinted glass. Crossing the muddy field against the wind, I stood with my back against the clock tower and noticed that an overhang at the top prevented the "screw" from seeing what the "pigs" did to each other within a strip some three feet wide at the base of the tower wall. Later I felt the cold air blowing through the plastic-covered windows of the eight-man cells, felt the gloomy, smoky hopelessness of concrete corridors lit with forty-watt bulbs, and saw the sheet of Plexiglas protecting the TV screen in the day room on Block D.

"Hi there, hi there, hello there," said a five-foot-tall, heavily bespectacled man who rose from a heavy chair and came wobbling toward me through the smoke, his little arms outstretched. "I said, HI THERE!"

"Robot," I muttered, backing out of the day room. I could imagine T.M. walking down the cell block at lights out, feeling that a death-follicle ray gun was pointed at the back of his head. I could imagine him alone in a dorm with the wind banging heavy sheets of plastic against the windows. Alone on a low metal cot screwed to the floor with seven men who, I had since learned, held him down and amid belching laughter made him drink their piss or stuck cigarette lighters up his ass and burned the hair off his cheeks. Each wanted a turn.

"I am in for the endless Black Crab Nebula death," I can imagine him saying to himself as he scrambled away through the twisted tunnels of his own imagination. "I am gone. Outer space. I am a piece of skin. Walking skin. Robot. Robot. Robot."

Rereading T.M.'s writings after my visit to Newtondale, his descriptions of torture seemed less delusional. It was not difficult to believe that they were highly symbolic accounts of life in prison. He was indeed a mole surrounded by hawks. He was a little girl. He was sexless and double-sexed. He was pulled into the bushes and killed. He was flattened against the brick wall of the clock tower on raw March afternoons and tortured with ordinary things like pens.

Although T.M. did not think that rape, masturbation, or the sadistic "experiments" that his grunting dorm mates performed on him at night were topics that should be written about in an undisguised form in front of a woman, he did tell me stories about "the bird man who ran the numbers" and about Mr. Paradise, who operated an illegal "store" where he "owned all the words." He would mention "the cuckoo room" frequently and the dreaded clock tower.

"Happy Valentine's Day," I once wrote as we settled in at our table in the cafeteria.

"V is for vengeance," he wrote back briskly. "Torture, vengeance and a whole bunch of s. rolled together that's impossible to count mainly because of the Newtondale Clock Tower and the Love Me Tender song."

"I don't get it," I said aloud. T.M. snatched back the pad.

"More than 7 times the size of the tower is the song and the impulse waves or whatever you want to call it that gives me the action to do it."

"What's 'it'?"

"The Love Me Tender Shit on this day or any day turns me into a female robot and that's not just screwing around," he scribbled. "I'm a little girl and all the rest of the world is MEN, and that's a G. D. F. kinda Love and so is the Clock Tower a G. D. F. thing."

"Glad it's over?" I wrote.

"Certainly I am, but I never stop swearing subconsciously."

I thought back to "How it all started."

"Who was Montgomery?" I asked.

"An old guy there. He used to sit in his bed all day. He wasn't the worst."

At the same time that T.M. was remembering Newtondale, he was telling me more about writing and how it made him feel.

"Why do you write to people?" I had written on the pad.

"I can't hold my end of the conversation up unless I write it or it at least seems like that to me at times," he wrote back. "I feel better when I write. It's easier to explain myself."

"Does writing slow your thoughts down?"

"It slows *everything* down. People talk too fast for me."

"I notice that you start writing when something upsets you. Does it calm you down?" I printed.

"No, it can get me *more* worked up, or at least it did when I was going to school. I sometimes believe that when you write it it happens," he replied.

"So can you write yourself to safety?"

"Of course not. The opposite."

Although his comments on writing sounded contradictory, T.M. seemed to be saying that under ordinary circumstances he could use writing either as a slower, more controlled method of communication or as a speeded-up barrier that blocked exchanges he didn't like. Similarly, in times of trouble, he could either write out ritualized, repetitive phrases the way someone else would repeat a mantra to slow themselves down, or he could symbolically outrun the danger by speeding ahead with words much as I had done in Italy. He was not investigating a too-intense reality as Cortazar had described, but he was holding the danger off as best he could.

I think there is a final, ironic advantage to T.M.'s writing. It allows him the luxury of being completely psychotic.

"Much of psychiatric endeavor, to a far greater extent now than in the past, is devoted to putting a stop to psychotic experience," wrote John MacGregor, "to preventing the spontaneous but slow processes of self-healing and self-knowledge. . . ."[4] Whether one argues that both writing and psychosis are ways to retreat temporarily from life to find something in the self that has been pushed aside, or whether one focuses more narrowly on the idea that writing is a way of learning, it seems possible that there may be a subtle usefulness in letting a person like T.M. write on.

After nearly three years in Mountain Valley Hospital, T.M.

4. John MacGregor, *The Discovery of the Art of the Insane* (Princeton, NJ: Princeton University Press, 1989), p. 269.

was moved to a halfway house. The transition was boisterous, and T.M., now called Tom or Tommy, reverted to writing almost exclusively for several months. Doom crystals and money bombs came back as did memories of Montgomery and the "Love Me Tender Shit," but he never retreated beyond reach.

"Are you safe at the new house?" I wrote the first time I saw him as an outpatient. "Are you as safe as you were in the hospital?"

Tom mumbled a while on paper, complaining of his medications and of time passing too fast, and it seemed clear (or as clear as these things ever get) that he would never be able to write himself completely free of the danger and estrangement that had accompanied him for so long. However, his old habit was still helping him to tolerate some large and rather threatening improvements.

"Of course the house is safer than the hospital," he finally wrote. "IT'S A HOME."

The time came when Tom rarely wrote. Now he reads or smokes, concentrates with touching intensity on making cookies or playing his guitar, and walks in the company of who-knows-what memories through the woods that surround his home.

"Why don't you write anymore?" I asked him several months ago.

"Too much trouble," he replied with a broad, rubbery smile, "but do you think you could get me a tape recorder? I'd like to hear how I sound."

It has been suggested that the sophisticated habit of telling stories to one's self about one's self in a journal or diary is uncommon among the profoundly mentally ill because their thoughts are disorganized and they are apathetic. A more important reason, I believe, is their lack of a proper audience. Unlike the lists, inventories of evidence, and defensive writings just sampled, journals are written for the sympathetic ear. Like interoffice memos, they are written to an aspect of the self that is interested in how life is proceeding; or, like letters, they are intended for an outside person who might read the account and be moved. Thoreau claimed he wrote his journal for the gods: "They are my correspondent, to whom daily I send off this sheet postpaid."

Rosina Venuto's diary was begun, much less ambitiously, for her mother, but brief as it is and simple as it is, it expresses the surprising power that the written word has for holding a life together. At twenty-five Miss Venuto found herself in a state hospital on a tough ward for patients who were both mentally ill and addicted to alcohol and drugs. In Miss Venuto's case, her troubles were further complicated by a splintered family, extreme poverty, and a brain that had never quite kept up, not even in third grade.

"I still have trouble reading," she confided to her diary. "I'm OK at the beginning of a sentence, but if it's too long, I get lost."

Rosina Venuto's diary was intended to convince her mother that she was still alive. The fragments that I have read begin with a dedication.

"For Mom. I would tell my whole day on paper so you can see I'm OK here in this place."

The charming Miss Venuto was as good as her word. "Took a shower," she wrote in a childish hand. "Lay on my bed." "Ate breakfast."

Miss Venuto did not bother to date her entries and I can only guess how long she continued to document her existence with the written word. "Smoked a cigarette." "Felt bad. Cramps." "Thirsty all day." Occasionally she would burst into song and not only describe but begin to arbitrate her predicaments.

"I don't understand why the stuff they give me makes me feel so bad. If it's good for you, why don't it make me feel good? I have such bad dreams, there must be a lot of bad inside me. I pray, but God is too smart to hang around this place, and I'm afraid I'll never get better and get out."

"Another fight. Ruth says I'll get the needle now."

Miss Venuto was apparently switched from the medication she had been taking in pill form to a much stronger one given by injection.

"Legs shook all night," she wrote in a hand that was deterio-
rating alarmingly.

"Arms don't work."

"Can't turn neck."

Miss Venuto's now spidery scrawl made it clear that she was
having a bad reaction to her medications. There is a side effect
that produces a restless, jerky stiffness that simultaneously
makes a patient feel trapped in cement *and* wildly agitated. She
was experiencing this effect and began suffering the waves of
panic that often accompany the reaction. She felt she would go
crazy if she couldn't break out of the invisible restraints. She
wanted to pace the corridors, flail her arms, and write all over
the walls, but the medication clamped her muscles into rigid
immobility. She could hardly walk. Her head shook so badly,
that her neck hurt and she had to lie down. The panic mounted.

"Please, God, take my life," her diary concludes in a barely
legible scrawl. "I can't hardly hold a pencil. I can't put one sentence down even with big letters."

Miss Venuto's medications were finally changed, and she
gradually regained her former agility in both mind and body.
She quit writing in her diary then, she told me, but still has the
sense that writing enabled her to survive fourteen months on a
locked ward.

"Writing is a form of therapy," Graham Greene once noted.
"Sometimes I wonder how all those who do not write, compose,
or paint can manage to escape the madness, the melancholia, the
panic fear which is inherent in the human situation."

Less poetically, psychologists who investigate the therapeutic
value of writing have noted that "in general, writers' emotions
change significantly when they write. Typically, positive feelings
intensify over the course of composing . . . [and] the Negative
Passive emotions weaken during writing."[5] By this, the authors
meant specifically that feelings of satisfaction, relief, and inspiration increased as feelings of boredom and confusion slipped away.

5. Alice Brand and Jack Powell, "Emotions and the Writing Process: A
Description of Apprentice Writers," *Journal of Educational Research* 79
(1986): 280–85.

"Writing can be as good as a cup of coffee," Bob Anderson agreed:

> My mind in the morning
> Is not good. Madness takes over.
> I wait in a cup of coffee—
> Careful not to oversip and erase the essentials.
> I add a cigarette, a poem, and after that
> Life is a high wire,
> One slip of the tongue between up or very far below.

And Miss Venuto adds, "That book of mine was the only one I could talk to, and when I saw the pages I knew I was alive, not locked in some shitty dream. All those words on the page meant I had a life even if I couldn't remember it. I mean writing isn't as good as speed, for Chrissake, but it's all right. It's an upper."

And so the writers on the back wards hang on to their disturbingly unstable days and months. With lists, evidence, notebooks full of ruminations and unhappy memories, letters, and diaries they express, conceal, explore, and figure out what goes on inside and out. They write to stay in control and to slip out of control, to comfort themselves with lullabies of repetitious words, and to prove they exist by writing their names. "Owning all the words," as T.M.'s cohort, Mr. Paradise, does, is often the only power they possess.

But what of the effect of these writings on the wider world? Are the lists, poems, and diaries comprehensible enough to negotiate with other people on the writer's behalf? Can they inform and enliven a psychiatric record? In my experience with the chronically mentally ill who are cared for at public expense, the answer to these questions is mainly a discouraging no. On the one hand, much of the writing I encounter is so full of private meaning and so short on anything resembling fact, that it is not understandable to anyone save its author. Whatever its virtues may be—such as containing anxiety—such writing does not reconnect a person to others, nor does it constitute a reliable enough record of action and reaction to teach its author the

consequences of his behavior. This is simply another way of saying that any writing or speech that ignores *all* conventions
becomes a private language. On the other hand, even the writing
that makes sense, and expresses a patient's fears and desires in
dramatic terms, is likely to be ignored in public clinics and hospitals. Although dream journals, diaries, and other forms of
writing used to be a big part of analysis, their usefulness has
declined with the rise of the medical model of mental illness.
Nothing in writing, save possibly the handwriting itself, points
toward brain chemistry or genetics. Further, if a patient is
encouraged to write, his or her therapist will need to read—or
even write back—and few have the time to follow the outrageous creations of our fantasies.

"Why or how do poets write," began Peggy Stein who writes
all day the way other women used to knit socks and now smoke
cigarettes.

> I work inside myself to achieve clarity.
> I question if I am seeing.
> I dig the light in my eyes so it will surface.
>
> .   .   .   .
>
> I create art with a broad positioning of words.
> I write for myself, together and alone.

14

THE RECORD KEEPERS

What is your warrant for valuing any part of my experience and rejecting the rest? . . . If I had done so, you would never have heard my name.

PYTHAGORAS

THE WORD *RECORD*, AS IN T.M.'S RECORD OR ANY OTHER PATIENT'S record, comes from the Latin *recordari*, to remember, which literally means to go back again to what was in the heart or mind. The definition is apt. The voluminous records now kept on mental patients indeed reflect what their clinicians remember, and show, often with embarrassing clarity, what was and was not in their hearts and on their minds as they worked with these people.

Several days before and after T.M.'s move from Newtondale Hospital to Mountain Valley Hospital, he was interviewed. The first interviewer wrote four questions in large letters on a sheet of paper, which T.M. then answered.

HOW ARE YOU DOING TODAY?
Infinely radiant.
WHERE ARE YOU NOW?
In jail without bail.
WHAT IS YOUR FULL NAME?

Miselaneous Super Hell
WHERE IS HOME?
in Super Hell.

The second interviewer escorted T.M. to a quiet office on the hospital ward and read him a standard list of questions. At the time, T.M. was talking nonstop about pain rays, death springs, and endless torture. He was afraid it was another one of those "Come here, Honey" days when they would "beat the shit out of me."

During the interview the client's demeanor was withdrawn, apathetic, immature, unresponsive, distractible, and bizarre. Based on the character and coherency of the client's responses, spontaneous comments, and behavior, the information obtained during the interview is very likely unreliable. Nevertheless, the professional opinions offered in this report are believed to be reliable and valid. . . .

Mr. M. appears to be best characterized as passive, dependent, aggressive, obsessive, paranoid, explosive and, schizoid. . . . It appears that his prognosis is poor.

This remarkable report, which runs on for nearly three pages and which introduces the patient to his new caretakers, is, I believe, best characterized as hostile, passive, aggressive, obsessive, empty, biased, grandiose, and verbose—or rather, "given to verbigeration," as is stated later. Worse, it is only slightly more flatulent than the run-of-the-mill reporting found in hospitals, clinics, and halfway houses today. Why would anyone write this way? (Not to mention think this way and see other people this way.) There must be powerful social and economic forces pushing clinicians to adopt such a disagreeably standardized and impersonalized stance vis-à-vis the mentally ill. What are these forces? Who do they help? And who do they hurt?

As we saw in the cases of Chuck Willet and Angie Savalonis, more than one story or explanation of a life often springs from the same set of facts. Each observer or record keeper sees what he or she is used to seeing, which springs in turn from that individual's training and experience. But not from just any training or experience. Today the people who work with the mentally ill are trained within the medical model of mental illness, and those with no specific training acquire, nonetheless, a typically late-twentieth-century-American approach to the emotionally troubled. In other words, the basic plots of the stories we tell about ourselves and about other people come ready-made off the shelf of our culture. We all know the outline of a successful entertainer story, an unhappy wife story, a precocious child script, or a juvenile delinquent scenario. Inhabitants of the Amazon jungle have a different set of plots available to them today, and three hundred years ago Colonial Americans had yet another set. Likewise, the story of any life that is presented in a psychiatric record will be shaped to fit the plots that clinicians learn are "appropriate" for the mentally ill, and these, unfortunately, come from a less rich and varied tradition. There is the scenario of the bright, promising boy who first gets into trouble at fifteen. This story goes on to describe seemingly inevitable entanglements with courts and institutions. Then there is the story of the quiet young woman who functions well until the birth of her first child. This story progresses through loss of husband, child, job, friends and points toward permanent residence in a subsidized housing project. Of course, no one gathers all the would-be clinicians together and says, "Look, the chronically mentally ill have broken brains. They aren't able to think or feel the way we do, so give them short, simple stories." Nonetheless, the pervasive condescension that prunes T.M.'s story into such a constricted list of pejorative adjectives is common. Strange as it may sound, this unpleasant readiness to deny the depth and complexity of the lives of the seriously mentally ill generally takes hold of the clinician during training.

To see how this occurs, let us look at one of America's most famous child psychiatrists, Robert Coles, and see how he was trained in the 1950s on the psychiatric ward of the Massachusetts General Hospital. Adding to his account anecdotes from my own training in the 1980s, we may be able to see how the cautiously restricted range of relationships that connect "those people," as one of my supervisors called them, to "us" are handed down through successive generations of clinicians much as the eccentric patterns of living described in Frankie DeMello's family are handed down among the mentally ill.

Robert Coles had completed the first phase of training, namely his course work, when he arrived at Mass General. The second part of training was an apprenticeship. This is the time when the trainee acts like a doctor, psychologist, or social worker, then brings the results to a more experienced clinical supervisor for guidance. It is in these weekly meetings that clinical legends are passed on and the qualities seen to be essential for good therapy are inculcated. It is also in these meetings that the new clinician in the "adolescence" of his or her career begins to voice opinions that test the status quo.

Coles describes his training in *The Call of Stories*, and in his account he focuses on the divided loyalty he felt for two supervisors.[1] One was a brilliant theoretician who represented the latest word in scientific thinking. The other was an old, partially deaf humanist whose methods seemed old-fashioned. Not surprisingly, Coles gravitated toward the more modern of the two. From this doctor, he learned to be aggressive. Taking control of therapy sessions from the very beginning, Coles drove toward the heart of the problem. Like both Miss Savalonis's and T.M.'s doctors, he asked questions generated by a theoretical framework that assumes that various kinds of deficits are the root cause of insanity. Does the patient know where he is? he learned to ask. Can he remember both distant and recent events? Can he reason? What's missing? In this way Coles looked for physical, cognitive, and what are called functional deficits—namely all those things that a patient has the physical and mental equipment to do but can't or won't do.

"Patient unable to care for self," wrote a social worker in T.M.'s Discharge-Oriented Service Plan. "Poor verbal communication skills limiting appropriate social interaction. Short attention span. Poor social interpersonal skills."

Putting all these inabilities together—in T.M.'s case they are

1. Robert Coles, *The Call of Stories: Teaching and the Moral Imagination* (Boston: Houghton Mifflin, 1989). See chapter 1, "Stories and Theories," pp. 1–30.

listed on the dark yellow Discharge-Oriented Psychiatric Assessment and the white Discharge-Oriented Comprehensive Assessment, not to mention the pale yellow Discharge-Oriented Team Assessment and two others—clinicians come up with a diagnosis based on the breakdowns of normal functioning. Because all these descriptions are couched in medical terminology, clinicians like Coles and his fellow residents naturally think of their patients as sick or broken rather than as sad, rebellious, or lazy. As Coles later realized, a gulf was already opening up between sick patient and well doctor.

Coles also learned to take his patients' personal history, family history, social history, and clinical history, and from these to come up with a case history that, as we have seen both with Miss Savalonis and T.M., miraculously points directly toward a standard diagnosis. In my internship, we even figured out *how much* to think about each kind of history by the amount of blank space there was in the chart under each heading. Now some agencies use checklists, and as the client speaks or stares silently out the window, the clinician checks off adjectives in little boxes under mood, memory, thought, and so forth.

"Part of the trouble in the training of psychotherapy [is] that psychotherapists don't learn enough literature, enough drama, or enough biography," said James Hillman in his discussions with Michael Ventura, which became *We've Had a Hundred Years of Psychotherapy—And the World's Getting Worse.*[2]

"You're right," Mr. Ventura replied, "it's weird that people whose work will largely consist of listening to stories aren't taught anything . . . about how people tell stories."

Unless, of course, you truly believe that the emotionally ill only suffer from broken equipment and have no stories to tell, or unless you don't want to get caught up in stories that could wrap themselves around you and not let go.

The latter seemed to be what the professors at Mass General feared. Coles copied their approach and became "cautious, politic, and meticulous." He learned not to get too close or

2. James Hillman and Michael Ventura, *We've Had a Hundred Years of Psychotherapy—And the World's Getting Worse* (San Francisco: Harper-Collins, 1992), p. 28.

become too involved, phrases he heard mentioned every day as signs of incompetence. He found there were many ways besides theory to maintain a safe distance. The language of psychiatry was one. He learned the jargon quickly and soon spoke of "phobic" instead of fearful, "positive and negative transference" instead of like or dislike, and "affect" instead of emotion. Adding graceless neologisms, such as biopsychosocial, and punctuating his speech with impenetrable acronyms, he effectively transformed his patients' troubles into "things"—like "nuclear neurotic processes"—that regular people don't associate with their lives. One of Coles's peers, Leston Havens, once wrote that "For the most part, language does our thinking for us. . . ." Rather than saying a person has mastered a language, he continued, be it English, slang, Greek, or psychiatric jargon, "It would be more accurate to say he was mastered by it."[3] This seems particularly apt in clinical settings, and once Coles's thinking had been mastered by jargon, he found that he could easily transform a person into a case. No one, he realized, gets too close to a case. And this was not all. Using jargon, Coles's voice soon became indistinguishable from all the other residents. His "adolescent identity crisis" was everyone's "adolescent identity crisis," and they all pretended that they saw and heard exactly the same thing whenever such a term was used. Looking at Mass General as a system, a family therapist might say that there was precious little differentiation going on. All the new clinicians seemed to want to be clones of their supervisors. And the more closely they agreed with each other, the further they seemed to drift from their patients.

Take my description of Franny O'Leary. As an intern, I had been asked to describe my first meeting with a middle-aged man whose wife was upset by his increasing absentmindedness. After I'd written the usual "45 y.o. white, Catholic, married male" business and had informally tested the man's short- and long-term memory, which seemed to be working pretty well, I noted:

3. Leston Havens, *Coming to Life* (Cambridge: Harvard University Press, 1993), p. 29.

Mr. O'Leary has the curious habit of singing to himself during therapy. When I ask him a question, he talks for a while, and when I ask him another question, he sings. It is not, strictly speaking, a true song, just a melodious, high-pitched doo-dee-doo-da-da repeated several times. It reminds me of a computer that chimes when you ask it to do something it is not programmed to do. Five or six times in the hour Mr. O'Leary looks out my window and chimes.

After a kind and thorough scolding, this passage was corrected to read, "Patient exhibited inappropriate singing behavior during interview." Quicker? Yes. Anonymous? Sure. But which description makes you want to meet Mr. O'Leary? Jargon, I concluded, expresses not only wretchedly simplistic thinking but an acceptable form of hostility as well—linguistic callousness, as Hillman put it.

So, too, with "proper boundaries." Coles was told, "Don't get too close." His contemporary, Leston Havens, was told "not . . . to express affection for many convincing reasons. . . ."[4] I was instructed, "We are never their friends. A parent substitute, but not a friend. We don't use the word." Later I heard references to "those unfortunate therapists who fuse with patients in the belief that what they call their affection is more powerful than their knowledge base."

"What the hell is a fused therapist?" I remember asking shortly after completing my training. I was sitting with one of the psychiatrists at the Hillsdale Clinic.

"Ah, fusion!" Dr. H. shot back, suddenly sitting up in his chair and sticking his legs straight out in front of him. "A fused therapist *beats* his patients in the first hour. No, no, no, wait. A fused therapist has lunch in the nude with a patient who was released from jail that morning—a picnic in the nude on the first day. Yes," he went on briskly, opening a drawer in his cluttered desk as if to look for picnic supplies, "with finger food and let me see—"

"Whoa, whoa," I pleaded, as I moved a pile of books and

4. Havens, *Coming to Life*, p. 195.

papers that threatened to collapse into my lap. "Seriously, I don't get this business of boundary issues. Whose boundaries? Who decides?"

Still rummaging through his desk for props, Dr. H. galloped on over my objections, as he always did, with more descriptions of outrageous scenes. Scribbling arrows and dots across his lunch bag, gesturing broadly, and performing a kind of theater all around the small office, he described fences and moats, permeable and semipermeable membranes, white coats, last names, kilometers, chairs with arms and insignia, clocks and watches until everything around me seemed capable of being a boundary.

"You look as if you want a rule," he finally said, climbing down from his desk, where he had been standing to demonstrate height as boundary. "Here it is. *Never use the word*. In fact, never use any of those interpretive words like 'inappropriate' or 'boundary,' which depend for their meaning on a secret code among clinicians of a certain color and culture. You write down, 'Mr. Jones walked into my office in July wearing four woolen shirts, two pairs of trousers, five hats, and bright yellow cowboy boots.' Then you let anyone reading that decide for themselves whether Mr. Jones is appropriate.

"And here's another rule, the one you came for, I imagine. Never be afraid of those words. Don't let 'boundary' make you stupid."

Now on his hands and knees pulling a pair of dusty galoshes out from under his desk, the wiry Dr. H. went on to tell me a story from his own practice. It was a parable about boundaries, and it involved a man who could not understand why he was treated so poorly in spite of his efforts to be liked. At some point in the man's therapy, Dr. H. asked to exchange coats with him, then hats.

"For a week I walked around town in this man's enormous trench coat and in a hat that just about covered me up. I wore these galoshes, too," he continued, setting them pigeon-toed on his desk, "because this man had enormous feet. Huge feet. Very big. And, you know, I got talked to in a different way in this costume. Without making any change in what I said or how I said it, people treated me differently. I could not have predicted the kinds of responses I got. Now is that crossing the boundary?" He stopped to laugh at his own question. "Of course it is." He waved his arms in mock despair. "I don't know anything about boundaries. Nothing. Only they're not a 'thing.' They aren't like stone walls that sit in the same place for years. Like a lot in life, you can't figure out boundaries once and for all."

As with boundaries, so with waiting. Coles was taught that his time was more valuable than the patients', who had nothing to do all day. We were taught that if a patient keeps a doctor waiting, it is a sign of unwillingness to engage in therapy. If a doctor keeps a patient waiting, however, it is a sign of importance—another marker along the gulf that separates the two. When, in order to meet my patients on time, I began excusing myself from a weekly meeting at two o'clock when it was scheduled to finish, I was reprimanded for being too eager and "too . . . "—my supervisor searched for the word—"too involved.

"You don't want to get the reputation," she said kindly, "of being sorta soft instead of . . . well, smart."

"You can't be both?" I wanted to ask, but didn't.

"Even pediatricians . . . talk like that," roared William Carlos Williams when Coles asked him about doctors who cross boundaries. "How you have to be 'cool' and keep your 'distance' and not become 'overwhelmed' by all the emotions that come your way. Of course, it's a clever setup: who in hell is suggesting that anyone should be overwhelmed, or should get soft in the head or self-indulgent emotionally? Why should we always be told that the alternative is between a doctor who really knows what he's doing, even if he doesn't have much time to be with his patients . . . and a doctor who has all the time in the world for his patients, but he's a first-class idiot . . . ?"[5]

Williams believed the answer to be that a few callous physicians bully others into thinking that being fascinated by patients is dumb so that their own callousness won't be seen for what it is. I would add that fascination is dangerous. I would say that the new, more egalitarian and responsive therapist is up against her own fears of seeing and feeling too much and against the

5. William Carlos Williams, quoted in Coles, *Call of Stories*, p. 109.

health care industry's fears that such responsiveness will lead to less effective regulation of her patients and her practice. As one clinician who attended Bruno Bettelheim's and Alvin Rosenfeld's Stanford seminars on children said, "I had to accept a world [and a self] with greater cruelty, pain, fear, and violence than I ever wanted to face. Understanding that world has left me with a sense of sadness about the way we live and who we are."[6]

Boundaries, waiting, diagnoses, anonymous notes in humorless charts—we were all learning to jump through the hoops of hospital protocol, ostensibly to become professional, additionally to keep us at a safe distance from our patients.

You're forgetting the life, Coles's older supervisor said when Coles began listening to his unfashionable point of view. "What ought to be interesting is the unfolding of a lived life rather than the confirmation such a chronicle provides for some theory."[7]

"How do you get to be a person like T.M.?" asked Dr. H. "That's what his record ought to explain."

If training doesn't teach the young clinician to regard compassion as unscientific, then the billing office will get the point across that it's not cost-effective. The idea that good therapy for the seriously mentally ill is a luxury rather than a necessity has been going in and out of fashion, driven largely, but not exclusively, by economics. Until the 1950s, the majority of the profoundly mentally ill were either cared for in private hospitals or warehoused in state institutions where they received little or no therapy. The annual cost of such care within a state system was only $636 per patient in 1949, but the price was rising at a rate of well over 200 percent per decade, almost twice as fast as the consumer price index.[8] (By 1984, custodial care had risen to $41,651 per patient per year, and at present, the full cost of a year of treatment, not just housing, in a state hospital in the

6. Bruno Bettelheim and Alvin A. Rosenfeld, *The Art of the Obvious: Developing Insight for Psychotherapy and Everyday Life* (New York, Alfred A. Knopf, 1993), p. 102.

7. Coles, *Call of Stories*, p. 22.

8. Ann Braden Johnson, *Out of Bedlam: The Truth About Deinstitutionalization* (New York: Basic Books, 1990), p. 90.

Northeast is between $290,000 and $547,000 depending on which bells and whistles are included.)

Because the states bore these costs alone until the 1960s when Medicare and Medicaid provided some federal relief, there was tremendous pressure to find a cheaper way of caring for the mentally ill. Deinstitutionalization seemed the best bet. If the senile elderly, the chronically mentally ill, and the retarded could all be returned to the community, they could be cared for at roughly a twelfth of the cost that hospitalization required. (At today's rate, for example, it costs about $36,000 annually to provide each client with therapy, medications, a small allowance, and room and board in a halfway house, rather than some $300,000 for a year in an institution.) With such dramatic savings in mind, it made sense to pour money into clinics, day programs, and residential "homes" and to give clients all the therapy they needed to support them in a less sheltered environment. At the same time, new antipsychotic drugs became available that controlled some of the more florid symptoms (like hearing voices) at least some of the time. This allowed talking therapy to begin its work, although not everyone agrees that this is particularly useful.

In the 1960s and 1970s deinstitutionalization became common policy across the country, and a swelling stream of chronic patients shuffled back into the community. In Massachusetts alone, the number of patients in the state system fell from 21,000 in 1969 to a mere 3,262 only eight years later. Costs were expected to plummet. Instead, the commonwealth's budget for the mentally ill doubled in this same period, climbing from $116 million to $233 million.[9] With hindsight, it can be seen that part of this unexpected rise reflects the greater numbers of mentally ill who receive services. The rise also reflects the fragmentation of care; that is, it costs a lot more to buy all the kinds of care a hospital provides—therapies, general health care, law enforcement, social services, transportation, and so on—from separate sources. The rise also reflects the rapidly increasing regulations that have been driving up the administrative overhead

9. Johnson, *Out of Bedlam*, p. 103.

of both outpatient and inpatient facilities at an outrageous rate. At the Hillsdale Clinic, for example, secretarial overhead has increased some 500 percent over the past dozen years, while clinical salaries have risen a mere 10 percent over the same twelve years. To look at it another way, throughout the 1970s, T.M.'s record grew at a rate of approximately one inch per year. By 1990 it was growing two or more inches *per month.*

Massachusetts was not alone in discovering that deinstitutionalization by itself does not hold down costs, and soon many states were devising strategies for cheaper treatment. Primary among them was, and is, privatization. Privatization is the turning over of state mental health clinics and other community facilities to profit-making companies, and it is at this point that listening and real therapy goes out the window for all but the well-to-do.

There are not too many ways for budget officers, who are now the actual directors of mental health facilities, to cut costs and turn a profit. One way is to pay low wages for the least skilled workers—interns and counselors as opposed to psychologists, for example, or health aides rather than nurses. Although this practice doesn't work in hospitals where labor is largely unionized, it can save large amounts of money in rest homes, halfway houses, and clinics. If, as a result of low pay, the turnover among staff is high and the morale low, that is the price that clinicians and clients alike pay for somebody else's profit.

Another way to stay in the black is to concentrate on billing and collecting rather than on treatment. Even at the Hillsdale Clinic, which remains a nonprofit organization, we are now required to produce a diagnosis and a plan for treatment in the first fifty minutes so that billing can begin. This is the kind of therapy that Bruno Bettelheim maintained was embraced only by idiots and megalomaniacs who think they can plan the whole game in advance.

Still a third way to cut costs is to abbreviate or even eliminate therapy itself. At Hillsdale we now have a sliding scale for the uninsured that doesn't slide below $40 an hour for long-term therapy—too costly for many. Another innovation is the "prior approval," a kind of permission slip that is filled out every three months and sent to the managed care company that administers Medicaid. My "prior approval" sheets plead in advance for the therapy sessions I guess I am going to need over the next thirteen weeks. Like other waves of paperwork that have come flooding into the clinic, prior approvals not only cut into our time with clients but hand over the management of treatment to some secretary or retired nurse who sits in an office building far, far away from the mentally ill.

Hardly less upsetting is the new emphasis placed on inadequate methods of treatment, which are increasingly given fancy names like "brief, problem-focused therapy." No one is yet arrogant enough to claim that six sessions can accomplish what two years of treatment tries to do, but the proponents of brief therapy would like to believe that it is more "adult" and more efficient for a person to dip in and out of therapy as problems arise than to form a close relationship with a therapist within which one's most intimate fears and needs can be discussed and possibly modified. Long-term therapy, they argue, fosters mutual dependence between therapist and client, and allows their discussions to spill over sloppily from "the presenting problem" to a "diffusion of content."[10] Of course it does. The fashionable quick fix is exactly the kind of therapy that stares so narrowly at the problem that the life slips away. It is the kind of therapy that slaps a coat of paint on dry rot. It is the kind that produces statements such as: "Patient will demonstrate a verbal understanding of medications. Patient will attend and participate in all assigned groups. Patient will be able to be redirected from word salad production to coherent speech with all treatment providers."

"Fido, bark once when I say Thorazine."

"Do you see how much harder all this bureaucracy makes T.M.'s life?" Dr. H. once asked me as he pushed off from his desk and rolled backwards across his office. "Today we are being asked to devise strategies—you know, a treatment plan

10. James Mann, M.D., *Time-Limited Psychotherapy* (Cambridge: Harvard University Press, 1973), p. x.

with medication, weekly visits, and so on—that take the *system's* needs into account first and the client's second. Say we reduce Tom's medications." The doctor spun his chair toward the window. "Away he'd go. Whoosh, into his private movie theater, and off down the road on those little excursions he's famous for. Good-bye, good-bye." He turned to face me again. "We know he'd stop checking in with his case manager. Maybe stop going to his day program at the clubhouse. Predictable. But now this starts a ruckus. His caretakers get upset because *they* don't feel safe."

"So now we sedate Tom to the point, not where he feels most content with his life," I suggested, taking up the theme, "but to the point where the Department of Mental Health and Medicaid feel solidly in control. No surprises at all."

Dr. H. grimaced as if he'd bitten into a lemon.

"But if the new goal is to contain costs," I continued, "and contain anyone who acts funny, contain therapists who might do things differently, who actually benefits?"

Dr. H. sighed deeply, and turned away as if to hide some portion of his frustration. "Well," he began, "superficially, I suppose you could say that the taxpayer benefits because management makes it so frustrating and time-consuming to get money out of the system that many of us don't charge for some services, or we even go out of business. Not that managed care is a smart or efficient way to control money, but it is a control. However"—he paused again—"I don't think that's the main, you know, the main force, motivation." He shrugged and seemed to look for an answer among the books and papers that littered his desk. "I suppose," he said slowly, "the real winner is anyone who convinces himself that you can substitute a regulation for your own conscience or your own common sense. If you think your job is finished once you've filled out the form that says you called the client after he threatened suicide, then I suppose you can go home and not worry."

Dr. H. tipped back in his squeaky chair and looked into the corner of his office where a poster of an erupting volcano hung cockeyed on the wall.

"The calls that come in from Wyoming," he began, nodding

to himself, "always from a phone booth. Middle of the night. 'Well,' the voice says, 'I've decided to end it all.' Something like that. I got enough of those calls to practice being suicidal myself. I don't know exactly how you dress if you're suicidal," he continued, then after a pause cut himself off from that line of thinking with a characteristic slicing motion of his hand. "But back to the phone booth. I'd walk to a phone booth at three A.M. with several lists of symptoms. I'd write them out on index cards so I'd know what to say." He frowned, remembering back to what I imagined were curiously peaceful nights for him.

"I'd hold the receiver close, right in by my chest, and read the lines with a penlight. 'Can't go any farther. Can't take another step.' Then I'd try to imagine what kind of response would increase or decrease the desire to kill myself. I tried, 'Wait! You're not alone. We can—something.' But, you know, that's promising help that can't be delivered. Wyoming! We are not in this thing together, and I will not be with you to pull you back or knock the gun out of your hand. Not in Wyoming, and actually, not anywhere.

"So I tried hearing the doctor say, 'Killing yourself? Wrong. No. Sorry, I only deal with the living. Call me if you choose to live. Good-bye.' Click. A medicine ball right in the stomach. Bang. Feel it? Now it feels like 'I have the problem. It's not the doctor's and it's not out there between us, hovering over the water somewhere.' It sounds like a tough response, and it is, but it's not misleading. It doesn't tempt the person to see how far he can go or how far the therapist will go to save him."

I pulled myself back from a phone booth on the side of a mountain and from another lit by a penlight on a dark street in Hillsdale. "And the regulations?" I asked.

"Exactly. The regulations either manage the therapy and get everyone saying the same not-very-well-thought-out things, or— and this is interesting—they prompt you to act 'as if something else is going on.'"

"Meaning?"

"If you don't let the managers manage your therapy, you learn to lie. *Not* document. *Not* write down much. Become dishonest. We're asked to act as if something else is happening. It's a funny way to do therapy—underground."

"Reminds me of what we often do to our clients," I mused, "asking them to act as if they wanted to be clean or as if they wanted to attend groups."

"Yes. We put a lot of pressure on the mentally ill to pretend they're doing better than they are. You might say that management of all sorts—with therapists, clients—leads away from the truthful response. If you don't like the truth or you can't afford the truth, you know, you start to manage and manipulate. And I think that's as close as I can get today to the motives behind managed care. It manages our money a little, our worries, our reality. Manages what we think and do. That's plenty." He rose from his chair. "They should get the word 'care' out of there."

Although the truckloads of recent regulations that are tolerated by some and infuriate others have combined with privatization and economic hard times to create a more standardized, less personal kind of care for the emotionally disturbed, there are other forces that add to the deterioration of compassionate care and, more broadly, to the disrepair of our communities. In particular, I am referring to a fearfulness, an uncharacteristic meanness of spirit and lack of confidence that I feel are on the rise among us. It is as if the residents, struggling with doubts and problems of their own, are becoming increasingly intolerant of any "extra" disturbances. Ten years ago a big, overweight client who shuffled around town with a pink baby doll in a bag would receive an occasional handout of food or clothing. Now she is picked up by the police after someone dials 911 and complains. Ten years ago the residents of Hillsdale tried to outwit the raccoons that raided their garbage cans and gingerly moved dead cats and squirrels from the streets into the bushes. Now someone calls the conservation officer every week demanding that the town "deal" with raccoons or screams that in five minutes a school bus will discharge itty-bitty children thirty feet from a squashed chipmunk. Are we that fragile? Have we become that intolerant of what we cannot understand or control?

Whatever the forces may be that are pushing us to seek safety by excluding the strange and the wild, they are significantly affecting the mentally ill. Not only do the residents of a town like Hillsdale not want to see these people on their streets, they do not want to pay for the kind of respectful care that would empower these eccentrics to challenge the rigid conventions—internal and external—that stifle their spirits. Hillsdale wants the mentally ill managed, not encouraged. It wants its tax dollars spent on short-term, lukewarm therapy that provides conventional answers for those who wish to rejoin our work-oriented and consumer-oriented world—although this is therapy that cannot help those who reject the way things are and wish to find new ways to live. Nevertheless, it is not only more cost effective but, more significantly, safer to control rather than to understand and support the alienated. This holds true for most people—whether one is a mayor, a restaurant owner, or a street sweeper. It is also true for a therapist.

This story of fearfulness and mediocrity is one that can be told about the care of the mentally ill, and it is a truly discouraging account. But just as there are other trends developing in our culture besides our growing fearfulness of each other, so there are other stories to be told about how schizophrenics and manic depressives manage to fit into a community—how anyone with any differences at all fits in. A hint of what is at stake here and of what needs to be done to reconnect individuals to each other may sometimes be found in improbable places. Take the Newtondale Hospital for the Criminally Insane, for example, and take the lives and even the worlds created there by the manic ex-convict, Johnny Paradise.

15

THE MYTHMAKER OF NEWTONDALE PRISON

In the beginning, Tséitsinako, Thought Woman, thought of all things, and all of these things are held together as one holds many things together in a single thought. So in the telling . . . the story- telling always includes the audience, the listeners. In fact, a great deal of the story is believed to be inside the listener; the storyteller's role is to draw the story out of the listeners.

LESLIE MARMON SILKO

"YOU DON'T GET IT, MAN," JOHNNY PARADISE SAID IN FRUSTRATION, pushing strands of gray hair off his face. "*Every afternoon* at three o'clock, the men in the yard called Cherubino a bad name. See? It was predictable. Like they knew what he would do.

"'*Tetona,*' one of the cons would say, sorta cupping his chest, like this. His line would double back along the guys coming out of Building B, and they could say anything they wanted about Cherubino's boobs without the screws hearing them. Then, oh man, the guy would explode.

"'*Zurullo!*' he'd shout—that's a kinda hard lumpy turd— '*Zurullo, zurullo, zurullo,* you motherfuckers!' And even though the guy was short, the fight was on. *Every afternoon.*"

Mr. Paradise slumped back in his chair with a big grin stretched across his thin face.

"You gotta admit prison is interesting. There's always something going down."

Johnny Paradise came to the Hillsdale Clinic from the Newtondale Hospital for the Criminally Insane. He never called it a hospital, nor did anyone else. It's simply Newtondale or prison. When I met him, he had just been moved from this institution to a small mental hospital and then to his first halfway house.

Johnny was a flexible switch of a man—thin arms, thin legs, thin neck—and he had about him a snappy quality, as if his reflexes might match the speed of his mind. He looked both older and younger than his stated age of forty-eight. His narrow New England face was weathered and beat-up, and it looked somewhat out of place riding atop such an energetic body. The overall impression was of an engaging old hippie, still smoking pot, still idealistic, still camping out on the edge of nowhere.

But beyond his age, his thinness, and his trickiness, it is useless to look for the beginning of this story, not Johnny's end of it, nor Cherubino's, God bless his short little soul. Johnny has plowed under both their pasts so completely that nothing remains. He once told me that he came from a family of writers—his mother wrote out recipes, his father etched names into trophies—and that he majored in drama until he OD'd on heroin twice in one day—but even quasi-historical facts such as these succumbed long ago to his imagination. Not even his real name—John Paradi—escaped artistic improvement, and before very long guards in the tank and docs in the clinic all called him Johnny Paradise: the one and only.

"It was like this," the ex-con explained as he danced into my office like a boxer on speed, ready to knock out therapy in a single round. "I got three to five for A and B with a dangerous weapon. Like a knife. And a policeman." He perched on the edge of a chair but immediately sprang up again. "Kicked his fat ass, and ended up in the slammer. But I got thrown in B. Good house. Smart guys. Shit, man, y'ave coffee?"

Mr. Paradise fired himself out the door like a squirrel jumping between two trees. Hardly had his old high-tops disappeared around the corner than I heard every door down the hall open and shut until he found the kitchen, three offices and a mop closet away. When I caught up to him, he had cooled off a quart of coffee with cold water and was pouring it down his throat without swallowing.

"OK," he said, bumping the pot hard on the counter and wiping his mouth with the back of his sleeve, "do your thing."

Christ, I thought, adopting Mr. Paradise's vernacular as we jogged back to the office, *what* thing?

Mr. Paradise had been sent to me for therapy. When New-tondale's officials finally realized that hell would freeze over before their man would burn out, they had managed to transfer him to a small experimental program for difficult men. Mr. Paradise was more difficult than anyone had bargained for, however, and he was enrolled in therapy both to calm him down and to help him fit in. For his part, Mr. Paradise detested the move. He missed the cons, "out to get you every minute," missed his buddy and protector, Cherubino Sentina, and missed being "KING, man. The best! The most! The *cagatintas* of the whole fucking yard! The one who shits ink, get it?"

And so the rowdy, homesick Mr. Paradise had started coming to the clinic bringing his prison along with him. Having visited the barren, self-contained complex at Newtondale myself, I was familiar enough with its layout to follow Mr. Paradise's telegraphic descriptions. When he said "hangin' out," I could picture him dressed in baggy prison grays kicking the tops off the dandelions that grow along the periphery of the gently sloping yard, or slouching in the shadow of the foreboding clock tower. When he said "wall," I saw sixteen feet of chain-link fence with neat coils of razor wire rolling along the top. And when he said "ice time," I could imagine him yanked from a restless crowd of cons and stuck in solitary for a few days for starting trouble. Trouble was what I usually got at the beginning of every hour. Typically, Mr. Paradise would arrive in such an agitated and disagreeable mood that I got a stomachache just thinking about our meeting.

"Fuck, man! Do we have to do this shit all over again?" he'd shout angrily. "What do you want me to say, huh? Hello?

Hello." He struck a ridiculously dramatic pose as he sat down. "'Tis no art to see the mind's construction in the face.' Shakespeare. So look at my face and you've got the answer, right? The big picture." He slumped back, sullenly hugging himself with his arms. On one I could see silver hatch marks made with a razor, running right up his forearm. "DIE" and "KILL" had been crudely printed in cigarette burns on either side. "Look, I'm . . . " he sighed deeply and closed his eyes as if in pain. "Fuck, the stones in my stomach are turning green."

At about this point, as he glowered ominously in the direction of the kitchen and I wondered if I shouldn't spend the rest of the hour in a commercial clothes dryer for relaxation, Mr. Paradise would moan a bit and finally throw himself on the floor. Then, with a great effort he would haul himself down the hall to drink whatever coffee remained in the coffeemaker. Sometimes he'd add a quart of water to purge from his system the medicines he took each morning. Depending on what he drank, a new man returned. I tried a little deep breathing while he was away and wondered if I could rub my stomach when he wasn't looking when he returned.

"So where did I learn to believe in God?" he asked, slouching back into the office and flopping into the corner chair. "From the prison high and my old buddy Bino." For a few moments Johnny Paradise sat back in his chair and waited. He crossed his skinny legs, half-closed his eyes, and let a bit of a smile tug at his mouth. "See, I have this quest like you can't imagine. I get this unreachable star shit and . . . DAMN, it's working. *Yes!*"

Eyes closed, hands gripping the arms of his chair, Johnny Paradise prepared for launching. I watched for the quiver of excitement that would run through his ropy limbs.

"Jesus!" he suddenly exploded, eyes snapping open, body jerking upright in the chair. "The best was the first in the morning. We'd line up to leave the block—Vinnie, Cherubino, me, the dozen of us—and we'd get Stelazine, Artane, Navane, melloroll—*all* that stuff—all the pills to start you off. So we tramp down to the chow hall," he continued eagerly, "for eight cups of coffee. Eight"—he shook ten fingers in my direction. "We drank outta these huge metal pitchers, like this high"—he demonstrated—"or bigger, man, like the biggest coffee pitchers. So I'm talking to Zeus and Agamemnon. I am impressing the shit outta them. And I end up Number One. But we had to get cigarettes, see?" And here he jumped up and frisked all his pockets. "Smoking activates the Artane, and with the first drag I'm flying, man. Flying."

Arms out, Johnny Paradise soared around my chair, narrowly missing my head, banked along the window wall then flew back toward his chair.

"I am defining North, South, East, and West." He pointed vaguely side to side. "Defining God and Jesus." Now up and down. "And all around me these real Steinbeck kinda guys are listening to me amid the banging and clanging of cannery row. Chow's *over*," he continued, his voice rising higher still, "and I watch them march out of that black chow hall. Every one of them bastards smoking, all in prison grays. Marching and smoking five and eight across. Jamming through the doors. Pouring out into the yard. A hundred steaming pistons, man, like a human machine.

"And there's Cherubino!" he shouted excitedly, his hands flying to his head as if astonished. "He's leading them outta the chow hall and back to the block and . . . and right into the john. Cherubino! Hey!"

His voice and arms dropped together, and he looked at me earnestly and a little sadly.

"He'll go into that john *alone* with the most dangerous men in the world, and . . . and I wanna help, but oh, Christ." He paused, giving me time to imagine the gray men storming in through the dim, low-ceilinged corridors of Building B, through the tall wire gates that cut the cell blocks off from one another, and into a damp room with low, seatless, stainless steel toilets. "Nothing to rip loose, nothing to drown in," a guard had told me. "We keep it real simple."

"And outta that good experience every morning," Mr. Paradise was saying slowly, "out of it I got, ah . . ."

He sat down again as if confused.

"Oh, I got adventures," he remembered. "Wonderful adventures, like the Treasure Island shit and Daniel Defoe. Like Cherubino and his tattooed boobs. What faith that man had." Mr. Paradise paused reverently. "Maybe it's the coffee talking, but the mornings were an adventure I've lost. Can't make it work here. Can't make anything work on two tiny fucking cups of coffee and no yard."

He fell silent for a while. "Maybe . . . no, I shouldn'ta drunk that coffee."

On good days Mr. Paradise leapt into my office in worn jeans and a T-shirt and told me Cherubino stories. On bad days, he slunk in with no coffee in his veins, looking beat, and told me nothing at all. He sat in the corner chair reading *Time* or sleeping or obsessively chewing his fingernails with a nasty crunching sound.

"I'm down now," he would say once or twice in an accusatory tone. "So go fuck yourself."

"Mr. Paradise . . . " I would begin.

"Lay off," he would mumble before trundling himself out the door and down the hall.

Ordinarily, this is not what is meant by a therapeutic exchange, and after even fifteen minutes or so of sleeping, reading, or swearing, a therapist would question what was going on. But with Mr. Paradise it seemed a shame to give up. For one thing, he was so vulnerable to the chemical highs and lows that his inconstant metabolism produced, that it was difficult to know where "genuinely depressed" left off and something ordinary like "rude" or "self-centered" began. For another, his highs were worth paying for. When he was "peaking, man, riding as high as I can go," he was outrageous. I think his best stories were about the bartering that went on in the yard—cigarettes being Newtondale's basic currency—and about Cherubino, the five-foot-four-inch Latino who in every other saga ended up in the john. I doubt that I would recognize him from Mr. Paradise's exaggerated descriptions, unless, of course, the man were bare-chested and I could see the Lamb of God and the *corazon sangrante* tattooed on either of his slightly pendulous breasts. But the credulous, uncomplicated Cherubino I had been led to imagine was all that the skinny Mr. Paradise was not.

"'Ay, man, you want protection?' he would shout at me after chow. 'Two pack! Two pack!' And if I had it, I'd give it. He was tough, like his cousin Vinnie. Short and tough. Fearless."

On this particular afternoon Johnny Paradise was wearing a new red- and white-striped T-shirt with the tags still on it, and he was grinning so happily that I was fairly sure he'd ditched the difficult men during their monthly shopping expedition and found some coffee.

"Whatcha gotta understand," Mr. Paradise was explaining excitedly, "is that the cons get together in the middle of the day to sell things. We steal coffee, hustle cigarettes, trade bullshit, and then we deal. Two-fer-one if you got no cash. Two pack for protection. Like that."

"And you'd sell this stuff right out of the dorms?" I asked, trying to imagine where a person could hide five pounds of coffee in a room so barren that even the bedclothes were stripped from the cots each morning.

"Stores are people, man—walking, talking supplies. I'm a store if I'm lying in the sun with my shirt off. Cherubino's a store when he hoses down the floor in the mess.

"So Cherubino works in the chow hall and he has coffee. I work nowhere and maybe I have nothing. But, hold on," he said, dramatically moving to the front of his chair and holding up his finger, "I have this Bible, man, and I know my way around it. So"—he paused again, smiling broadly—"I start telling them stories.

"One afternoon, see, I'm crazy—out of control, hallucinations all over my body—and I start playing the voice of God as Cherubino feeds me these packages of coffee." Here Mr. Paradise adopted the booming voice of a Pentecostal preacher. "'And I stood upon the sand of the sea and saw a beast rise up with seven heads and fourteen horns, and upon his horns were fourteen crowns and upon his crowns the name of blasphemy.'"

Johnny Paradise doubled over with glee at the memory. "Cherubino would sweat till there was water all over his face.

'You mean me, Johnny?' he'd say, scared as hell, sweat pouring off his face. He was in for murder, see, and afraid of the electric chair. Worried. Like really suffering. Vinnie, too, only Vinnie was uglier than a fart. We'd send him to castrate rats. So at just the right time I'd say, 'Lift up thine eyes, Cherubino, man, and have faith in Almighty God.' And he'd turn it right around— start laughin' and punchin' me and givin' me more coffee. Such spirit in that guy, you know. Such muscle. Such *bravery*! And all. . . ." And here Mr. Paradise nearly choked on emotion. "And all in such a short guy who don't even know about Magellan." He shook his head in disbelief and his stringy, shoulder-length hair flopped back and forth like a wet mop.

"So you trafficked stories. That was your 'store'?" I asked, hoping he'd elaborate a little on Vinnie and the rat business.

"Yeah, you might say that," he replied, suddenly tired. "I'd tell stories. We'd drink water to sober up. Then back to the block in time for the two P.M. blues to hit us like lead pipes."

"Up and down, huh?"

"Bravo, Doc. You got a way with words."

Once or twice, as what we were calling "therapy" staggered forward, I tried to get him to tell me about his childhood, but his imagination wouldn't let him. He could remember Gramercy Park in New York City—a swing, a fragrant patch of grass, a fix—but each picture from the past vaulted him into a novel of high adventure. You could say that his imagination overwhelmed all his other modes of thinking and was not charitable. It pursued him with relentless animations. It turned the pastrami sandwich he wanted to eat into a mangled corpse and the straight blue chair he wished to sit on into Niagara Falls. It turned his twelfth birthday party into a scene from *Lord of the Flies*.

Further, his relentless imagination demanded release, and he told me that it was uncomfortable for him to go for more than a day or so without spinning a yarn. He truly had the habit of words, this man, and if he did not tell a story for others, about others, he would find himself ambushed by plots that imposed themselves on his personal thoughts. The sight of dry leaves

pushed him to start an adventure story under his breath, and a
square of sunlight on my office floor once pulled from him glit-
tering sentences on love.

"Sometimes I turn my whole life into a story," Mr. Paradise
was saying in one of his rare pensive moods. "That's what writers do, you know."

He walked behind me to a window that looks out across a
parking lot and into a small park of oak trees, and began.

"'What does it all mean?' Bennett asked himself as he stood
by the window and looked out across the parking lot into a
small park of oak trees. Outside, a wind had sprung up and
brown leaves flew down from the sky like blackbirds settling on
an empty field of corn. The sun was going down. The cars were
leaving the parking lot one by one.

"I don't know," Mr. Paradise continued, extricating himself
from his story with a shake of his head. "Do other people wonder like this all day? Do they always want to know about this
wind, this bird, this parking lot . . . this small show?"

Several days later, I learned that trouble was brewing in the
halfway house where Johnny Paradise had lived now for about
three months. Although always a moody, difficult man, he was
apparently losing what little self-control he had and was becoming increasingly intimidating. He began leaping onto chairs and
angrily shouting poetry at his housemates then racing upstairs
and locking himself in the bathroom. He talked incessantly, and
he refused to talk. He could suddenly turn obsequious. He could
just as easily start a fight on the stairs.

"—Time for the slammer," he said to me, after being put on
restrictions. "Time for the third door."

Concerning these troubles, I had met several times with the
mental health aide from the halfway house who had been
assigned as Mr. Paradise's advocate or ombudsman. Raymond
was a gentle, slow-moving man who saw in Johnny a quickness
and a sensitivity that he believed was associated with genius. He
admired those portions of Johnny that he could understand and
charitably suspected that the rest was "philosophy." We both
agreed that the "Death be not proud shit" that came out of

Johnny's mouth and the "bare ruin'd choir" business "where late the sweet birds sang" could not be dismissed as psychotic noise.

"I think the men envy your way with words," Raymond once suggested when the three of us met in my office.

Mr. Paradise looked up at the ceiling and gave an exasperated sigh. "I'm walking up the stairs in front of Our Lady of Heartbreak," he said pointedly. "I reach the top and start to turn. Suddenly, I am *overwhelmed* by the certainty that nothing good will come of my life."

"That's being in a bad mood, isn't it?" asked Raymond tentatively.

"That's me going off my fucking rocker," Mr. Paradise shot back. "My mind is definitely not a steel trap. It's got holes, Raymond. It's a fishnet. An empty fishnet, and whose fucking fault is that?"

Raymond and I were slow to get the hint, nor was there much we could do even when he made his predicament clearer by goosing a resident of the halfway house with a lighted cigarette when the latter laughed at something Mr. Paradise said.

"I think you make them uncomfortable," Raymond said when the three of us were together again. "They don't understand what you say."

"All around him there were *nuts*," said Mr. Paradise, rising grandly from his chair as he often did when in a literary mood. He stood absolutely still, his skinny arms outstretched. "Here, there, and everywhere. The actor wouldn't move. He was frozen in a long yellow Monday. He knew that when darkness comes, the road stops. The nuts were frozen, too," he enunciated motionlessly. "Frozen nuts. 'I am performing for cubes,' the actor told himself and could not move."

"What's a storyteller to do without an audience?" I asked as Mr. Paradise dropped back down in his chair, a look of complete disgust on his thin face.

"You tell me, Doc. You're the expert."

Raymond and I looked at each other helplessly.

"He's right, you know," I finally said with a shrug. "He needs listeners."

Several days after Mr. Paradise had spelled out his curiously ordinary problem, I learned that he had broken a coffeepot at the halfway house and stomped after his roommate with a piece of broken glass.

"He's headed out," Raymond told me over the phone. "As soon as we can find a bed, he's off to the hospital."

Although not before showing up for one last appointment on the following day, hand wrapped with filthy gauze. He seemed to be in a somber and curiously reasonable mood.

"I hear you're leaving," I said, as he sat down carefully and crossed his tube-like legs.

"Yeah."

"Know where you're going?"

"Some hospital. Saint something."

"Good place for stories?"

Mr. Paradise looked at me briefly and smiled. "No. No good stories in the hospital. No energy." He sighed as if deciding whether or not to let me in on the problem. "See, in a hospital they drive a man's energy out with pills," he explained. "Big-time downers. If they can make you hate yourself"—he shrugged— "then you don't give 'em a hard time." Mr. Paradise collected what little energy remained in his decaffeinated system and leaned forward.

"It's like this. You can't tell a story to someone who's asleep or crazy, because he's gotta *know* how the story goes. You know what I mean? He's gotta know where to light up. Now Cherubino and Vinnie—Christ, what a noiseless rocket that Vinnie was—"

"A what?" I interjected.

"A fart, man, but they both knew how to fly. Short guys, but they could get right up there with you and give the story a lift. Lotta sadness in their lives to build on.

"I remember one time when Sentina was down. Scared from some transfer papers they'd given him—so scared he got the shits. So in the middle of the night I find him taking a crap, an' I say, 'Hey, man, let's sneak a butt an' I'll tell you about Ron and Don.' We all knew those stories about the fat-assed twins who wanted to play in the movies."

Mr. Paradise was smiling now at the recollection. His blue eyes squinted into moons and his wide mouth revealed the customary mosaic of gold- and ivory-colored teeth. The giddiness was returning.

"So I hustle back to the dorm and steal a butt," he continued, elaborately lighting an invisible cigarette, "and Cherubino and I sit on the crappers and get high on stories. I tell him about the time we catch the twins trying to shoot the Lone Ranger on television. An' I play the voices and do my Tonto routine. He had a high little laugh for a brave man, Cherubino did. A kinda 'heee, heee' little laugh. But it was good. We could generate the heat."

"And then?" I asked.

"And then the screws start yelling"—he laughed—"and back we go. But I gave Cherubino a good heee, heee. Bullshit and laughs, man. That's my store."

"So," I said slowly, to no one in particular, "he gives the lift. You give the laughs. But in a hospital or a halfway house, no listeners, no laughs, no deals . . . no nothing."

Mr. Paradise thought for a while. "That's good," he said. "That's about right. It's like ice time, and they know you can't survive in ice."

And then, as if I might be the last listener he'd encounter for a while, Johnny Paradise leaned farther forward still, rested his forearms on his rail-like knees, and told me one last time about Cherubino Sentina and the john.

"I remember one dark, rainy, son-of-a-bitch afternoon," he began, frowning dramatically. "Cherubino and I had been hangin' out in the mess hall. He was hosin' the place down after chow, an I was eatin' coffee with a spoon, see? So it's still pouring, an we get fucking soaked walking back to the block.

"Shit hole," he added.

"We hated afternoons," he went on, shaking his head. "No energy. Deep pain. But this time we went to the day room where

Bert, Vinnie . . . Gorilla Montero, Larry—a bunch a' guys—
were playing cards *and*—this is where it gets interesting—
Cherubino decides to deal himself into this game."

Johnny Paradise straightened up and slid to the edge of his
chair, the better to pantomime the action. "Now picture these
guys around the table. Cherubino and Vinnie on one side—
short, thick necks, man, real thick necks, like . . . like Aztec
kings or something. And Larry across from them—fuckin'
dumbo, that guy, a regular lot lizard—and Gorilla on the side,
sorta controlling things. You know what I mean, you could tell
he was in a pissin' mood by the way he sat all crouched forward
an' wound up. There was bad feeling on that block as long as
that ape was around.

"So I'm sitting three chairs off reading some old Carl Sand-
burg shit about smokestacks when I hear Montero say, 'Whasa
matter, Sentina, your ass won't sit right?' An' Sentina says right
back to this big guy, 'That'll cost you a ball, faggot.' And in *one
second*—holy shit!—the four of them are up and out the door,
heading for the john. Four hot men, hot men." Mr. Paradise was
rattling along now like an auctioneer. "Boiling inside, man, boiling, and all in for murder. Gives you that don't-care style, and
these guys didn't." He leapt from his chair and ran toward the
windows, his tattered high-tops slapping the floor.

"I run down the hall after them an' stop at the door, see? I'm
lookout." He grabbed the cranks that open the office windows.
"Je-sus Christ! It was murder. Those men went at it in the back
stall like stallions. The kicking was thunder. Bang! Crash! Crack!
Slam!" He was shouting now. "A murderous fight. Holy shit!
Fighting on medication, man, with the most dangerous men in
the world." He paused for an instant. "An' then I hear Cherubino"—Mr. Paradise pressed his head tight against the louvered
windows—"I hear, 'Get away from me, faggot!' Grunting and
then this horrible, high, kind of pig-sticking scream that . . . oh,
Christ!"

Johnny Paradise remained pressed against the louvered windows, his scarred hands gripping the cranks and tears running
down his face.

"*Fucking son of a bitch!*" Paradise exploded, whirling away from the window and socking the back of an empty chair, which went sliding across the bare floor.

I leapt for the door, but he stopped where he was, doubled over and holding his bandaged hand. "Oh, shit, what the . . . ?" Mr. Paradise straightened slowly and stood as if dazed in the middle of the office. Still holding his hand, he walked back to the corner chair.

"So I . . . they jumped him . . . Cherubino," he continued hesitantly as he sat down and tried to find his place in the story. "Bastards." He was silent for a minute and a curious argument seemed to run back and forth across his features. His mouth tried to make words, but he was losing ground.

"Johnny," I said quickly before he drifted out of reach into his other mood, irritable and despairing, "you got that story all mixed up."

He said nothing.

"What happened to *you*?"

Mr. Paradise looked past me. "Me?" He paused. "I wrote 'Death and Insanity' on the bathroom wall and flew through the window."

"Who got you?"

"Montero," he said flatly, giving a little twitch to his shoulders. "Happens to everyone. You take pills, your head flies off, you get hustled by queers. Then noises go off in your head."

"Johnny, who stands up to this guy?" I finally asked.

Johnny Paradise dipped his head to the side as if casually ducking a wrecking ball that had been swinging in his direction. He looked me in the eye.

"Why, Cherubino," he said with relief. "That was the point I lost track of. He was *fearless* even when the booty bandits took him on, sons of bitches. '*Zurullo!*' he'd shout at those mother-fuckers. And even though the guy was short, he fought *every afternoon*.

"So Cherubino and Vinnie go back to playing cards. Can you believe it, man? They sat right down at that table with their thick necks and big brown hands that could lift a fucking tank—human forklifts; Marlon Brando kinda guys—and Bino says to me outta the side of his mouth, like this, he says, 'Watch me beat this dumb-assed son of a bitch'—and he could, too.

"Cherubino with cards . . . ? Let me tell you what was going down. . . ."

Johnny Paradise rode off into another story. He had forgotten his bandaged hand, forgotten the bed waiting for him in St. Something Hospital. He was the king again, and beneath sparkling banners of electric obscenities he led me, as he had led so many before, out of the dark humiliations of prison life back toward the victories of skill and spirit. As he continued to speak in his death-defying way, I pictured him sitting on a cot in one of the low-ceilinged dorms with half a dozen men sprawled around him. The plastic sheathing on the wire-covered windows dimmed the light and gave the room a hazy blue cast. Brittle mattress covers crackled each time a body shifted. And there was Johnny Paradise, describing the fight of a lifetime between men who, with the help of his vision, turned into wild stallions, who broke through walls and galloped over every fence in the world. He was reliving that daily escape from prison for his listeners and telling them a deeper truth about themselves than they had the courage or imagination to grasp. For me, as for the others, Mr. Paradise turned Newtondale into a great arena. And so it remains, because in my mind I cannot separate the misery I have seen there from the stories that Johnny Paradise loved to tell.

"And *that*," he concluded, "if you get my meaning, is why we were afraid of *nobody*." He sat back in his chair with a look of satisfaction I had rarely seen on his face before.

Later that week Mr. Paradise and his inconstant memories went off to the hospital and there, with more medications but still fewer listeners, he slid into the kind of arm-cutting, word-burning depression he had known lay ahead. I heard that he didn't speak at all for several weeks, and that they thought of giving him shock treatments to start him up again.

But he has reemerged, this man who reels with the shock of ordinary experience and who turns everything he encounters into tales of amazement. After six or eight dreary months, he left the hospital and reluctantly moved into another halfway house, where he is again attempting to bully his listeners into a legendary world. Knowing Mr. Paradise, it will be a crazy world—an imprecise, exaggerated world—but one that makes of battered men heroes who can survive present insults and former disappointments.

"Do other people wonder like this all day?" he had asked. "Do they always want to know about this wind, this bird, this parking lot . . . this small show?"

"No," I should have told him then, "not everyone has to work so hard to stay in touch. But the few who do," I might have added, "are the singers and the storytellers—the explainers. And when these people weave themselves back into the world, they often mend a larger community as well."

GOOD STORIES,
GOOD THERAPIES

*I am myself and what is around me, and if I do
not save it, it shall not save me.*

ORTEGA Y GASSET

JOHNNY PARADISE SPENT A GREAT DEAL OF ENERGY TRYING TO
weave himself back into whatever community he found himself
in. Whenever he was displaced, either physically by being moved
to a hospital or emotionally by being pulled up and down by his
inconstant moods, he groped around like a stranger for a time.
He did not know where he was, and he did not know *who* he
was in this new place or state of mind. Like a person suddenly
widowed, he was at odds with his own identity until he could
talk his way into a slightly different and better-fitting version of
himself. It is a curious fact of human nature that a person cannot make sense of himself unless he feels understood by someone else. It is more curious still that this process of seeking to be
understood through storytelling is the same process that makes
of individuals a community.

"Where does the healing power of the story lie?" Bennett
Simon asks in his book *Mind and Madness in Ancient Greece*.
He considers the story's power to lull and comfort—perhaps it

reminds us of being read to as children in our mother's lap. He notes that stories awaken, intensify, and clarify many of our own feelings. In ways we do not fully understand, the experience of listening to a tale that is to some degree uncanny—simultaneously familiar and strange—releases painful feelings. Finally, he talks about shared experience. He believes that when people—alone or together—listen to "a tale that expresses the group's fundamental values, beliefs, and aspirations," the experience serves "to restore us to and reintegrate us with that group."[1] Hearing a story invites the listener to "rejoin the larger community." Although Simon is specifically talking about great stories—the epic poetry of ancient Greece—he believes his ideas hold true to some degree for all storytelling in every age and culture. Each time we are truly caught up in a story that is more than merely a complaint, we have the chance to redefine and restore, if only slightly, our relationship to family, community, gods, heroes, "and ultimately all human beings."[2]

And yet we have seen that there are many and varied barriers to this kind of doubly directed understanding. In the world of the mentally ill, if there are no listeners who already understand the gist of the schizophrenic's or depressed person's story who can say, "The same thing once happened to me," clients who feel like strangers are not likely to reconnect either to the community or to themselves. We have also seen that a great deal of what is called clinical training further widens an unfortunate gulf between client and therapist, and that this pattern of mutual distrust is passed on through generations of clinicians. Economic constraints and the supposedly efficient but actually controlling, impersonal, and disrespectful treatments that are developed to balance budgets and meet regulations are yet additional obstacles to any real understanding. In short, there are many walls blocking the kind of free and impassioned exchange of stories that holds a community together. Listening is no longer cost-effective; passion is not professional.

1. Bennett Simon, *Mind and Madness in Ancient Greece* (Ithaca, NY: Cornell University Press, 1978), p. 79.

2. Simon, *Mind and Madness in Ancient Greece*, p. 79.

But "something there is that doesn't love a wall," as Robert Frost says. Thus some of the barriers to understanding that we have considered in chapter 14 are being undermined both by our culture's cautious willingness to extend respect to minorities, whose views have not always seemed to lie along the road to progress, and, within the clinic, by therapists' growing readiness to build more egalitarian relationships with these same people. As Leston Havens writes, "The work of psychological healing rests on the resources of the emerging culture."[3] We are not without resources.

At the risk of oversimplifying a complex situation, let me suggest that the forces that best break down walls are respectfulness and responsiveness. I don't know to what extent these can be taught—after all, both require courage and self-confidence—but they can be encouraged or discouraged. Training programs, clinical settings, regulations—all the things that together make up the context of clinical work—either encourage a therapist to go off on her own into the always uncharted territory of an individual's life or to hold back and stick with the group. My own feeling is that many therapists, *if left alone sufficiently*, have enough innate curiosity and kindness to get deeper and deeper into their occupation. They become increasingly willing to see the world from different perspectives and increasingly able to develop intensely personal relationships with a wider and wider variety of people. If given the chance, they put aside formulas and diagnoses, risk traveling alone, and become enthralled with what they find.

The poet and pediatrician William Carlos Williams argued early for a truly passionate connection between doctor and patient. Dazzled and fascinated by all kinds of people, his goal was to resonate like a tuning fork to the poetry of their lives.

"I lost myself in the very properties of their minds," he wrote. "For the moment at least I actually became *them*, whoever they should be. . . ." He adopted their conditions as his own, he maintained, and although this was not easy, and the

3. Leston Havens, *Coming to Life* (Cambridge: Harvard University Press, 1993), p. 70.

union was sometimes blocked by disliking or distrust, more often the merger resulted in a flash of deep, mutual recognition and in what Williams bravely recognized was love.

"I sure met a wonderful girl," he said to his wife in a story in *The Doctor Stories*.[4]

"What! Another?"

"Some tough baby. I'm crazy about her."

Or again, with a different patient, "I had to smile to myself, after all, I had already fallen in love. . . ."

Yet another, for whom he had "a sort of love," captured him with "the peculiar turn of her head and smile" by which he knew her.

Leston Havens seems to point to this same willingness to be captivated when he describes the therapeutic bond as "this liking, so like a loving."[5] And Bruno Bettelheim discussed these feelings, although less flamboyantly, when he spoke of sinking into his patient's position and actually feeling the patient's perspective. He used words like "fellowship" and "allegiance" to describe the "intensely personal relationship" that hopefully develops as doctor and patient embark upon a mutual journey of discovery. He was against feeling superior to patients. He was for the realization that "we are all alike in one most fundamental way, in our need to be loved and cared for."[6]

It is rarely possible to point with any precision to the experiences that deflect an eager student away from the exciting business of chasing down pathological states and toward the far more difficult and dangerous activity of responding to a life. In Robert Coles's case, however, he has reconstructed the events that pushed him from his early aspirations as a theoretician toward his lifelong career as listener and storyteller.

Coles's older supervisor, who initially seemed rather dense and old-fashioned, kept telling the young resident, "What ought

4. William Carlos Williams, *The Doctor Stories* (New York: New Directions, 1984), p. 51.

5. Havens, *Coming to Life*, p. 4.

6. Bruno Bettelheim and Alvin A. Rosenfeld, *The Art of the Obvious: Developing Insight for Psychotherapy and Everyday Life* (New York: Alfred A. Knopf, 1993), p. 235.

to be interesting is the unfolding of a lived life rather than the confirmation such a chronicle provides for some theory." This was surprising advice for Coles. Revolutionary, in fact. His supervisor was suggesting that doctors ought to pull up a chair and listen, that they ought to follow rather than lead, that they ought to get right in there and empathize rather than hold themselves aloof.

To Coles's credit, he gave the advice some thought, and when he asked his patients for an old-fashioned story, he was astonished by what he discovered. For one thing, his patients changed, right there before his eyes. This one smiled and asked if she could get her cigarettes. That one said, "You tell me your story, and I'll tell you mine." Then, from this new atmosphere of camaraderie, flowed streams of stories. Coles was told about ordinary fears and disappointments that didn't fit terribly well into diagnostic slots. He was told about a particular beating on a New Year's Eve, about two happy moments in an entire life, the memory of this cluttered kitchen and that dented car. He was intrigued but uncomfortable.

"Maybe I was committing the sort of error all first-year residents make," he thought to himself, "an error one older psychiatrist had in fact described: I'd allowed the patient's 'agenda' to take over, had become bogged in a morass of circumstantial detail. Where would I go now, anyway, in the further sessions that awaited both the patient and me?"[7]

Worried that he had become a follower instead of the leader, Coles wasn't even sure he'd have time to pack all these stories into the next supervisory hour. Their very size made them awkward to work with.

"I did manage to tell it all," Coles remembered, and his supervisor's response "marked an altogether crucial moment in my postgraduate education."[8]

"Each patient will tell you a different story," the old-fashioned Dr. Ludwig said to him, "and you're an all-day listener."

7. Robert Coles, *The Call of Stories: Teaching and the Moral Imagination* (Boston: Houghton Mifflin, 1989), p. 13.
8. Coles, *The Call of Stories*, p. 13.

"Then what?" asked Coles, in effect.

"Write brief biographies of the patients," Coles remembers him saying, rather than listing their symptoms.

"The upshot of that weekly experience with Dr. Ludwig was a turnabout in my way of working," wrote Coles.[9]

Not only did he become captivated by the concrete details of his patients' lives, he also became interested in capturing the vitality of their stories. But at first he could not. In fact, his early reports, although no longer oriented toward theory or pathology per se, still lacked spirit. When his wife criticized him severely for turning his young polio patients, whom she described as their friends, into soulless cases, Coles was jolted and annoyed.

"I was upset at her reference to friendship. True, we'd all become quite familiar with one another, but they were *patients* of mine, I hastened to remind my wife. Her response boiled down to 'So what?'"[10]

Coles challenged his wife to show him how she would present a better portrayal of a person. Two weeks later she handed him a description of a young woman with polio.

"The story was deeply affecting, and in its own way poignantly 'psychological,' full of the girl's memories, her hopes and fears, her constant worries. I was surprised; I felt ashamed; I was envious; I got angry. . . . After I cooled down I went to see Dr. Ludwig with a copy of my wife's chronicle. He was quite taken with her project and wrote to tell her so. I was beginning to be convinced. . . ."[11] Convinced, that is, that the power of description comes from one's willingness to respond to and be moved by the patients. To connect passionately, as Williams used to say. Or to sink into the patient's position, and let yourself be gripped by stories, as Bettelheim and Simon put it, respectively.

Coles's training, ordinary in its intent, unusual in its results, anticipated the changes in psychotherapeutic thinking that are

9. Coles, *The Call of Stories,* p. 14.
10. Coles, *The Call of Stories,* p. 28.
11. Coles, *The Call of Stories,* p. 28.

unfolding today—albeit in the face of great resistance. His willingness to immerse himself in the life, rather than merely document its problems, and his respect for his patients led him away from the old role of scientific expert and toward the newer stance of a biographer of valuable lives. The result, documented in Coles's forty-some books, is not a new theory of knowledge or a new standard of rigor in the documentation of lives. It is vitality.

That vital therapy and vital case histories spring from a wholehearted responsiveness to one's clients comes as no surprise to biographers who, over centuries, have adopted many kinds of relationships to their subjects—many more than therapists have experimented with. Biographers have tried amassing mountains of facts. They have also praised uncritically and exposed unmercifully. Currently, however, there is a growing realization among them that a biography is a joint production of two lives, the result of "a contest of singers," in James Hillman's felicitous phrase. For the portrayal of a complete, convincing, and vital life, the quality of the biographer's response to his or her subject is all important: "It is only when he fails to respond fully . . . that he truly betrays that life by robbing it of its vitality and produces one of those vast mournful compendia that add, someone once said, a new terror to dying."[12]

Marc Pachter, editor of Telling Lives, a collection of essays written for a symposium on biography, goes on to say that biographers must have "a passion for life." They must have an intense desire to chase after, fight for, respond to, and contend with another person's experience. The best have a "near-missionary drive to save, if not a soul then a personality for the company of future generations."[13] Here, in literary rather than clinical terms, is that persistent, respectful manner of working together.

As an example, Pachter quotes Catherine Drinker Bowen, biographer of the famous American physician, Oliver Wendell Holmes.

12. Marc Pachter, ed., *Telling Lives: The Biographer's Art* (Washington, D.C.: New Republic Books, 1979), p. 7.
13. Pachter, *Telling Lives,* p. 4.

The more I learned about Oliver Wendell Holmes, the more insupportable it became to think of him as dead, cold, and motionless beneath that stone at Arlington. I found myself possessed of a witch's frenzy to ungrave this man, stand him upright, see him walk, jump, dance, tell jokes, make love, display his vanity or his courage as the case might be.

Even biographers whose subjects have "tough personalities" and were not well or widely liked find themselves enthralled.

"I was alternately attracted and repelled by Leo [Szilard, the Hungarian who envisioned the atomic chain reaction and helped design the first atomic reactor]," said William Lanouette, author of *Genius in the Shadows*, "and I think a lot of people were. He was his own worst enemy. I'd be praising him and then say, 'Oh, Leo. Why did you do that?'"[14]

The list of intrigued biographers could go on and on. After all, said Victoria Glendinning, one of Anthony Trollope's recent biographers, "I think you are fond of anyone you spend time with. People shut up in prisons get fond of spiders."[15]

In short, biographers already accept the idea that they will enter into an intimate and dynamic dialogue. They will applaud and later despair. They will get too close to their subjects then find themselves too far away. They will work at absorbing a lifetime of experience then try to distill it into a complete, convincing, and vital portrait of a life. They will, if possible, save a personality.

Bettelheim and Alvin Rosenfeld take up the case for the

14. William Lanouette, quoted in Lynn Karpen, "A Dream: Szilard and Liverwurst," *New York Times Book Review*, 24 January 1993, p. 23.

15. Victoria Glendinning, quoted in Lynn Karpen, "She Sat Down Beside Him," *New York Times Book Review*, 31 January 1993, p. 23. In all likelihood Glendinning was referring to Nien Cheng's account of solitary confinement described in *Life and Death in Shanghai* (New York: Penguin, 1986). As Cheng worried about her own safety and the dangers that ultimately proved fatal for her daughter, she befriended a small spider who lived beneath her toilet seat. "My small friend seemed rather weak. It stumbled and stopped every few steps. Could a spider get sick, or was it merely cold? . . . It made a tiny web . . . forming something rather like a cocoon. . . . When I had to use the toilet, I carefully sat well to one side so that I did not disturb it" (p. 155).

fearlessly empathic therapist in more conventional terms. In *The Art of the Obvious*, they seek to pull young interns and residents back from the impersonal world of charts, facts, and treatment plans and push them toward the development of intensely personal and respectful relationships with their patients. Urging them to prepare for a new patient the way you prepare for an honored guest in your home, they stress the importance of the therapist's willingness to learn from the patient, to follow him or her on a long journey that only the patient can direct. Like a biographer in some respects, Bettelheim's ideal therapist is driven by curiosity to see the world from the patient's perspective. To do so, such a therapist is willing to resonate to the anxiety, uncertainty, and tumultuous emotions that the patient experiences. Again like a biographer, such a clinician finds him- or herself standing too close one minute then holding the patient off the next as both their anxieties and desires rise and fall.[16]

James Hillman is still another who sees parallels between biographer and clinician; in fact, he has called therapists the new historians. But that was yesterday—today, he has gone a step farther. He feels that those who wish to help heal the troubled psyche must follow the ideals of respect and responsiveness to their logical conclusions; that is, *therapists must clarify rather than modify* the essential eccentricities that are brought to them. As his coauthor, Michael Ventura, says, "We are not trying to discover and treat a disease, we are trying to invent and speak a language. *That* is the treatment, to speak and listen to the life; and the goal isn't that the life heal, or become normal, or even cease its suffering, but that *the life become more itself*, have more integrity with itself, be more true to its daimon."[17]

This is indeed revolutionary (or as a family therapist might say, this is the ideal prescription for negotiating adolescence, for allowing a person to break away from the family or group and

16. Bettelheim and Rosenfeld, *The Art of the Obvious*, p. 214.

17. James Hillman and Michael Ventura, *We've Had a Hundred Years of Psychotherapy—And the World's Getting Worse* (San Francisco: Harper-Collins, 1992), p. 151.

become different). Hillman wants therapists to *"encourage,* maybe even inflame—the rich and crazy mind."[18] No more cooling out the symptoms as if every paranoid thought and anxiety was an error in judgment or a screw working loose. No more shutting down the imagination by returning disgruntled patients to the kinds of lives that made them unbearably restless in the first place.

"We have to work on cures that are beyond *my* cure. That's revolution. That's realizing that things out there are dysfunctional. That's the therapeutic task. It's not to tell a person how to fight or where to fight, but [to give him] the *awareness* of dysfunction in society, in the outer world."[19]

So Hillman maintains that therapy's job is to help people protest against the elements in society (as well as in their minds) that imprison them. Especially when conventional styles of living are no longer moving our society in salutary directions, it is time to encourage new ways of living—not time to enforce conformity. Seen from this perspective, every case of what we call a mental illness is also an unwitting experiment in imaginative adaptation—a new way of getting along in an increasingly confusing world.

"Too black and white," said Dr. H., shaking his head and leaning back in his squeaky chair. "You're making it sound as if there are two kinds of people, normal and abnormal. Ha!

"Imagine, for a minute, that you're climbing a mountain. You're walking along wearing a pack—you and a companion— and you're on a well-marked trail. . . ." Dr. H. paused, and we each constructed a mountain range of rocks and trees that rose unevenly into the blue summer sky outside his office window.

"You're on the red trail," he continued, scribbling dots across his blotter with a red pen, "when your companion says, 'Will you look down there! A little canyon. You want to ah . . . ?' And you say 'Well, I'm not . . . , but yeah, OK, a little ways.' So the two of you leave the red trail," and here he walked his chair

18. Hillman and Ventura, *We've Had a Hundred Years of Psychotherapy,* p. 75.

19. Hillman and Ventura, *We've Had a Hundred Years of Psychotherapy,* p. 219.

across the office very cautiously, "and you start down this narrow canyon. 'I wonder where this branch leads?' one of you asks, and off you go in still another direction. Sometimes you agree to stop the experiment. 'Look, we have to get back to the trail,' you say. But perhaps the next time you don't. You like the sense of adventure. You like this needing to be aware of what's going on, which you don't have on the trail.

"'Oops,' you say. 'May have stayed out a little too . . . Shadows getting long and . . .' And sometimes that's a real mistake—people get hurt or hospitalized. And sometimes you'll find a person who is simply superb in such a situation—inventive, practical. He's useless on the trail. Keeps wandering off. Gets bored. Doesn't make sense. But let him lose his way in a canyon at nightfall . . . and he comes to life."

Hillsdale's wandering psychiatrist shoved off from the far wall of his office and came rolling back to his desk.

"Do you see what I'm getting at?" he asked. "There are hundreds of ways to climb a mountain. Some people always stick to the trail, but others experiment. They never climb it the same way twice. I wouldn't want to generalize and say that everyone on the trail is normal and everyone in the bushes is crazy, or that all experiments are good ideas. I would say, however, that if a person sticks to the road and walks right along the white line, very carefully, he will *never* think for himself. Every experiment is better in that one way; it involves thought."

There is an unexpected and exhilarating corollary to Hillman's proposition, which becomes easy to see using the metaphor of the mountain. If troubled clients are in some ways restless inventors of unusual ways of thinking, and if their attempts merit our respectful attention rather than our immediate disdain, then the responsive therapist will find that a great deal of his or her day is spent off the beaten track. Rather than plodding along the white line in the middle of the road, unimaginatively writing out behavioral contracts that encourage compliance to "normal" standards, mornings will be spent walking into overgrown fields to admire models of the Concorde made from toothpicks or to watch large holes being dug. Afternoons will be spent in a swamp sampling the black ooze of psychotic depression—figuring out if it's good for something. And evenings? With luck, evenings will bring that liking, so like a loving, that lets you travel along the faint trail of another's memory and lets you light the pathway as you go. This is what respectful and responsive therapy can give to therapists—if they are left alone, and if they dare. This is how they learn to *think*— about the patient, the illness, and themselves. Trips into the canyon are the payoff.

And what of the stories that are told as two people leave the road under the hot afternoon sun and set out along the canyon's rocky floor? How do these tales differ from those told by travelers who stick to the road?

Early one summer morning a young woman came into my office having just been released from a hospital where she had spent three weeks recovering from a manic episode and a serious attempt to kill herself. Still shaken and divided, she sounded like a person who has been awakened abruptly from a dream and is embarrassed by the fragments of fantasy still caught in her voice. Sitting down in my office, she tried hard to relocate the white line in the road.

"Did you see the episode coming?" I asked her.

"Well, sort of . . . but not at first," she answered hesitantly. "I really thought I had the flu. I couldn't sleep. I was throwing up. I was just getting . . . depleted, I guess. I knew something was going on when I, ah, saw Gordon's face in . . . But I didn't hear voices," she added quickly, "just these images of Gordon."

The young woman turned away from me and gazed raptly into an empty corner of the office. Then, with the slightest shake of her head, she brought herself back.

"The lithium must have been out of my system by then— what with the throwing up and all. My mind wasn't working right. I mean, I hadn't meant to go off the meds, but when I do"—she exhaled suddenly—"thinking falls apart."

We sat in silence for a minute or two, and it seemed to me that she went right back to the empty corner of my office and to her memories of her former boyfriend, Gordon.

"If you had never been ill," I finally said to her, "and had no label struck to your forehead saying 'manic-depressive,' do you think your friends might have interpreted your vision as a sign? That when you saw Gordon in—"

"In my date, in Dennis," she said excitedly, picking up the theme. "I'd gone out dancing with Dennis two days before the hospital, and it was *weird*, I mean really *creepy*, but Gordon's face just, like, appeared. And his arms, his chest, even his shirt— the shirt I'd given him the Christmas before he died. I was dancing with Gordon, like he was . . ."

Out came her own story then, tumbling over the barriers that "lithium" and "psychotic thinking" had temporarily placed in her way. God had indeed given her a sign, she believed. He had allowed Gordon to come back from heaven for a day so that she could decide whether or not to remain on earth.

"THIS IS THE DEAL," intoned the voice of God over music so loud that it was hard for her to know exactly who she was listening to. Yet into this confusion and out of this confusion she spun, twirling around the dance floor with Gordon and Dennis wrapping their arms around her pink-flowered dress, one pulling her toward earth, the other toward heaven. "LEAVE NOW WITH GORDON, OR STAY AND MAKE A LIFE FOR YOURSELF."

"Only the deal wasn't nearly that clear," she continued, her eyes beginning to fill with tears at the memory of that beautiful and terrifying night. "God said it was a sin to . . . to *want* to die so bad, but when Gordon talked to me . . ." She stopped and looked me straight in the eye. "I had him back, you know. I really did."

I told this sobbing girl the story of Orpheus and Eurydice then—as well as I could remember it. I said that Orpheus was longing for his girlfriend who had died, and he wanted to see her again so badly that he risked "passing beyond the terrible threshold" to get her. Finding her in the underworld, he told the rulers there the story of his love. They were moved, and they let him take Eurydice back to the ordinary world. But he must not look at her directly. He was only allowed to sense her presence behind his back. When he turned by mistake to make sure she was with him, she was taken away.

"That's it," my client breathed in astonishment. "That's exactly what happened to me."

The conversation didn't end there, as I believe it would have had we stuck to the old "take your meds and you'll be fine" routine. Instead, the young woman—almost frantically relieved to learn that someone else had been given the chance to embrace a person he thought he had lost forever—began trying on alternate interpretations. Had God or the Devil sent this vision? What had it meant, she wondered. Would Gordon come again? Did she want him to? Without formally saying good-bye, the manic episode slipped from the office, and was replaced by an event that was intriguing, significant, and personal—an event that fit this woman's picture of herself, that joined her to the traditions of the Western world, and that gave her the right to consider having a life rather than a disability.

It is indeed a curious fact of human nature that a person cannot make sense of himself unless he feels deeply understood by someone else, unless he can stand in for the hero of some story other than his own. And it does seem more curious still that this process of seeking to be understood through storytelling is the process that creates the bonds we call community.

"Conversation is the socializing instrument par excellence," wrote Ortega y Gasset, "and in its style one can see reflected the capacities of a race."

Learning a great variety of stories that are passed back and forth among ourselves in conversation connects us to history. Being part of those stories gives us an identity and a life within the family of man.

17

DANGEROUS LISTENING

Go right on and listen as thou goest.
DANTE, *DIVINE COMEDY, PURGATORIO*

What we do is intimate. Good therapists play at the net—very fast, very close.
WILLIAM HALLSTEIN

MAGGIE BISHOP LOVED TO WALK. THE DAY I MET HER SHE HAD walked four miles to the Hillsdale Clinic from a small apartment on the edge of town where she both lived and worked. She had come, she stated, because at fifty-four she could no longer afford to be ill.

"You've read the chart," the gray-haired, rosy-cheeked woman said with a grimace, waving a weathered hand in the direction of my desk. "Every year or two I have a terrible episode. Manic. Unbelievable. I can't afford to have them anymore."

The attractively energetic Miss Bishop began to enumerate the costs of manic-depressive illness, as she obviously had done before.

"Education, career, marriage, family." She counted them off
on her fingers. "The first attack positively blindsided me. I was
a novitiate at Marymount studying to be a high school teacher
when this illness . . . " She paused briefly. "All my life I've
wanted to be a nun and a teacher," she said thoughtfully. "My
sister Beth and I used to drape towels over our heads and belt in
our nightgowns to look like the sisters at Our Lady of Loretta.
We even had a shrine in the barn among Uncle Nunzi's extra
castings of the Virgin Mary."

Miss Bishop went on to explain that she had grown up
under the influence of a powerful grandmother who, having
given up on guiding her own bookish daughter toward a life in
the church, had pinned her hopes on the next generation. In
other words, Nanna DiLupini had set out to make Maggie a
nun. With the benefits of hindsight, Miss Bishop thought she
could see that the result was a three-way tug-of-war. She had felt
drawn to the church with its seductive drama safely contained
within a rigorous order, drawn toward her mother's fantasy of
academe, and drawn reluctantly toward a bright and bitterly
disappointed father who always talked of "possibilities." Before
the illness had begun to batter her hopes, Miss Bishop said, she
had survived the tension pretty well. Her older brother had been
a runaway, her younger sister the underachiever, while she herself had been, "Well . . . the one with possibilities."

With an appealing earnestness Miss Bishop went on to
describe her not insignificant accomplishments. Sitting forward
in the corner chair, her hands miming the story she had begun to
tell, she outlined her struggle to complete college and serve in
the church. Withdrawing from Marymount due to her illness,
she had transferred to a state university where she not only completed her undergraduate degree but eventually earned a master's in English which equipped her to teach. As for the church,
she had hovered around the fringe for a decade, volunteering in
a parochial school, but never feeling welcome. She didn't blame
them for being wary, she explained, for in those days, she simply
blasted her way toward her goals.

"It was a happy time," she said uncertainly, still sitting forward in her chair, "but scrambled. Even the most intense . . . I

mean the most memorable things just, I don't know, evapo-
rated."

"Like what?" I asked.

Miss Bishop blushed slightly as she gazed intently over a
troubled landscape of reflections.

"Like certain experiences in church, I guess," she said
vaguely. "Like dating." For the moment, at least, she declined to
comment further.

But there were many experiences she did remember, and each
had an undercurrent of excitement running through it. I particularly remember one of our early meetings when we played catch
across my desk with the memories of cathedrals. Just before
becoming my client, Miss Bishop had made a winter visit to her
old haunts in Florence, which had so excited her that it had
brought on one of the worst bouts of mania she had experienced
since her twenties. Upon her return, she had been hospitalized
for several months at great expense. Although she had emerged
from this ordeal with a fierce resolve to abstain from excitement
and return to a "constricted and utterly boring life," the after-
glow left by all the ideas that had snapped and popped through
her mind as she trembled in the hollow darkness of churches
and cathedrals still played across her face.

"*Mysterium tremendum,*" she whispered with a broad,
straight smile as she rested the darned elbow of her sweater on
the side of my desk. "I was on the other side of the Arno in the
little church below the Pitti Palace, the one with the painted crucifix that seems to bleed, and I . . . " She hesitated. "I believed I
could actually see a patina of prayers glowing along the dark
oak rails and benches. And I could sense—almost feel on my
skin—the millions of petitions that had been sent upward along
that crucifix toward heaven." She sat back in her seat, still smiling at the memory of her transport. "I stood in the transect
before the Christ, looked up, and the tears . . . " She shook her
silver head in amazement. "Sweet tears. Nothing sweetens the
mouth, you know, like a good cry.

"And then there was the convent of San Marco where the
works of Fra Angelico have been collected. It was originally the
monastery of the Silvestrini monks. Did you know that?" She

continued quickly, as if afraid to linger too long over her memories of delight. "I was assaulted by beauty."

As Miss Bishop paused, I found myself remembering a long-
forgotten visit to a Belgian monastery where a double line of
darkly clad monks had, one by one, turned back their black
capes revealing heartbreaking triangles of magenta silk. I
smelled again the old stone and sputtering candles, glimpsed
again a mysterious world of which I was not a part. I liked Miss
Bishop already.

Leaving Belgium abruptly, I hurried to catch up with this ter-
rier of a woman, who had already moved from Florence to
Livorno where she was superimposing the memory of dead rabbits, which she had seen in a market hanging by their feet and
bleeding into plastic bags, onto a spectacularly bloody Christ
painted by Fra Angelico.

"It's the accumulation of emotion that is so affecting in
Italy," she was saying, her compact body leaning into the idea
she wished to get across. "Blood on Christ, blood on rabbits.
Skinned goats, naked statues. Cats hunting pigeons in the park.
Men hunting. Women . . . Mary holding . . . " Her voice caught,
and she struggled a moment to continue. "Mary always holding
her son." She lifted her chin defiantly and frowned.

But quickly she was off again on the wings of association to
a story about a visit made by the Pope to Paris, and although
she now seemed to sit quietly in her chair, legs crossed, head
thrown back as if to read reminders printed on the ceiling, I
sensed that she continued to fly gracefully and artfully through
some of her favorite memories. "Immersed in riches," she mur-
mured, "assaulted by beauty."

Thoughts of the Pope led to daffodils by a route I have forgotten and, still reading from the ceiling, Miss Bishop quoted a
line or two from Wordsworth's "I Wandered Lonely as a
Cloud." I answered with a rough approximation of Edna St.
Vincent Millay's poetic observation that it is dangerous to find,
at the end of winter, too much yellow all at once.

"Heady stuff," nodded Miss Bishop, giving a shiver and
crossing her arms.

"Heady stuff," I agreed, and my arms crossed themselves, too.

The session ended on a polite and rather formal note, as I learned was her way, and I turned my attention to other people and other questions, sure that I would enjoy the months or even years ahead with the able Miss Bishop.

I was not mistaken. Every week Miss Bishop walked to the clinic in all weather and delighted me with stories. At times they were about her family—her silent and unremittingly alcoholic father who set fire to the grass around their house twice a year rather than cut it, or her sweet, beleaguered mother who retired each evening at seven to read. Other stories were about long, idle summers spent reading or winter afternoons in bed with asthma. But most often Miss Bishop wanted to talk about recent books and travel, not family or childhood. She never wanted to talk about mania.

It soon became apparent that Miss Bishop was not on speaking terms with what she referred to disdainfully as "this illness." "This illness" got her kicked out of Marymount. It wrecked her chances for marriage. It spoiled everything.

As far as she was concerned there was a well-intentioned although mystifyingly lazy Maggie who failed to live up to her family's expectations, and there was also a crazy woman who thought she was omnipotent and went crashing through the woods near her home in a rage when the chemicals in her head went bad. The two were unrelated.

"It's chemistry, that's all," she once said, shaking off a glistening yellow slicker and tossing it on the floor behind her chair. "I have never been able to establish anything with anyone because of this illness. When it strikes"—she shrugged—"I turn mean, and people are offended. I can't remember what I say most of the time. But I'm told it's angry and unpleasant." She made a wry face. "The Mother Superior finally said to me, 'Maggie, I can't turn you loose on the other students, because I just never know.' That's when I left for good."

"Can you remember what you did at Marymount that got you kicked out?"

"Not really," she said with annoyance. "I've been over this a million times with other therapists. I get depressed. I get excited. Then my chemicals go, and my mind falls apart."

"How did your chemistry get so mixed up?" I asked, sensing that she would not talk about her problems except in mechanical terms at this point.

"Oh, genes," she answered quickly. "My mother's family is crazy. They made statues of vegetables."

"Statues of vegetables," I repeated.

"Cement tomatoes. My mother's uncles started a business making the Holy Family and birdbaths. You should have seen their lawn. Then they branched out into zucchini, pumpkins, and of course hundreds of *lupini*—the butter beans—in all different sizes." She smiled to herself. "Finally they started building a motel using the same method. I'm not kidding. The first unit was in the shape of a pumpkin. Then they made a tomato and an eggplant, I think. The project failed when Uncle Nunzi died, but that's where I get it."

That evening, before leaving the office, I wrote out two pages of notes on Miss Bishop. I noted the happy, scrambling quality of our hours together. Many of her memories reminded me of my own.

"'That reminds me of a story,' I find myself saying to her. 'But I have one to tell you first,' she insists. And her stories are vivid," my notes continue. "I can't help seeing and feeling what she describes. She creates a yard cluttered with cement tomatoes and holy families that I pick my way through, or dark churches that I walk into at noon right off the street. It's as if her descriptions pull me into her memories, and even now as I write down what she says, there is a curious temptation to sharpen the story and change it as if I had been along on the journey myself and had seen something she was trying to ignore."

As spring turned to summer, I prompted Miss Bishop to tell me about her "twelve-by-twenty life"—namely her strictly curtailed regime of walking and working. She lived alone, she said, in a tiny apartment some twelve by twenty feet in size located above an accountant's office on the outskirts of Hillsdale. From there she trudged into the town forest both morning and evening for a four-mile hike. Between walks, she sat at a rolltop desk that had been her father's and wrote single-paragraph reviews for an out-of-print bookseller in Ohio. This pattern did not vary. Every day of every week and every season of every year, the routine was the same.

"There is much I can't do," she said flatly. "I know I have the potential—the gifts—but no ability to realize them."

"What do you mean by no ability?"

"Well . . . two things," she answered. "For one, I'm lazy. I don't do any more than I have to. And for the other?" She shrugged. "I can't afford the excitement of anything that's . . . well, that's interesting and real."

"You don't look lazy," I replied, glancing at her well-worn running shoes, but not understanding the predicament she was trying to explain. "And bored?"

"Well, I don't *do* anything."

"Whereas if you lived a *good* life," I replied, "you'd be, ah—"

"Teaching full time in the church and devoting my life to communion with Christ—doing the things I'm prepared to do instead of nothing."

We sat a moment in silence while in my mind the concept of communion tangled with thoughts of excitement and fragility.

"Would you say," I began tentatively, "that you planned on a life of active, loving care then found yourself robbed of the strength—or rather the constancy of mind—to love?"

She made no reply.

"I mean," I continued, "it's difficult to celebrate divine love without some form of human . . . intimacy."

Miss Bishop flushed crimson. "I'm trying to say," she said sharply, "that I can't afford the excitement of a productive life. And yes, even small things like thinking or daydreaming cause trouble. In that, however, I don't think I'm any different from anybody else."

I waited a minute or two, wondering whether to explore what sounded like her grandmother's and probably her father's inflexible prescriptions for the right kind of life or to risk asking further about something—probably some deep yearning—that was apparently on speaking terms with both the manic and constricted sides of her life.

Miss Bishop made the decision. "I have a dentist's appointment," she said, standing up abruptly, and with that she was out the door.

A week later, as the hot July sun began to bake the grass and ripen the corn in the fields surrounding Hillsdale, Miss Bishop returned to talk of love. She had an active imagination, she told me, and when combined with what she called her "extravagant responsiveness," the result was a vivid, yet cautious, interweaving of fantasy and experience.

"Like everyone else," she said pointedly, "I think a lot about love."

She told me then about a man who walked by her apartment and carried himself in a way that signaled his interest in women.

"He is very tall, and I can imagine how he would have to bend down to put his arms around me."

There was also a lithe young postman, a mustachioed bank teller, a grocer who put the accent on the second syllable of her name—Mag-*gie*—and Martin. In all Miss Bishop's disquisitions on love, a librarian named Martin figured prominently. She had met him in the Hillsdale library the year before, and by now the silver-haired, bespectacled gentleman was embellished almost beyond recognition by streamers and garlands of deliciously aching fancies.

"We are truly soul mates," she began, "and last week—the afternoon of that dreadful thunderstorm—Martin and I spent twenty minutes in the basement looking through old magazines. We stood face to face . . . and close, close enough to catch his smell and to see he'd missed a patch on his neck when he shaved. It glittered, that white stubble, like tiny glass beads."

Miss Bishop raised her eyes as if to refocus on the scene in the library. "Perhaps I was talking and just don't remember," she said more to herself than to me, "but I have a picture of Martin standing squarely in front of me and looking so . . . so open, so attentive, just soaking me up like a sponge. He stood there looking like he was sixteen and I was a girl who ... or rather I was *the* girl.

"He tips his chin up when he's listening," she continued with a smile, raising her chin in an exaggerated version of one of her own gestures, "as if he's sort of daring my words to reach him. It's those moments I take home with me—those treasures."

Miss Bishop went on to tell me that during her morning and afternoon walks she carefully replayed and expanded upon these moments—carefully because too potent a fantasy could take on a life of its own in her head and cause trouble, and carefully because too many replays could "drain the juice."

"On my walks I seem to be listening to music that no one else hears," she said rather dreamily, "or rather I feel like I'm riding on a bus at night with the reflection of the inside lightly imposed on all that passes by. I can't tell you how many times I've watched my own image ride with the moon."

And so she apparently walked and read and ate and slept within a haze of companionable fantasies that shifted almost as she moved. In one variation, for example, the look that Martin gave her in the basement during the thunderstorm led the two of them to reach simultaneously for a magazine. Their fingers touched. Lightning shot from the sky. The lights went out. Without warning, Miss Bishop was enfolded in the passionate embrace of a man who, like herself, had ached for years for love.

"And if I let myself play the music," she continued, "or drink a glass of wine ... "

My own recollections of passionately ordinary fantasies joined hers then, and I think we stared past each other into separate thunderstorms for several moments.

"I suppose you've been told not to drink," I said matter-of-factly, breaking the spell.

"Many times," she answered quietly.

"And yet," I said for her, "and yet ... "

A few weeks later, Miss Bishop arrived at the clinic early, greeted me with a big smile, and walked so briskly down the hall that I had to jog to keep up. As usual, we spent ten minutes talking about books and, having thus fallen in step with one another, she proceeded to tell me about a bad trip to the dentist.

"'Who can open the doors of his face? His teeth are terrible round about,'" she began, leaning forward in her chair and firing a line from the Book of Job smartly across my desk. "I developed an abscess behind one of my teeth—right here," she tapped, "and my regular dentist was out of town. I located another, rather too young for my taste," she said with an exaggerated grimace, "but he explained what was going on and began to give me novacaine with *complete* disregard for my reaction." Miss Bishop's eyes widened and she came forward in her chair.

"I cannot express the pain I experienced as that fire was injected into the abscess. *And* it didn't work. I sat there in agony, feeling myself sweating and starting to pant. Horrible," she said, worked up again at the memory. "I was coming apart at the seams."

Miss Bishop sat back with a sigh and passed her hand tenderly over the side of her rosy face. She had on a new teal green sweatshirt and faded jeans. With a tarnished-silver barrette holding back some of her hair, she looked like an old kid.

"Pain can do that, you know," she continued, "pull you apart just like fear." She paused. "Or pleasure . . . or anger."

As I watched, it seemed to me that Miss Bishop had hurried into the office only to dash off to someplace else. Apparently she was flying through a maze of associations as she remembered all the ways she had ever come apart.

"'Yet nothing can to nothing fall, nor any place be empty quite,'" she recited with feeling. "'Therefore I think my breast hath all, those pieces still, though they be not unite.'"

"Lovely," I said hesitantly, "but how fragmented do you feel right now?"

"John Donne was ordained at the age of forty-two," she answered, continuing her own train of thought, "in one of those great stone churches. . . . But back to my teeth. I had a difficult time sleeping the first night, and I'm still worn out, but Tylenol helps. I feel steadier now. But what an ordeal."

The rest of the session swung rhythmically between real pain and imaginary pleasures, which did not seem odd given Miss

Bishop's familiarity with both. The abscess, as well as the stress of dealing with a new young dentist, had obviously revved her up. After all, she told me, with a particularly direct smile, life was so generally boring that she rather enjoyed "these little times with their rushy thoughts."

On the ordinarily rather formal Miss Bishop, a gentle rush was charming. She cocked her head to one side and wondered how many times she'd *really* been in love, didn't wait for an answer, and admitted she had enjoyed feeling the dentist's arm against her cheek.

"Don't like the rubber gloves," she rattled on. "You can usually tell so much about a man from his hands. And the way he smells." She chuckled.

"How did he—"

"I love to watch them move," she broke in. "There's a man on my street with a proud walk which I find wonderfully attractive."

On she went to review the postman, the grocer, and others I had heard about before. "I fell in love with a man once for the way he took off his shirt," she continued, "and with another who had the most sensual way of patting my dog."

The warmly glowing Miss Bishop sat in her chair talking of love. Her pale blue eyes sparkled. Her wide, flexible mouth made a line that dipped and rose as symmetrically as a bracket. In her mind, she roamed the world, harvesting memories of imaginary seductions. As she described her attraction for a black-haired Italian in the Leonardo da Vinci airport who had beautiful shoes and manicured hands, I suddenly thought of Miss Bishop as a farmer living at the base of a towering dam. Clearly, this woman needed water in the most desperate way, but to open the sluice, even a crack, meant risking no ordinary flood.

"What are the warning signs of your manic episodes?" I asked, as Miss Bishop sat back in her chair, fanning her face with her appointment card.

She blushed. "I'm carrying on, aren't I? For me it's sleeplessness," she continued with a sigh, "and irritability. It's as if my thoughts take on a life of their own, as if they spin faster and faster until they sort of launch themselves into another . . . not orbit, another form, another way of fitting together that's"—she laughed shortly—"wrong and dangerous. Shameful. But I'm all right now," she said quickly. "As long as my tooth doesn't hurt, I can sleep fine."

"And if you couldn't sleep tonight?" I asked. "What would you do?"

Miss Bishop looked annoyed. "I'd take Tylenol, and of course I'd continue my medications. I'll call if I need you."

A few minutes later she left, and although she assured me she was in no danger of an "episode" and had extra medication should one begin, I could not help adding to my picture of her as a farmer under a towering dam another, in which she herself was the angry waters behind the dam. I was beginning to see how she might wash everyone away with her wrong thinking and her wild emotions if the dam broke. That danger, I suspected, placed a great deal of guilt and shame on her shoulders no matter how she explained "this illness." There were a lot of things about mania that Miss Bishop wanted to ignore. As she had said to me several times, "You won't recognize me when it happens. I don't recognize myself."

I wrote another note that evening.

"Miss Bishop says her illness is caused by a broken brain— the old twisted molecule, twisted mind idea—and in my presence, at any rate, she isn't willing to consider that her heroic, but only partially successful, efforts to lock away 'bad' emotions have a lot to do with her upbringing. Her mania seems to be an extreme way of regulating intense emotions. Presumably, in the DiLupini-Bishop household unregulated emotions posed so great a danger (eternal damnation? father's retaliation? sexual abuse?) that self-inflicted emotional repression was preferable. I wonder what or who she is like when the controls are removed?"

I did not have long to wait. Several evenings later I received an emergency phone call from the clinic. Miss Bishop was sitting in the middle of Silver Pond in a stolen rowboat taking off her clothes. Would I please do something?

The insect sounds of a late summer night grated and clicked as I walked down the driveway to my truck. Overhead a three-quarter moon rose through the barely moving branches of black-leafed oaks. The police had apparently received a complaint from the owner of the boathouse on Silver Pond when a woman had come onto the dock singing something funny and untying the skiffs.

"*Ave atque vale*," she had sung as one after another she pushed the rental boats out on the dark waters where a gentle breeze started them across the pond. "Hail and farewell. . . ." When the boatman had confronted her, she had hopped into a skiff and splashed awkwardly off using a bailer as a paddle. She was somewhere out in the middle now, watched warily by a boatful of policemen.

As I approached, I could see on the water a jittery pattern of light and shadow that came from the lights of a cruiser parked next to the dock. Beyond this circle of nervous flickering, the water lay rippling quietly in the warm night.

"Dr. Baur?" It was the boatman's teenage son. "I'll take you out."

Oarlocks rattled for a moment and then with a few easy strokes that sent the reflections swirling, we pulled out into the pond. For a minute all was quiet, and then my ears picked up the low sounds of men conversing. The rowboat swung slightly to the right, and we headed for the path of corrugated moonlight that drifted across the pond with the smell of fresh water. A rhythmic splashing sound came from still farther to the right and my heart began to pound, as I sensed from the pressured cadence the presence of Miss Bishop.

We drew nearer still until at last my eyes made out the shape of a gently rocking person. Sitting in a boat too dark to see, Miss Bishop's white torso seemed to float above the water catching what little light there was on her wet and at least half-nude body.

"Maggie," I called softly.

She turned abruptly as if startled.

"Maggie."

"No!" she said loudly, and turning her back, she bent over the side of the boat and began to scoop moonlit water out of the pond and pour it over her head.

"Hail, Mary, full of grace, the Lord is with thee. Blessed art thou among women. Blessed is the fruit of thy womb, Jesus," she intoned as she scooped and poured, scooped and poured.

"Maggie, what's going on?" I interrupted. "Please talk to—" "Hail, Mary, full of GRACE!" she shrieked suddenly, drowning out my voice. "The Lord is with thee. Blessed, blessed, *bless-ed!*"

Abruptly Miss Bishop lurched to the bow of her boat and began paddling away from us with her hands. Instantly, three beams of light shot out across the water from the police, whose boat was downwind.

"Get out! Get away from me!" Miss Bishop screamed furiously as if they were already in her boat. "I don't need any of you swine. Just clear out!" She threw herself back toward the stern, paddled for a moment, then resumed her angry baptismal mutterings. The police modestly extinguished their lights.

For twenty minutes or so I tried to talk with Maggie Bishop, and at first I thought I might bring her back. When I suggested that she seemed caught in a terrible struggle, she understood me well enough to cry out in pain, and when I said simply, "Scary, scary thoughts," or "So little control," she looked in my direction and groaned.

"It's hard right now, Maggie," I told her, "but you'll come out the other side."

Not without making the voyage. As the minutes passed, I could almost see Miss Bishop leave. The threads holding her to the ordinary world broke one by one, and very gradually she became louder, faster, and harder to understand. Now she began to pray again. When I interrupted her, she swore. When I called her name, she took a bite out of her shoe. She threw some article of clothing overboard with a wet slap. Her demeanor changed, not minute by minute but almost second by second. For a moment she would sob, then abruptly break into humorless laughter. Almost immediately her head would jerk to the right or left as if startled by a voice. Sometimes she would start to whisper a reply, change her mind, and return to my world just long enough to mumble a kind of running commentary on my words.

"Sure, she can say that," I heard her say under her breath. "One for you, one for me."

Although I could not see her face clearly enough to be stunned as I always am by the blank and totally uncomprehending stare of psychosis, which I know alternates with extreme but at least familiar expressions of terror and turmoil, I knew Maggie was letting go. I asked to be rowed over to the policemen.

"Talking's not going to do it," I whispered. No one spoke.

Naturally, we were all afraid that Miss Bishop would throw herself overboard and either disappear beneath the black waters or fight viciously with anyone who tried to pull her out. However, there was no safe way to take her into protective custody from a tippy skiff. Finally, as we listened to her banging on the seats with the bailer, we settled on a nerve-racking plan. I would try to keep her occupied for approximately an hour while the breeze continued to push us slowly toward the willows on the northeast shore. We would drift into a shallow, muddy cove and once there the police would close in behind her while I tried to reach her bow line and take her in tow.

The moon was higher now, and as we rowed back toward Miss Bishop's boat, the water sparkled darkly around the blades of the oars. I tried to think of something to say.

"My mind is a centrifuge," she had told me. "My thoughts spin faster and faster until I'm flattened against the inside of my own head."

I'll sing her a lullaby, I thought. But it was so quiet out on the lake, so open, that I didn't think I could.

"I'm a volcano," she had said on another occasion. "I have difficulty talking about my resentments. Eventually, all the stuff I've been sitting on boils to the surface."

I'll encourage her to be angry, I thought briefly, but I knew that would not be helpful now.

"I am defeated, like my father," she had said, and I considered sympathy.

"We all have imaginary lives," I remembered her saying, and, as our boat drifted to within ten feet of hers, I could see that she was on her hands and knees doing something on the bottom of the skiff. "Imaginary lives," she had said. "That's where I store the love I need." How many times had I heard that? Chuck Willet's guardian angel, Mr. Isabella's Indian guide, Mr. Bartlett's insatiable lover, Natalia. Mr. Bartlett, who said for us all, "There are times in my life when the illusion of love is necessary for my stability."

The boats lay quietly in the water. Miss Bishop sat up, her wet shirt draped seductively across one shoulder.

"Maggie," I called softly, "tell me again about Martin."

There was a long moment of silence, and I was suddenly terrified that she was going to jump. No one moved. The breeze stopped. The moon stopped.

At last Miss Bishop shifted slightly, and her skiff sent ripples like small coded messages across the water.

"Well," she said deliberately, "well, Martin and I are playing basketball."

"Who's got the ball?" I asked quickly.

"Martin."

"I can't see him. Where is he?"

Miss Bishop chuckled malevolently and whispered a few quick words to an invisible companion.

"With me!" she shouted abruptly. "We're together! Martin and I are together!"

And as we drifted for the next three-quarters of an hour across Silver Pond and into the cove curtained with dark willows, Miss Bishop told the world about Martin who stood across from her in the Hillsdale library and on the basketball court and in this little rowboat and listened to her words as if he were in love.

"Good for Martin," I said thankfully as our boat cut across her bow and I reached for her line.

"Yes, good for Martin," she agreed, and with that she stood up, stepped to the stern, and capsized the skiff.

A light blazed on revealing a splashing, gurgling Miss Bishop rising from three feet of muddy water, covered with lily pads. One of the policemen leapt agilely from his boat and came wading ashore with a pair of handcuffs. There was a brief skirmish among the willow fronds, and then a simple command for a blanket. A cruiser lit up in a nearby driveway, and my last memory of Miss Bishop that night was seeing a wet teepee wading out of the water between two muddy policemen.

Four days later I visited Miss Bishop on the acute ward at Mountain Valley Hospital. Driving over I thought back to an earlier conversation.

"What you don't understand," she had said, "is that once I've gone manic on someone the trust is gone. When I've screamed at them or torn off my clothes, they are forever on the lookout for signs of craziness. In their eyes I'm contaminated.

"*You* are normal," she continued vehemently. "*You* can say to someone, 'Oh, be quiet!' or 'Stop.' I can't. If I say something like that, I get 'the look.' 'Now?' it seems to say. 'Is she going off her rocker now?' No therapist knows what that is like."

She was right, of course, and I felt foolish not to have appreciated her feelings of contamination. It made sense, and as I parked my truck under a tree laden with green crab apples, I sat awhile and thought about the stages of a breakdown, and the different kinds of damage that each inflicts. I had first learned about acute psychosis from a patient with whom I had a solid connection—two kindred spirits. When he laughed and played, I did the same. He yearned. I yearned. He grieved. I grieved. He wound up, and I did, too—both sleepless on the same train. And then he began to lose control over his mind. First the ordinary inhibitions we call courtesy gave way, and he shouted at me. He told me I wasn't helping, or not enough, and this was painful to hear. He told me he was drowning all alone, and at that time I could not sit for very long with that suffocating sadness. It was threatening, and it was embarrassing. Finally, he crashed into psychosis, and I could not follow. He changed before my very eyes, not breaking down as much as breaking away—turning away from me, betraying me in a way that a broken leg or a physical illness could never do. He turned his back on me and laughed. Howled. Shouted at me. In my helplessness, I hated him, and I wanted him back. Although useless and wrongheaded, it would have felt good to scream, "Don't you ever do this to me again as long as you live!" And perhaps, I thought, as

I climbed from my truck, this was the problem that Miss Bishop was trying to explain to me. To the observer psychosis does not feel like something a person has or doesn't have—imbalanced chemicals, a faulty blood supply—but like something he or she *is*—a man or a woman retreating into an acute self-consciousness, a laser focusing back on itself, incandescently powerful, willfully disconnected from everything and everyone. It is a kind of rejection that few can either forget or forgive.

With these thoughts I walked into the hospital and stopped by the nurses' station to read Miss Bishop's chart. I expected sadness and was half-appalled, half-delighted to learn that she had torn the place apart in the first twenty-four hours. Of course, flamboyant disregard for the rules was not the key to release, but neither was her characteristic obedience. I was glad to see she was angry.

"She appeared irritable bodily and facially," wrote a nurse who, I sensed, carried a lifelong grudge against the English language. "Client repeatedly throws garments down toilets and clogs the same. She turned over two tables and ripped cover off mattress on ward. She was verbally threatening to staff."

Predictably, Miss Bishop was given extra amounts of medications.

"Client exhibiting stiffness of arms and legs, poor balance and confusion," the chart stated, listing the drugs' side effects. "She exhibits unsteady gait, shaking, and delayed motor reactions."

For some reason, I hadn't counted on finding Miss Bishop "roped and doped," as the saying goes, and I was enraged at the idea. No longer as put off by emotional turmoil, I now *wanted* the naked sadness that is so upsetting but so necessary an accompaniment to any major realignment of the heart. I slammed the chart shut and stormed out of the office. I took a deep breath and walked apprehensively to the dorm.

I found Miss Bishop sitting at the end of her bed, staring blankly out a window that looked out on a grassless courtyard where other patients walked around a track like robots. She looked tired rather than angry.

"OK if I come in?"

She didn't move. I drew up a chair.

For a long time Miss Bishop and I sat in silence, she staring out the window, me trying to find in her face a clue to her present state of mind.

"I remember almost everything," she finally said, still staring out the window. "All the stupid, horrible details."

Miss Bishop told me the story then of her mind's betrayal. How she knew after her visit to the dentist that she was headed for trouble as thoughts of love flew through her head like the scrambled pieces from six or eight different puzzles.

"There's a whirling first," she tried to explain, "which is exciting, like flying. Yet underneath I always sense the presence of anger . . . and terror. But I go on anyway," she said flatly, "into the woods or down to the pond—on with my great adventurous thoughts, truly expecting to be able to outrun them or control them this time. I *always* think I can make it work. I can do it, I tell myself. I can show everyone how strong and . . . special I really am."

She turned toward me very slightly, and I could see that tears were starting to come to her eyes.

"And then the story goes crazy," she continued, her voice shaking. "Random ideas just slam together and lock, trapping me in. . . . I mean, a memory of Martin will connect with a thought of Silver Pond, and I become *sure* that he means to meet me there. Then another idea will connect—a book jacket I saw in the library—and it's further conviction of love or danger. I can actually feel myself being sucked into this morbid way of thinking and trapped in expectations that my mind just . . . just makes on its own. Even when I tried to pray out there in the boat . . . " Her voice caught. "It's such a *shameful* process."

"Shameful?"

She turned to face me fully, tears now streaming along the lines of her weathered face. The look of anguish in her eyes wrenched my heart.

"Can't you understand?" she whispered. "It's my fault. It's *my* mind, and I can't stop it from destroying me and destroying everyone around me."

One of those curious drops occurred in my heart then as I

understood again, yet more deeply than before, the magnitude of the betrayal, the complexity of the trap. Miss Bishop was acknowledging not only the dangerous unreliability of her thinking, but also the impossible position that this placed her in with the people she wanted to love. She assaulted these individuals with the force of her pent-up emotions—explosions of anger, love, and frustration, as real as they were exaggerated—but she also assaulted them with a barrage of beautifully turned, rigorously logical arguments that were not true—were crazy, in fact. Who could be asked to respond sympathetically to her intense feelings year after year while at the same time holding off the dangerously incorrect constructions of her powerful mind? She did not feel like an innocent farmer at the base of a weak dam. She felt like a trap.

Over the next several days an amazing story emerged from Miss Bishop. Either her dunking in Silver Pond had brought back memories from childhood, or she was now ready to talk about things she had not felt comfortable discussing before. As we sat in her room or walked through the grounds, she remembered sitting on the edge of her bed as a child, hands on her knees trying to exhale against great pressure during an asthma attack. On numerous occasions, she was sure she was going to die. She also remembered feeling afraid every time her father set fire to the grass under her bedroom window—so afraid of her father, the fire, and the smoke that she wasn't able to breathe. She remembered praying in the barn before the mottled gray castings of the Virgin and felt again her grandmother making a cross with oil over each of her lungs.

"And what did you pray for?" I asked as we strolled along a drive lined with crabapple trees.

"Air," she replied.

"What did you give in return?"

"Nothing."

"What was the bargain you made with God?" I persisted.

"Oh," she said with a sigh, "to be a good girl, I suppose." She was silent a moment. Then, still unaware of the import of her words, she added, "I did make a kind of a deal with God. I promised to give my life to Him, if He'd mend my lungs." She laughed humorlessly. "God's good little girl."

We walked on in silence.

Finally I asked, "Are you telling me that as a young child you agreed to lock up all your anger, your fear, your noise, your excitement in exchange for air?" I paused. "Were you hoping that as long as you were good, you'd be able to breathe?"

Changes in how we explain the very centers of our personalities do not occur easily or quickly, and probably not for the reasons we think are important. Autumn walked purposely into winter, the days grew short, and Miss Bishop and I explored how growing up with weak lungs in a tense and rageful household might prompt a person to adopt a desperately restrictive regime of self-control. We did not ignore the present, either, but found in her current life parallel vulnerabilities and fears. By Christmas there was a satisfying sense of determination about our meetings. We could see and agree upon the job ahead—the gradual reintegration of this divided woman and a cautious return to many kinds of love. I would be willing to say that remembering the deal she made with God was the beginning of Miss Bishop's recovery, except that my notes suggest that something else was at work.

"Curious as it may seem, I think success depends as much on the joint creations of our imaginations, as on historical discoveries," I wrote after a session in February during which we had talked of the colors of European winters. "We seem drawn to a 'walking together' through each other's lonely memories. It sometimes feels as if we were two old expatriates telling stories that grow more wonderful and more confident with each retelling. Or maybe it's that we find each other's stories so irresistible in some peculiar way that we add their quality of transparency, or I want to say grace, to our own accounts. Can stories deepen and enhance each other? Can people give each other grace by talking? It is so difficult to know what goes on beneath the words."

It was, I decided later, as if a second conversation—not real in the ordinary sense, yet not trivial—was being carried forward in our imaginations without regard for our conscious intentions. It was as if the energy for therapy was coming from a deep matching—of common hopes, of common desires, and of fears as well. In other words, it seemed to me that there were two kinds of talk and two kinds of listening that were going on between us. One revolved around the sad and angry things that people need to tell each other. Miss Bishop needed to admit that her brain betrayed her, and that she felt sordidly implicated in its crimes. It was heartbreaking to hear her describe her battles. Again and again she would go up against deep habits, imbalanced chemicals, old, old wounds, and again and again she would lose the contest without either understanding or consolation. It hurt her to reveal the secrets of her mania. It hurt to listen.

Yet the second kind of conversation that twined itself in and around the first, that held and captured every honest revelation, had an incandescent beauty that illuminated and transformed the first. Outside the reach of reason and control, her words of sadness were so to the point of being alive, so nakedly descriptive of the human condition, that I fell in love again and again with being human. And what a dangerous thing that is.

But that is what therapy is composed of for me—two kinds of listening, two kinds of danger. And it is this that I have been trying to say both to Miss Bishop and myself, that dangerous listening is what it takes to change a mind. At least at this moment, it seems perfectly clear to me that there is no shortcut or safer route in therapy or in love, no way to listen to the deepest sounds of the heart—its yearning for love or greatness or retribution—without being moved to the very edge of our tolerance and our abilities. To adopt anyone's condition as my own is to agree to live among the vulnerabilities that shadow every life. It is to know that there is no way for anyone to sail home in safety.